YOUR VIGOR FOR LIFE APPALLS ME

YOUR VIGOR FOR LIFE APPALLS ME

ROBERT CRUMB LETTERS
1958-1977

Edited by Ilse Thompson

FANTAGRAPHICS BOOKS 2012

Robert and Dana Crumb   Aline Kominsky, Crumb, Marty Pahls

FANTAGRAPHICS BOOKS
7563 Lake City Way NE
Seattle, WA 98115

Published by Gary Groth & Kim Thompson
Associate Publisher: Eric Reynolds
Ilse Thompson: editor
Dan Dean & Evan Sult: layout & design
Additional production & design, 2012 edition: Emory Liu & Paul Baresh
Marisa Corso, Gil Jordan, Matt Silvie & Frank Young: proofreaders
Thanks to: Robert Boyd, Bill Schelly, Mark Thompson & Frank Young

Special thanks to Don Fiene for collecting and organizing these letters.

Second Fantagraphics Books edition: July 2012

For a full catalog of Crumb comics, magazines, and books, call 1-800-657-1100 (outside
U.S., 206-524-1967) or visit the Fantagraphics website at www.fantagraphics.com

ISBN: 978-1-60699-560-0

PRINTED IN CHINA

EDITOR'S NOTE

Over ten years ago, Dr. Don Fiene conceived an ambitious project — a follow-up of sorts to his painstakingly researched, meticulously compiled, and utterly indispensable *R. Crumb Checklist*. He envisioned a multi-volume compilation of Robert Crumb marginalia, including interviews, articles, photographs, introductions, miscellaneous correspondence, and reviews of both Crumb's art and his musical performances. For years, the reams of material Fiene had collected were shunted from editor to editor at Fantagraphics Books: while each of us was acutely aware of the relevance of the project, we were somehow unable to tame the behemoth into some publishable form. Hundreds of permissions had to be obtained (and, as years went by, re-obtained) while publications went defunct, ownerships shifted hands, and writers and photographers slipped off the face of the earth.

After the project had languished in the files for most of a decade, Fantagraphics decided to salvage the centerpiece of Fiene's unwieldy treasure: this collection of 50 letters, written by Robert Crumb to his comics fandom friends, Marty Pahls and Mike Britt, between 1958 and 1977. These letters span the years during which the pensive high-school reject emerged into the limelight as America's most celebrated and controversial countercultural cartoonist.

With a few typed exceptions, the letters are hand printed in upper-case letters. They contain the misspellings and grammatical floundering typical of a high-school kid. Punctuation is haphazard and relies most heavily on the ellipsis, so there's often no clear indication where one sentence ends and another begins. Needless to say, the process of transcribing the originals into regular typeface, while maintaining the integrity of Crumb's idiosyncrasies, has been challenging. Although my focus was on remaining true to the original, the very nature of the task required a bit of editing. So, because the final product is conspicuously different from the original, I've provided an outline of my editorial m. o.

Crumb's punctuation and grammar remain intact, as do his spacing, indents, and documentation formats. However, since his phrases tend to run on or trail off into ellipses, I've imposed some structure, with context, readability, and Crumb's apparent intent in mind. This entailed simply opening certain phrases with a capital letter, after determining what was a complete, incomplete, or run-on sentence. Also, Crumb's ellipses have been standardized, except in cases where he makes an issue out of them, by, say, having them stretch on for half a page. You will notice that certain words are reproduced in upper-case letters and sometimes in boldface, indicating that Crumb printed them bolder and larger than the rest.

I have corrected Crumb's spelling errors, except in instances where (a) the misspelling is clearly deliberate, usually to suggest casual pronunciations (e.g., "discusted" for "disgusted," "gummint" for "government," "nemmine" for "never mind," and "jellies" for "jealous"); (b) the misspellings are idiosyncratic ("alot"); and (c) he refers to his misspellings or expresses doubt about the meaning or spelling of a word. My justification for correcting general spelling errors — aside from giving a break both to the reader (those misspellings are hard on the eye) and to myself (proofreading a text for "correctly misspelled" words is a near-impossible task) — is that most of the errors are more characteristic of any kid who's struggling to pass English than they are of Crumb. Aside from spelling corrections, the text has not been altered. For instance, I do not add words that he appears to have left out, or replace words that seem out of context. This policy allows for some remarkably awkward wording, but a line had to be drawn.

All of the artwork that appears in the margins of Crumb's letters has been reproduced and placed appropriately throughout the text. The more heavily illustrated letters have been printed in their original hand-printed form. Regrettably, a few pages were missing from the letters I had to work with. Fiene informed me that, for the most part, these are pages in which Crumb catalogs his collections of comics and records or details his latest finds. For collectors and those who were avid members of fandom, this is an unfortunate omission (of course, many readers may be grateful). I indicate missing pages with the notation: [...]. Since Crumb devotes much space to cataloguing titles, his references have also been standardized: titles of comics books, comic strips, books, records and songs, etc. have been placed in quotes or italicized according to academic regulation.

I. T.

v

Robert Crumb is the most autobiographical and self-revealing of artists, so the extent to which these letters illuminate his life, specifically his early artistic and intellectual development, is perhaps surprising. The first letter is dated November 20, 1958, when Crumb had just turned 16; the last letter is dated September 20, 1977, almost 20 years later. Most of the letters cover a five year period from 1958 to 1964, with only a handful of letters between '64 and '77. The majority, therefore, chronicle his thoughts and preoccupations from the age of 16 to 21, certainly among the most volatile, bewildering, and formative years of a young man's life, particularly so for an artist as driven as Crumb was even then.

All the letters are written to two friends, Marty Pahls and Mike Britt, who shared his passion for comics and cartooning, his interest in art and music, as well as his groping for a philosophy of life. It was also the time when Crumb was defining his sexual identity and formulating his attitudes toward romantic love. "I went to school with Mike Britt for two-and-a-half years, something like that, in eighth and ninth grades," Crumb told me in a recent interview on the subject of this book. "When I was in tenth grade, he moved away. We were classmates, and he was the only other guy that I knew that was a comic nerd." About Marty Pahls: "I got to know him through correspondence when [my brother] Charles and I did *Foo* magazine. He got ahold of a copy of it through this other fanzine. It was the early days of comic fandom, like 1958, and he was impressed and wrote to us, and we got into a long correspondence. Then he came to visit us in '59." Pahls was a couple of years older than Crumb, attended college when Crumb was in high school, was more academically inclined and more worldly than the socially awkward Crumb, with a quick, articulate intelligence. Crumb clearly felt a deep and abiding connection to Pahls (who later wrote the introductions to the first three volumes of the *Complete Crumb Comics* series before he died in 1988). "He was a mentor to me for a long time," Crumb recollected. "Even still, I'll sometimes be thinking about something and wonder what Marty would think about it."

Comics fandom was a loose network of fans who kept in touch with each other through fanzines and letter writing and the occasional (but expensive) phone call. It was truly a grass roots social milieu, hugely unprofessional in its "organization"; there were no fax machines or e-mail, of course, or even comics conventions at that time, and no profit motive, either. Fandom was mostly about friendships and passionate argumentation predominantly among adolescent males. Comics fandom originally coalesced around EC comics (Entertaining Comics)[1]. The EC line as a whole was arguably the most literate line of mass market comics to have appeared in the history of the medium, and, not surprisingly, engendered the most literate and passionate response from fans.

Crumb was specifically inspired by *MAD* and its creator Harvey Kurtzman. "At that time," Crumb said, "there was very little interest in, say, Carl Barks, or the other stuff that Charles and I were interested in. But there was a lot of interest in EC and *MAD* and Kurtzman." Crumb was feeling increasingly isolated in late adolescence and comics fandom was for him, as it was for so many other high school kids who couldn't fit into the rigid and conformist and exclusionary hierarchy of high school, a "place" to meet kindred spirits who shared his interests and passions. "Fandom was a way out of this isolation." Crumb confirmed. "Marty was the first person I knew outside of my immediate family and people I met in school. Fandom was part of some larger cultural force that existed outside of whatever local place you happened to be in. That was an amazing discovery for me, that there was this network of people with the same cultural interests. That was a big turning point."

The subject matter of these letters presages to a remarkable degree the themes that Crumb was to obsessively chronicle, investigate, and return to throughout his career. He was most interested in cartooning and music. He grappled with the big philosophical questions, mostly of an existential kind, that continue to run through his work to this day. He analyzes his own motives, reveals the stresses and fractures of his family life, and even touches upon the inchoate love-hate relationship with women that would fuel so many of his stories. Despite the doubts and anxieties he expresses, what is revealed here is a presiding intelligence; precocious critical acumen; uncompromising, occasionally petulant, self-assurance; alienation from, and skepticism of, social norms; contempt for the boondoggle of mass culture; and, even then, a yearning to become a great artist.

He was, at the age of 16, something of a connoisseur of cartooning. There appears to be no nostalgia for the mediocre-but-captivating comics that most kids read and remember fondly as adults. He repeatedly affirms his love of Walt Kelly, Carl Barks, and Harvey Kurtzman, three of the unquestionably greatest cartoonists working at that time. He enthusiastically tells Pahls that he plans to collect every one of Arnold Roth's new syndicated newspaper strip *Poor Arnold's Almanac* (letter 8). At the age of 16 he's aware of classic illustrators and cartoonists Charles Dana Gibson, John Held, Jr., H. T. Webster, and Harrison Cady. (His effusive references to Alex Toth, he said, reflected Pahls' enthusiasm more than his own.) EC Comics had ceased publication in 1952 (although *MAD* continued in an increasingly diluted form) and as the intensity of focus on EC withered ("You must admit that even now, EC fandom isn't as enthusiastic and fiery as it used to be... All the older EC fans are growing up and going into the world to make a living, leaving EC behind for the time being." — letter 7) fans' main interest shifted to super-hero comics from DC and, later, Marvel. This was certainly not a direction Crumb was interested in, and he even takes a swipe at it in letter 35: "Have you received your copy of [the fanzine] *Alter-Ego* yet? Ghod... What a waste of good paper! Don't see how anybody could devote himself to DC comics.") This may sound like a subtle shift in emphasis, but it denotes a declining intellectual maturity in fans' critical acumen, from discussing Bernie Krigstein's use of splintered panels to "imitate" cinematic technique or Harvey Kurtzman's satirical impulses, to the internal sub-plots of super-hero comics. This would only have alienated someone as astute as Crumb, who was even disenchanted with post-Kurtzman *MAD* (from letter 17: "*MAD* is now made to suit the average teenage tastes... It's funny, but... Well, something about Kurtzman's humor that's much funnier... It doesn't make you laugh out loud like *MAD* does, you get a deep inner enjoyment...")

He was completely unmoved (except to revulsion or contempt) by the popular music of his time. His taste in music was, if anything, more esoteric than his taste in comics. These letters suggest that he did not let music wash over him, as pop music is wont to do, but, rather, listened intently and critically, and searched out then-obscure musicians. For example, he writes in letter 27: "I've never heard of the name before... and I doubt if you ever have... It's Tal Henry & His Orchestra... A good band. 'My Little Old Home Down in New Orleans' is really a great number... Arrangement-wise and solo-wise... Really a joy to listen to." And later: "I found two records by this Tal Henry & His North Carolinians on the 2000 series. Neither of them live up to that one ('My Little Old Home,' etc.) These two I got are '28, the other two are '29 and much better... The '28 ones sure weren't worth the fifty cents apiece. They have a weirdly sickening quality about them... This quality is relieved by only one short fairly good trumpet piece on one of the four sides... Which is also the best of the sides arrangement-wise..." This is not sophisticated, of course, but the language is sober, respectful, discriminating. Note, too, that even then Crumb didn't use the subjective "I like" locution much; these are objective judgments — he seems not to be saying this music is good to me, so much as this music is good, period — which suggests how important art and music were to him then (and continue to be throughout his life). "I was never able to understand it either," Crumb said when asked why he was so attracted to music created 20 to 30 years before he was born, "but from a very young age I was always attracted to old music that I would hear in old cartoons or old movies. It always got to me, reached me deeply, and I started when I was about 14, 15, searching for music that sounded like that. I bought these LPs of Dixieland jazz, Peewee Hunt, and stuff like that, and it just didn't satisfy. Then I discovered 78s, and there were 78s laying around all over the place in these second-hand stores, and that was a big revelation. Marty Pahls got into it at the same time I did. It was kind of funny, we got into it together, discovering what there was on 78s, and you'd find these records that were spectacular, and the names were completely forgotten. Unknown people just made the most amazing music. You'd find Duke Ellington or Louis Armstrong, [artists] that were still known and talked about in books about jazz, but there were so many of the names — who's this? You know, I was bewildered. The music was so great, and yet the names were a total mystery. That whole thing was so intriguing, it was like discovering buried treasures. There was no discussion over these guys in the culture at all, none, nowhere, zip. And Marty and I would exchange letters — who's this, what do you know about this guy, whoever heard of him? After [Marty] died, I looked at those letters that I wrote to him later, where I would list these records I was finding, and [discovered] he had checked off certain records that he wanted to get from me. He would come out and wheedle these records out of me."

Crumb's parents were not music aficionados. "My mother liked music, but she liked the most standard middle-of-the-road crap of the time. She liked Mario Lanza and Perry Como and Frank Sinatra." I was surprised to hear Sinatra lumped in with Como and Lanza, and since Sinatra is generally considered one of the greatest popular vocalists of the century, I pressed him on why he never appreciated his voice. "I hate Sinatra," Crumb said emphatically. "I can't stand him, his attitude, the whole gestalt, to me the sensibility of that music is just repulsive. The whole sensibility of all that '50s, '60s pop music of the middle class, that bourgeois element that tended towards admiring and liking this kind of sleazy, almost gangster-Mafioso kind of lifestyle. Even the liberal intellectual side of it as represented by *Playboy* and Hefner is repugnant to me and always was. I much preferred the contemporary music of the '50s, like down-and-out rockabilly, criminal juvenile delinquent music. I couldn't stand [Stan] Kenton and all that slick Las Vegas sounding big-band jazz. Ugh! I just can't stand it!"

Crumb's refusal — or inability — to separate Sinatra's voice from Sinatra's public persona, or the social context his music represented, is a particularly dogmatic example of Crumb's rejection of inauthenticity, especially of the manufactured reality of the mass media. A belief in and search for authenticity, for the real, is, in fact, practically a leitmotiv that runs through these letters. Crumb didn't know it at the time but he was intuitively groping his way to the same conclusions that public intellectuals were reaching at approximately the same time, in David Reissman's *The Lonely Crowd*, in Herbert Marcuse and the Frankfurt School, in Dwight Macdonald's famous animadversions against mass culture. "Market analysis be damned!!!" Crumb practically bellows in letter 29. "It's choking art to death in this country. Not only comic strips, everything... movies, TV, magazines... 'Tis a pity. That's the chief reason I'm reluctant to sell anything. Alot of market-analysis people have to get their noses into it and smother expression..." Or (from letter 26): "Have you seen that new series *The Roaring Twenties* on television? Ghod, what commercial crap! Violence, sex, the usual disillusioning baloney. They have inauthentic 1920s style music. Very bad exaggeration, stereotyping to the extreme. A real letdown... Disgusting."

Crumb's conception of authenticity was not applied only to mass media, but to human beings as well. He was, in his own untutored fashion, aware of the emergence of mass man, of what Marcuse called "one dimensional man," and he appears to intuit that the media, or culture, reflect human values — or their absence. In letter 30 he writes, "These college kids are nothing but impressions on other people, on each other. Their real selves got lost somewhere around the age of 11, 12, 13. It's all sad." He makes an important distinction between mere intelligence and genuine insight in letter 27: "How could you spend a week with [Carol] and not be unhappy... I know I would have been depressed having to live a week with a girl with false values such as she has... As for intellectual girls, as with many very smart males, they seem to lack insight and awareness, though they might be top-grade intellectuals. There's a girl here in Dover school like this. She's probably the top scholar in the senior class, but it is apparent that she has little insight. I think insight in a person is more important than calculating mind." And perhaps most poignantly, about himself (letter 28) he wrote: "I want to develop a strong inner life, so that I won't be easily swayed by the outside world and other people's opinions. I want to be something inside. A real person, not just a shell of a human being. That's vague isn't it... I don't want to be a half baked human being. I want to be a whole person. I want to have faith in myself, in life. At present, I don't... I can sense the lacking, the emptiness of my present state of existence."

Crumb attributes much of his propensity for reflection to his brother Charles: "So much of that is my brother Charles' influence. He was really into that stuff, and in a way, I think he had a positive influence. He was so attuned to the phoniness of popular culture, and how people just bought into it without questioning it. He was always ranting about that stuff. We would read different religious philosophies, different writers, and try to ask questions — what are we doing here? what's this reality about? why are we here? — and all that. You know, I'm still asking those questions."

Much of his reflection is devoted to venting the demons of frustration, depression, dissatisfaction, or simple acquiescence to the prospects of a dismal and unfulfilling future (he even refers to his desire to commit suicide, and to a suicide note by his mother that he found by accident). In letter 17, he writes: "I may end up being a philosophical bum... Even (horror of horrors!) a white collar accountant... (choke!) How could anybody stand such a job... I dread the thought... but that's life... cold, harsh life... looking at it realistically..." In an uncharacteristically hyperbolic flourish, he writes (letter 41): "DAYS OF SUNSHINE? What in the hell are you talking about? Days of sunshine shit... Days of sunstroke would be more like it... days of screaming agony in the Devil's pit of living nightmares... That's what I'd call it... I think the sweetest days I can remember spending with you were in Northhampton that time... But those years in Milford were nothing but a hell of a mess... A continuous and destructive state of anxiety prevailed over our lives..." Passages such as these suggest that Crumb subscribed to the Czechoslovakian writer Josef Skvorecky's "idea that the world breaks almost everyone, and those it cannot break it kills."

By the age of 21, he was intent to put as much of himself and as much as he knew of life into his comics. (Was there a single professional cartoonist in 1961 who had such ambition for the expressive possibilities of the comics form?) In letter 30, he writes:

"Yes, I'm trying to put into my work the every day human realities that I've never found in a comic strip yet, though Feiffer has come the closest. It's an extremely difficult thing to do in the comic strip medium... There are so many delicate little things that, when I try to express them in comic strip form, come out awkward... Alot of things, it seems, can only be gotten across right when you write them down, explain them out with words... I consider it a challenge, though, to be as human, and real, but yet interesting and with my personal ideal toward life, as possible in a comic strip. Charles and I have had a few debates as to whether you can express reality to its fullest in the comic strip... He says it can't be done. I say I'm going to try it... So far, I haven't really gotten at stark reality, the bottom of life (as I see it) in my work... I might end up giving it up and going over to writing alone, if it doesn't seem to be doing any good to try to do it in comic strips. But, then, who knows, I might succeed?!" Little wonder, in retrospect, that Crumb was at the fore-front of the underground comics movement, which liberated the medium from the sterile and innocuously fantasy-based context toward which the comics industry had assiduously aspired.

For me, there has been an unresolved conflict between Crumb's serious attitude toward his art and his attitude toward seriousness. In letter 14, he writes, "I have a good art class here at Dover... It's an extra long period and the art teacher does a very meticulous job at teaching art... Of course it seems a little bit over-serious to me, but I s'pose I'll get over that." His famous dictum, "It's only lines on paper" is routine-ly invoked by marginal talents to justify frivolous or just plain mindless cartooning. When asked about this apparent contradiction, he said, "There's a tension between wanting to get as close to the truth in some form of expression as you can, and being too serious. After I took LSD, it struck me that I was being too serious about the whole thing. That's when I went back to what was considered a really dumb cartoon drawing style and kind of renouncing this more modernist Jules Feiffer approach. I decided it was better to have a more non-cerebral, less serious approach after taking LSD. It was part of the big turning point."

Although he certainly hasn't abandoned his attempts to get at reality through comics, he has, after nearly 40 years of intensely personal and revelatory comics, adopted a more prudent view of the medium's, or at least his, limitations. "I actual-ly did try to do a strip about [my relationship with Charles] about three years ago, about how we used to walk the streets, and all that. I couldn't do it, I couldn't pull it off, I quit. Somehow it just wasn't working. I had to stop. I don't know. I would-n't necessarily say that it couldn't be done, but..."

Crumb's views, preferences, and prejudices have remained astonishingly consis-tent from the time he expressed them in these letters to the present. Two examples are his views toward free will and literary expression. Crumb's assertions in late 1959 that there is no such thing as free will may puzzle readers who are familiar with his later social criticism, which would not have the force it does if its presupposition wasn't that people have the capacity to choose between right and wrong. In letter 18, he writes: "There is no such thing as free will. People aren't responsible for their actions. There is no such thing as sin. Man is merely a product of his environment and influences..." His reference to sin is a tip-off: he was abandoning the life raft of Catholicism and was trying out a new belief system ("Charles and I are leaving the Catholic Church. We've discovered some facts which pretty well prove it [...] to be wrong in many things," from letter 16.) It was Mark Twain (not Ayn Rand) who gave him an intellectual alternative. "I was just beginning to break with the Catholic Church, and I read a book by Mark Twain called *What is Man?* I think he said that man was a machine, that's how he put it. It was put in the form of a debate between an old man and a young man." Today, Crumb's opinion of the free will question has not changed so much as it's been refined. He now regards the concept of free will as "a real subtle matter. I think free will is something you [have] to cultivate. Very few people actually do. We probably have the ability, but that's a really hard thing to get to, the ability to exercise free will. Most people don't use it very much. That's why religions are based on the idea that we're responsible for our actions, and that's what mortality is based on. But actually finding and taking that responsibility is a very esoteric matter." In other words, free will is a state one should aspire to, but which most people don't reach.

Secondly, Crumb's attitude toward writing appears to have been frozen in 1960 and hasn't changed to this day. In letter 20, he complains to Pahls that "All through the writing I find this overly fancy wording... You should use more plain and simple language, like you do in your letters... But you ought to simplify your wording. In your letters you're not trying to show off, you're sincere and concise. That's the way you should be in your writing." And again in letter 27: "Your symbolism is good and the ideals behind it great, but I think perhaps you ought to try being a bit less complicated for the sake of the unwashed masses (like me)." This preference for straightforward, naturalistic prose (over and against experimental uses of language, ornate or intricate prose styles, in short, Bukowski over Proust) reflects Crumb's almost reactionary dislike of aristocratic forms of art, an intense dislike for anything smacking of pretension. An experimental use of language, Crumb told me, "is usually just a sophomoric pretension." What of a writer who couldn't be considered sophomoric, such as Joyce? "I can't read Joyce. That's the kind of literature that's only for those who really are willing to work at it. You have to work hard to appreciate Joyce." When pressed, Crumb elaborated: "I think [art] ought to be easy as well as truthful. It shouldn't be easy if it's not being truthful. A lot of popular culture tends to be easy without being honest. It's just trying to pander to the lowest common denominator by being simplistic in that way. That's dishonest. I was trying to read this William Faulkner book, *The Sound and the Fury*, and I found it infuriating because there's something obscure that he was doing there that to me was just like a self-conscious exercise in literary effect that I could have done without. It didn't add anything to the story he was telling... it was just a fucking straightforward story about these people, it's so interesting, who needs these literary pretensions? I just want to know about these people that he's talking about, which was interesting. I wanted it to be as clear as possible. I don't appreciate arts that pursue what you can consider mannerism, I guess..."

It is ironic that an artist who has had such an aversion to so much of modernism (forget post-modernism!) spearheaded, with his *Zap* collaborators — S. Clay Wilson, Victor Moscoso, Spain, Robert Williams, Rick Griffin, Gilbert Shelton — as well as his other underground comrades — Jack Jackson, Art Spiegelman, Justin Green, and so many other unparalleled artists — a revolution in comics that exploded all previous preconceptions of the limitations of subject matter capable of being explored in the medium, and that signaled a permanent change in how cartoonists perceived themselves. The artist who was congenitally wary of seriousness brought a new seriousness to comics. The artist who admired the past more than the present liberated comics from their past. The artist who reveled in sexuality, scatology, and vulgarity brought a new dignity to the form.

---

1 EC was founded in 1945 by Max Gaines and, as its original full name (Educational Comics) suggests, specialized in such morally uplifting fare as *Picture Stories from the Bible* and *Animal Fables*. Unsurprisingly, the company fared poorly on the marketplace. When Max was killed in a boating accident in 1947, his 25-year-old son, William, took over the company, re dubbed it "Entertaining Comics" and, with the help of editor/writer Al Feldstein, began delving into more dangerous territory. After flirtations with crime, romance, and western comics, the duo found their métier and meal ticket with the 1950 launch of their first so-called "New Trend" title, the grisly horror comic *Crypt of Terror* (soon renamed *Tales from the Crypt*). Gaines and Feldstein followed up their success with more horror, suspense, and science-fiction comics (including *The Vault of Horror*, *The Haunt of Fear*, *Weird Science*, and *Shock SuspenStories*), as well as two war comics and, in 1952, *MAD* — these last three edited by Harvey Kurtzman. Literate, boundary-pushing, and often staggeringly well-drawn, the EC Comics burned brightly until a campaign spearheaded by child psychologist Fredric Wertham (author of the polemic *Seduction of the Innocent*) forced them out of business in late 1955. Only *MAD*, transformed into a magazine, survived and thrived.

EC cultivated a fiercely loyal "fandom," partly because of the editors' jocular, familiar relationship with the readers, but mostly because of the craft and richness of the art and the cynical, taboo-busting verve of the writing. Virtually all of the underground cartoonists from the '60s and '70s (and many of the "mainstream" cartoonists as well) cut their eyeteeth on the EC line, and many were deeply involved in fandom — exchanging letters, trading comics, making checklists, trying to follow the subsequent work of cartoonists scattered in the post-EC diaspora. In this, Robert Crumb was but one of many.

EC Comics have been reprinted in a wide diversity of formats, and are still available in most comics shops.

YOUR VIGOR FOR LIFE APPALLS ME

November 20, 1958
Milford, Delaware

Dear Britt,

I s'pose I ought to wait about a month before writing, like you did, but I like to get mail, and I like writing to people, especially people I know well. Lee Owens hasn't written in a couple months, so...

Kinda thought you weren't going to write.

Best thing about your letter was that the pencil was so light that I had much difficulty in making out the letter. Also, I prefer your printing and on this kind of thin-lined paper and in ink.

Boy, you sure are lucky to see Marty Pahls' collection! What has he got besides ECs[1]? What year were the *Judge* mags?* I got that *Frenzy* no. 4 with the article about old lampoon... I mean humor mags in it, best article in any *MAD* imitation... Tells about Robert Sherwood's *Life* and *Ballyhoo* and *Judge* and *Peek* and *Time*. I've seen all the latest Davis work that you wrote about.

Haven't seen Wood's strip, altho I have seen Jaffee's[2] *Tall Tales* and Blechman's *Square Peg* (a regular strip in *Seventeen*, real good). Wow! ECs! Wow! LIES!

Lately, I bought *Whiz Comics*[3] with Captain Marvel, December, 1943, vol. 9, no. 49. Thought you might be interested or know someone who is. 68 pages. First story real good (got it at Poland's). Also got *Extra* no. four at Carroll's Market. Got the *Monster Parade* long time ago with Ivie[4] work. The *Extra*, by the way, is in VERY GOOD condition, in case you want to trade.

* Nemmine. I just found out at the bottom of page 2 of your letter (46, 47).

---

[1] See Gary Groth's introduction to this book for a brief history of EC and *MAD*.

[2] Jack Davis and Wallace Wood were two of the defining EC artists. Wood's polished graphics made him ideal for the science fiction comics, while Davis' lankily caricatural style took the edge off some of the more grotesque of the horror stories; both found a perfect working partner in writer/editor Harvey Kurtzman, on the war comics *Two-Fisted Tales* and *Frontline Combat*, and later in *MAD*. *Tall Tales* creator Al Jaffee became a regular artist for *MAD* in 1958, after contributing sporadically for a few years. He is best known for creating the "*MAD* Fold-In" and "Snappy Answers to Stupid Questions."

[3] *Whiz Comics*, published in the early 1940s through Fawcett Publications, debuted the character Captain Marvel, as drawn in a cheerfully cartoonish style by C.C. Beck. DC Comics currently owns the rights to the character, and continues to publish new, modernized *Captain Marvel* stories. Confusingly, Marvel Comics owns the name to the title *Captain Marvel* (DC's comics usually appear under the title *Shazam!*) and has published stories featuring an entirely different character of the same name.

[4] In the *Golden Age of Comics Fandom* (Hamster Press, 1995), Bill Schelly describes Larry Ivie as "one of the earliest fans to be considered an authority of sorts on the subject of comic book history. [...] His artwork appeared in a wide variety of fanzines of the 1950s and early 1960s [but] his real importance to comic fandom was that his apartment in New York was a mecca for literally hundreds of fans over the years."

Seen *Panic*[5] no. four? Davis did two articles. Perty bad. Also a new, odd lampoon mag called *Sporty*. Davis did neet picture of football player on first page.

That *Playboy* cartoon by Davis sure is good. Also in that issue neat Jules Feiffer[6] work.

This magazine wrote and told us they'd send no. 5 *This* for *Foo*[7]. So, what o' bunch o' clods!

Also, we received a copy of Sam Smith's magazine *Horny*... as bad as *This*, perty disgusting! Hectographed[8] mess. Pretty good typing though!

Speaking of typing, if our typewriter wasn't being fixed right now, I'd have typed this letter. Typing's pretty tough, huh kid? (hoo)

Also received a letter from Gary Delain, pres. of the Harvey Kurtzman[9] Fan Club, asking for the first four issues of *Foo*.

Also received *Fanfare* from Marty Pahls, and we got the COVER along with it, which you didn't! Yaahh!

I s'pose you want to trade the *Felix*[10] and *Pogo*[11] for somethin', eh? Well, besides what I already told you about in this letter, and what you already know I have, there's nothing else to trade, so if you want any of the aforesaid, okay, it's o' deal. (Except my *MAD* doubles, which I sold to Kenny Winter (clod who makes *EChhh* with Pavsner))[12].

There are alot of general things I'd like to tell you about, so... First... I have continued *R. Crumb Almanac* (no. 10). New lettering and all in ink. In number 10, November... I'm writing a biography of *Foo* up to the present. It's going to take more than one book too! Might send it to you one of these years (provided I get it back, of course).

---

[5] *Panic* was a *MAD* clone, first published by EC in 1954, and edited by Al Feldstein. The first issue, featuring a parody of "The Night before Christmas," was pulled from the shelves and landed Gaines in court for publishing offensive literature. The case was swiftly dismissed.

[6] Jules Feiffer's sparse, dynamic, socio-political comic strip, *Sick, Sick, Sick* (redubbed *Feiffer*), graced the *Village Voice* from 1956 to 1997. See bibliography.

[7] The first of three issues of the Crumb brothers' offset comic book, *Foo*, was created in 1958.

[8] Several of the titles mentioned herein are self-published fanzines which were produced with the primitive hectograph kit.

[9] After a dispute with Bill Gaines over the ownership of *MAD*, Kurtzman left EC to create the slick *Trump* for Hugh Hefner. *Trump* was discontinued after only two issues, for reasons that remain in dispute, and Kurtzman spent the rest of the '50s trying to rekindle the magic of *MAD* in other venues (*Humbug* — his current project when Crumb wrote this letter — and *Help!*, to which Crumb would contribute). Eventually, Kurtzman created (with frequent collaborator Will Elder) the strip "Little Annie Fanny" for *Playboy*.

[10] *Felix the Cat*, created by Pat Sullivan and Otto Messmer, debuted as an animated cartoon character in 1920. Messmer began drawing *Felix* as a newspaper strip in 1923 and continued until 1954. See bibliography.

[11] After a couple of incarnations in Whitman-Dell's *Animal Comics* (as *Bumbazine and Albert the Alligator* and *Albert and Pogo*), *Pogo*, by Walt Kelly, appeared as a newspaper strip in 1948 and was discontinued in 1975. See bibliography.

[12] Crumb contributed to the fanzine, *EChhh*, first published by Kenny Winter in 1959.

Things are in a droll state in school. 'Member Elisa Capehart, that real quiet girl with glasses that used to sit in front of me in homeroom last year… Well one day this week she was absent and somebody told Dennison that she eloped, so Dennison says "Swell" in a disgusted tone, heh, heh?

Stayton[13] got kicked out of art class, but talked Kunkle into letting him back in. That day was a million laughs!

Doug Johnson tole me about a week ago that he's heard from you and about you having a girlfriend and all (hak, hak)!!

I'm reading a little pocket book called *Life at Happy Knoll*, with artwork by Ron Wing of whom I have suddenly become an avid fan. His artwork has a real catchy style. If you ever get the chance, you ought to get the book. I think you'd enjoy his artwork. He also does work in *Harper's*, and has a cover on a book called *Tubie's Monument*, which I intend to get (35¢).

The *Golden Buc*[14] is coming along at a terrific rate of speed. They might even get one issue out before Christmas. Pretty disgusting. Nobody wants to do anything except sit around and talk, except maybe Sally Milbury, who pleads with everybody to write an article, and Sharon Hilt (recent staff member), and myself (who has written two articles and did a whole column of humorous classified ads). Are you planning on doing any work for the school newspaper up there? Are there any artists, cartoonists, writers, etc., in the school?

Yep, things are in pretty sad shape around here! The whole school is on one side, and me and Charles[15] and a few other clods on the other. So… How's Bert?

If you come across any ol' *Lulus*[16], *Felixes*, *N. Funnies*, *A. Panda*[17], *Life* mags (pre 1930), *Ballyhoo*, *Judge*, *New Yorker*, or anything you think would interest me, write to:

You know my name by this time.
603 N. Walnut St.

P.S. LIES!   Milford, Delaware

GET INNA BOX!

---

13 The mysterious letters WIS appearing throughout this collection are William Stayton's initials, according to Crumb — an in-joke.

14 Crumb's school newspaper.

15 Charles Crumb, Robert's older brother, was also an avid member of fandom. He and Robert collaborated on several comic strips throughout their school days. These "two-mans," as the brothers called their collaborations, as well as other examples of Crumb juvenilia, have been reprinted in the first two volumes of the *Complete Crumb Comics* series. See bibliography.

16 *Little Lulu* was conceived by Marjorie Henderson Buell ("Marge") as a one panel gag in 1935. *The Little Lulu* comic book, written and storyboarded by John Stanley for its first decade and a half, debuted in 1945. The daily newspaper comics strip was drawn by a succession of artists from 1955 to 1967.

17 *New Funnies* and *Andy Panda*: funny animal comics created by Walter Lantz, the creator of *Woody Woodpecker*.

Dear Britt

We stayed home from school today 'cause the snow was so deep. Boy, it's been snowin' somethin' awful down here! How is it in Mass.?

Got th' *Felix* and *Pogo* couple days ago. Sent *SSS* no. 6 and *WSF[1]* no. 28 same day. Used same envelope and put one stamp on it, so it might take awhile. By th' way, what did you receive from Joel Goldstein in that envelope? I know you used it just so's I would tear off your return address and see who sent it to you. So, who is th' clod?

Gee, toobad you can't get th' story done, but... oh well, thanks for the contrib anyway, even though we're not using it. Too much like *Dig.* (Where'd you get those old prints?)

Charles is writing a letter to your mother exposing YOU. Hah!

If Basil Wolverton[2] did that cover for *Spoof[3]*, I doubt if he did his best on it, bein' as I don't think he got paid. I wonder when that damn *Spoof* is coming out, also *Frantic* 3. When? When?

Thanks for Blurchman work, perty good, from *Esquire*, I presume?

What's your galfriend's address? I'm gonna write to her and see if she's really your girlfriend, not that I doubt YOUR word, but... Honest, you're a liar! All kidding aside (who's kidding aside) please send me her address 'cause I don't believe a word you write, just all the letters... wha-a-?

Well, damn, here's 50¢. That book better have a hard cover and nice expensive paper! And plenty pages! Hurry up and send it, RIGHT TODAY... NOW... Right after this sentence... Okay... Go get it... I said go get it... Well?... GIT!

Well, you got the book? Good! Now continue reading. Is *Rick O'Shay[4]* in the paper up thar? If it is, if you ever find any strips before Sept. second, send them to me. Th' daily strips that is. I got most of th' Sundays.

(Charles says for you to go stick your head in a big pile of sha-

---

[1] EC's *Shock SuspenStories* and *Weird Science-Fantasy.*
[2] Basil Wolverton's first strip, *Spacehawk*, was published in *Target* in 1940. By 1942, he was producing a strip called *Powerhouse Pepper*, showcasing a trademark cast of hilarious, obsessively rendered grotesqueries. He won the *Li'l Abner* "Lena the Hyena" contest in 1946 and became a regular contributor to *MAD* in the 1950s. See bibliography.
[3] EC fanzine published by Doug Brown.
[4] Syndicated humor / western comic strip by Stan Lynde.

ving cream. Hah, hah — oog)

'Member the Christmas play we had last year? Well, th' ol' lady (Mount Montgomery) decided to have the same play this year. Everybody plays th' same parts... 'cept Kay Isaacs is in it, Sharon Nauman plays Mary... some new girl... some clod named Bob Williams is th' lover boy, and Bill Hayt is Herod's man!

Clara May Kemp is engaged to some service guy. She don't speak to anybody anymore, and doesn't hang around with all those girls in th' halls and at lunch. Just goes around by herself with a far away look on her face. GOOD LAWD!

Charles decided to send back the filler you sent us. To make it real official and all, so's you can't send it to some other mag, he put a rejected seal on it. (Th' clod spelled REJECTED wrong)

Well, I guess that's it. WOW! ECs! WOW!

~ 3 ~   December 24, 1958
Milford, Delaware

Dear Britt:
Merry Christmas! We got out the 19th too, and only had a half o' day o' school. We go back the 5th of January. We put on that Christmas play on the 19th, what o' mess! Hayt forgot his lines and messed up everything! I had trouble getting back o' th' curtain to th' middle of th' stage so's when they

pulled back th' curtain (th' one back of th' stage) me and Mary (Sharon N.) would be standin' over th' manger. Well, I had to squeeze between Butch Walls and that curtain, an' almost fell out on th' stage, but I made it! It was really a mess!

Thanks for th' *Pogo* strips, but you sent me one that you already sent in a previous letter (stoopid!). So, I'm sendin' it back. You may need it! EChhhh! What o' clod!

I'll send you th' eight cents soon as I see th' *Sick, Sick, Sick* book, see? No sooner! Hah! You think I trust you or somethin'? Hah!

Big strike up at Carroll's Market! *Donald Duck* "Lost in the Andes" in brand new condition. *D.D. in Bigtop Bedlam* (you 'member Charles had it without a cover) in brand new condition. Middle page was missin' but Charles took it out of his old one and put it in th' new one. Also first issue o' *Popeye*[1]... WOW!... Old 1949 *New Funnies* in good condition, 'cept part o' the cover torn off... Ol' *Felix* (Harvey), original printing o' *Cinderella* ('49 or '50), ol' 1948 *Walt Disney* comic in perfect condition... 'ceptin' no cover... dammit! Also I got four issues of *Esquire* for 50 cents. Th' guy wanted to get rid of 'em. Included in this bunch the big 25th anniversary issue (one dollar) in good condition. I cut out all th' good stuff out of th' four and stapled all th' articles and cartoons into one big magazine. Threw th' rest away. Those *Esquire*s are too bulky to have around the house.

WOW! OBOY! I'm gettin' a 1920 something *Judge* magazine from Marty! Can't wait! Also he's lendin' me a copy of *Cartoons* to look over at my leisure. I hear he's going to visit you this summer. EChhhh! What o' clod!

WOW! We got *This* no. 5 today! (Ugh) What a rotten magazine. Terrible. It stinks! It's awful! I think those guys can't draw any better than Max[2]! The humor is rotten! Why don't they stick their heads in sh—aving cream (worn out joke, eh, wot?).

Stayton got kicked out of art three times since I last wrote you! He always comes back in and pleads with Mr. Kunkle to let him stay, and he says he'll be a good little boy and all that. Boy, after Christmas, if Stayton gives Mr. Kunkle any trouble with all that new equipment we're going to have, something terrible's going to happen in that art class! Mr. Kunkle is really fed up with Stayton! (WIS) Also Stayton got kicked out of driver's ed for speeding. What o' clod!

'Member last summer... I mean, the summer before last... I showed you *Humbug* no. 2 after I had just bought it... I met you on a street corner... You said I was stoopid for wasting my money and you walked off with that teenage catty strut you used to have that summer... So you ended up paying

---

[1] In 1929, E. C. Segar introduced Popeye into his already popular comic strip *Thimble Theater*, which had been running in the *New York Journal* since 1919. See bibliography.

[2] Artist Maxon Crumb, Robert's younger brother, recently illustrated a selection of Edgar Allen Poe stories for a book titled *Maxon's Poe*, published by Cottage Classics, 1997.

me eighty cents for eight *Humbug*s... har... har... Oughta have your face kicked!

'Member you tole me I was stoopid for wasting my time reading *MAD* magazines... So look who turned out to be all the stoopider... collecting ECs... har... har... Oughta have your ass kicked!

Just thought I'd refresh your memory a bit.

How's Bert?

Hey! Guess what! Carol's[3] planning to marry some clod from Philly named Bob Imperitrus... pretty nice guy... Italian... where's glasses... I mean, wears glasses... does blueprint work and has a partnership in a photography business... Carol's sickly in love with th' clod, and I s'pose the feeling is mutual.

Here's a rundown on my ECs. WOWEE!

*MAD*s one through 45... *Panic*s one through twelve... a couple others... My only interest in EC is *MAD* and *Panic*... I'm not a true EC fan... So eat shit!

Boy, that *MAD* 45... COPY! They had a *MAD* Driver's Manual, or something... They used our hand signals idea... (*Foo* no. 2... "Foo Driver's Test") They also used our idea of Nixon's visit to South America... They have a picture of Nixon... just like ours... (*Foo* no. 2... "Clod Award") with a "Yankee Go Home" sign behind him (just like ours)... a broken window... (just like ours)... Lousy rotten copycats!

Oh well, tha's the way th' world is...

Well, I guess I've written about enough... but mainly I'm gettin' a cramp in my forefinger...

P.S. I'd be sending you a *Golden Buc* only it didn't get out on time... It was all printed up and everything... and was supposed to be passed out the last day of school... but Milbury's father didn't get it to the school on time... Now it'll have to wait till next year... Boy, that aggravates the HELL out o' me!

[3] Carol and Sandra Crumb are Robert's older and younger sisters, respectively.

Dear Britt:

Enclosed Nebbish strips (three of 'em, and an issue of *Foo* no. three). I was in a hurry that night and forgot a <u>lot</u> of things! I had to write a whole BUNCH of letters!

Here's one for th' books: Butch Walls is going with Patricia Rogers. Gak!

In your next letter, describe in detail th' *Animal Comics*. What condition is it in? How much did Kelly do? Who drew cover, if it <u>has</u> one? If it's good enough, Charles says there's a remote chance that he'll trade *Walt Disney's* June 1946 for it, but I doubt if he will. (How 'bout tracin' cover)

No, Charles doesn't wanna send you the *Disney* comics to read, he doesn't want to let them out of his possession for any length of time. Say, where'd you get th' *Animal Comics*? From Marty Pahls?

Woddayamean, what the hell am I blubbering about!? You know damn well what I'm blubbering about! Usin' all those little quotes from Marty Pahls' letters for your own! HA!....... HA!!

On the *Disney's* cover (in 1941 pocket book) are the letters like they were in 1948? If not, copy th' lettering in your letter, okay?

Where you gits those ol' *Walt Disney* comics? (April 1949 and January 1951)

You says: "How come I never tole you *Foo* folded"... Well, I says: how come you never told me about this magazine of yours!? O' course, Marty Pahls is filling me in on it in his letters. In his last letter he said that you decided to call it *Squatront*[1] instead of *Festoon*. (They both sound pretty STOOPID). He says he's doing a war story (or maybe horror) in the first issue. I figure he was the one who suggested you call it *Squatront*, GAVE YOU THE IDEA, I should say! I quote from a recent letter (not the latest, just recent) written 3 January, 1959... "He likes the title *Festoon* which was *Fanfare*'s working title for awhile — but FESTOON is an actual word having no bearing on humor. I would prefer..." and I quote "... SQUATRONT or SPAFON..." etc, etc... I see you listen to Marty Pahls before you listen to your own mind... You are a FRONT... a SHELL for these people... Why don't you break AWAY... Do what you see FIT... REPEL BOARDERS!! (which was once furiously bellowed by a renowned one-legged rogue to a small boy who had recently received a flintlock pistol)

---

[1] Mike Britt published *Squatront* in 1959. *Squa Tront*, another EC fanzine published by Jerry Weist in 1968, is no relation to Britt's.

BIG STRICK... STRIKE, I mean... at Carroll's again... Boy, BIGGEST ONE YET!... Alotta good stuff up there recently, too bad you ain't here! Here's list...

WALT DISNEY'S COMICS

August	1952	Perfect Condition	
July	1952	"	
May	1952	"	
April	1952	"	*
February	1952	"	
January	1952	"	
December	1951	"	*
November	1951	"	
September	1951	"	
March	1951	"	
February	1951	"	*
January	1951	"	
December	1950	"	
October	1950	"	*

Charles had a few of these (*) in rotten condition

[...]

You heard from Fred von Bernewitz[2] lately? I think he's gaphiated[3] from fandom. The last letter we got is date Oct. 1, 1958. Yeah, he's gaphiated, withdrawn, gotten on, elicited... Never heard from him after we sent *Foo* no. 3 in late October or early November...

My father brought home a tape recorder t'other night... We had loads o' fun with it... recording our conversations... goofing around... what o' ball! It's really a laugh when it's played back to us!

---

[2] Bill Schelly says that Fred von Bernewitz was one of the "older and more articulate EC followers." His work appears in the fanzine *Hoohah* among others, as well as his own *The Complete EC Checklist* (1956), which has since become an invaluable resource.

[3] Crumb is here deliberately misspelling the fannish acronym GAFIA ("Getting Away From It All"), traditionally used to describe a fan who "defects" from fandom.

Thanks for consolations of the death of *Foo* (inside you feel good!) (no?). The offset at Latex is a possibility we've been considering. Only it can't be sold in town.

We wouldn't call the new mag *Foo*, it would be called *Joker*. Howzat sound? (Also it would be a sort of a different type of magazine. Charles isn't too much for starting a new mag, and we'll probably never get it out, but it IS a thought (we'd just print a hundred copies).

Lucky, corresponding with a cartoonist! Lucky, lucky! Ha!... So who ain't?... What's Johnny Severin[4] have to say? How many letters have you gotten from him so far! C'mon! Tell me your source for *MAD*s, kid! I got a new source! WOW! Lies!

Hey! Those bubblegum cards are real neat. They don't sell 'em here! If they sell them up there, how about getting me some more, huh, kid?

I saw that writing on Freberg in the February issue of *Esquire*... Boy... oh boy... Real neat artwork along the top of the page... Me thinks I'll swipe the issue out of Roten's when ol' Seb's in there... (Uncle George* is getting wise to us. We go in there when th' ol' guy's in there and stay around for about an hour reading all the magazines... No trouble from ol' Seb about this at all, but Uncle George is beginning to see the light!)

Thanks for the *Students' Review*. I haven't had time to read it yet, but I DID notice the cartoons. Do you know the guy who does them? Pretty good! What is his age? Fill me in on all you know about him... if ANYTHING!

Most likely there won't be another *Golden Buc*... Nobody gives a <u>DAMN</u> about it... not even Sally Milbury anymore!... Nobody's mentioned the *Golden Buc* in there for about the last eight weeks! They just sit around and talk about abuncha school SHIT that doesn't amount to a DAMN THING! I'm thoroughly DISCUSTED! I think I'll JUST QUIT!! Damn it all!!

As I recall, you had TWO (2) copies of June, 1951 *Walt Disney's Comics*, both in good condition. Charles will trade "Mickey Mouse and the Black Sorcerer" (in fair condition) for one of the copies, as long as it's in fairly good condition, okay?

If you agree to this, send it with next letter.

* That's Mr. Roten

---

[4] John Severin, an EC artist whose naturalism was heightened by a rough-hewn inking style that made him ideal for war comics, worked frequently with Harvey Kurtzman on *Two-Fisted Tales* and *Frontline Combat*... After EC imploded, Severin worked for Marvel and DC Comics (among others) before settling into a long-time relationship with the *MAD* imitator, *Cracked*.

5

February 7, 1959
Milford, Delaware

Dear Britt:

LOUSE! Y' seemed to be in a fairly rotten mood when y' wrote your last letter! ROTTEN LOUSE! I'm sending you another Nebbish strip. And I don't think the humor's on the *Pogo*-ish side, it's more on th' NEBBISH side, actchuwilly!

WOW! BIG STRIKE! OLD *WALT DISNEY'S*! This was REALLY A STRIKE! August 1947, June 1946 (those traced covers of *Disney's* we sent you are actually May and June 1948, LIES!) March, 1946, December 1945, and January 1942. Where and how we got 'em is none o' your damn business, and if you don't believe it, 's' tough! Charles don't feel like tracing anymore covers, he traced six Mickey Mouse covers as it is, kid! They are enclosed here, I think!

Hmmm! That *Animal Comics* doesn't sound like much! I dunno as it's worth anything! *Humbug* number eleven is about what I'll give ye, and if you don't agree to this, okay, you'll be out one *Humbug* 11, and I'll be out nuthin' much.

After much considering, Charles has actually decided to trade (against my will) June 1948 *Walt Disney's Comics* (one with Donald and nephews in boat on cover) in good condition! He's a sap if y' ask me, and you're gettin' a pretty damn good deal, kid! REALIZE IT. I can't figure out why Charles wants to trade, but that's his business! He says the March '49 (which he wants for it) has to be in good condition, and send it with your next letter if you want the June '48. Charles might change his mind if you don't. Believe me, kid, this isn't any gyp or anything... Don't worry, you'll get th' June '48 if you agree to the trade... So, if I were you, I'd do it!

What you gives for *Donald Duck* ("Sheriff of Bullet Valley")? It's still in good condition, but now it belongs to me! What you gives for "Mickey Mouse 'n' th' Black Sorcerer"!

Whatsis *Playboy*-type mag called *Joker?* Yer sick!

I forgot to mention — we got June and August 1949 *Walt Disney's* (in good condition), November 1946 *New Funnies*, March 1952 *Little Lulu*, and *Panic* number ten (which I promptly sold to Kenny Winter for 25 cents). Boy, Carroll's is payin' off good these days. NO LIE! Also July 1951 *Walt Disney's*.

Charles has decided to trace some more covers for ye! Yer lucky he's doing this, kid! Boy, those old *Disney's* are neat! Should I enumerate on the details? That '42 issue is all REPRINTS from 1939, real old strips! Beautifully drawn! Cover (January '42) is pretty potty, though. Plain blue letters and plain yellow background. I don't feel like going into a detailed description of the other covers right now.

Hey, kid! You forgot to explain that *Disney* cover that it shows in the Better Little Book[1] ad. All I want to know is: are the letters like they were in 1947?

Seen your work in *EChhhh* #two. Story is good, but artwork not too hot... Is it hard to draw on those stencils? That "John Severin was here" didn't exactly tickle me PINK! You gotta admit — even without your article, *EChhhh* two is a good magazine! Big improvement over the first issue!

Yah, I'm writin' to Stan Lynde these days.

Forget about th' bubblegum cards — no, wait — don't forget about them, get as many as you can, and I'll give you a penny for each card (you get to keep gum). Okay?

Yeah, we sold lotsa copies of *Foo* number three at school. We got 'bout 400 and 50 copies of all three issues together left, and yesterday a clod named Terry Tuchin sent fifty cents for all three issues and said he heard about *Foo* from Mike Britt... YOU, namely... Thanks alot for the help, STOOPID! (ha ha)

Don't want any *New Yorkers* from last year, got practically all of 'em from last year. Now, if you could get some from the '30s or '20s, okay!

'Member the days when you were here in Milford? Ah, those bygone days... Remember what a rotten louse you were sometimes, callin' me STOOPID cause I didn't know some damn girl's name and you did, or 'cause I didn't wanna get a D.A. haircut? Yechhh, wodda clod! Doug Johnson was God Almighty and I was nuthin'! Remember? I was dum 'cause I didn't know anything about pinball machines! Actually, Sirrah, I didn't CARE to know anything about them. But I was tryin' to please you, and just messed everything up. You, tryin' to act like some juvy... some tough kid... some DAM CLOD is all you were, and y' know it! Tellin' me to wise up all the time in

---

[1] Originally Big Little Books, Better Little Books are miniature illustrated novels made of recycled newspaper comic strips, first published in 1932 by Whitman. Narratives were developed based on the reprinted comic strip panels used to illustrate them. Naturally, the results were awkward.

those days... I guess you're beginnin' to WISE UP, huh? I ain't sayin' everything I did then was right... but I wasn't as wrong as you thought I was... about EVERYthing, was I? That accursed Chatterbox... Chatterbox... It makes me sick! Pile in there after school just 'cause everybody else did... It embarrasses me to think of the way I conformed to the big teenage world then... The only reason I ever go into that goddamned Chatterbox nowadays is to pick up magazines and start reading them until ol' lady Derrickson comes along and blows her top about it... I wait to see how long it takes her to notice me... I enjoy this, and take much pleasure in it... You, that time at th' damned Canteen in Lincoln... (I dunno why I ever showed my face in the place, boy, was I influenced!) I went over to you... You were with Johnson and the rest of those louses... Boy, you REALLY thought I was STOOPID... You snubbed me all that summer, and I tried to be friendly... to a certain point... It hurt my feelings because you ignored me... and I was miserable because I was being rejected by everyone... YOU, especially... I went around in misery... because I couldn't be a part of everything... I began to wake up last year... and now, when I look back on it all... I wonder... I wonder so MUCH... why did I even try? I realize now that I just can't make myself interested in teenage stuff... Cars 'n' sex talk, 'n' switchblades 'n' sports... I finally realize that it's useless for me to try to get popular in school, and ride around in a car nights... because I... I just don't get a kick out of it... I'd rather sit and read a good book... And to put on a big act, it just doesn't come out right, that's what happened in eighth grade... I tried to get into the big social swim... Why, I don't know... And I guess I just didn't do things right... because it wasn't what I really wanted to do... My interests were actually far away from th' teenage world. Now, I don't feel miserable or anything because I can't be in with the crowd... I just don't care at all... I'm content with my own interests and correspondents like you, Pahls, and the others. I guess I couldn't tell you all this by word of mouth, so I've just all of a sudden let it all out on this paper... Hope you understand it, if not, think about it.

R. Crumb

P.S. Enclosed is one *Pogo* strip... I
appreciate you sending me *Pogo* strips
an' all, but... DAMMIT... You've already
sent me this one twice afore... What're y'...
tryin' t' be funny or sompin'? I cut it
in half down th' middle just to be
sure y' couldn't send it back!

6

March 14, 1959
Milford, Delaware

Dear Britt (Th Ancient?... Marty's English comic books?)

Thanks for sendin' comics... The *Animal Comics* is real neat! Good cover by WALT KELLY, you clod. Wottaya mean, no Kelly work! That sure is a neat cover! ECHHH, what o' clob!

Well, for the *Three Pigs* comic, we are sending *Frontline Combat* no. 19, take it 'n' like it! We think you'll be happy with it, Sev-Eldo combination an' all. We'd trade th' no. four but we got a better proposition, January 1947 *Walt Disney* comic for it, which we promptly traded! Yuk yuk. Boy, that '47 *Disney* comic is neat.

Charles is very well satisfied with the April '49, but he's not too happy about its condition, but, anyway, he's still sending the June '48, though! Yer lucky, kid! Charles may trade you some more of his old *Disney's* if you get anymore stuff to trade.

Are you getting all those '43 and '44s from Kenny Winter? Lucky!

No, kid, all the *Western Cowboy Comics* of John Roberts are Dells, none that you'd want, he has a mess o' ol' war comics, though!

Love comics by F. Frazetta[1]? (Blurch) Lev Gleason[2], who the hell is Lev Gleason? Who cares, for that matter.

In some of your earlier letters, you say that you are glad you came here, that school is fun, you're sittin' on top o' th' world, and all that... Well, what happened? You had a girlfriend and everything, boy, what o' clod! You havin' much trouble with your studies?

Me, I get up in the morning, go to school, plod through the hallways all day, go to my classes, and at 3:00 o'clock I get out and go home and read the mail. Tha's all, don't do nothin' in school much anymore, go in the art room at lunchtime an' draw. Speaking of art, our art class has really gotten smaller!

Tommy Halloway isn't in it no more, Barbara Wilkens quit, Ruth Wing is gonna quit, so is Wilson Robinson and Bill Dennis. So here's who'll be left: (Stayton got kicked out) me, Charles, Gary Burlingame, Donald Ingram, Joe Gooden, Terry Yieser, Nancy McFadden, Joanne Lofland, Susanne Mills, M. Robinson, Nancy Dill, and Mr. Kunkle. Oh, I forgot Ruth Fiefer.

---

[1] Although he drew relatively few comic-book stories (and of those, only a tiny handful for EC) before moving onto a hugely successful career as the creator of cover paintings for new editions of Robert E. Howard (*Conan*) and Edgar Rice Burroughs (*Tarzan*) pulp novels, Frank Frazetta remains legendary for his lush, sensuous, painstakingly rendered penwork.

[2] Leverett S. Gleason, a politically liberal comic book publisher through the 40s and 50s, became a major force in comics with the violent and sexy *True Crime Comics*. In 1946 he was investigated by the House Un-American Activities Committee for having "communist connections."

You got any more ol' *MAD* mags lately? (no. 27, 29, 31 and 33). HEY! I got *MAD* 24! HAH!

It would be fun to exchange tapes, but we wouldn't be able to save each message. Also would be a hell of alot of postage, and we haven't got a tape recorder that handy ourselves! Marty's got alot of his own voice on the tape and some good music. He sure goes to alot of trouble for us. He got me a couple more old *Judge* mags, both of 'em are 1917. Boy, they are neat! One's got a cover by Norman Rockwell, the other cover is by James Montgomery Flagg, the guy who did the famous Uncle Sam "I Want You" poster. Also two old *Life* magazines from 1928. Only one has a cover, but it sure is neat, two guys (in cartoon) dancing on a stage with th' spotlight on 'em, up in the corner it says "VAWDVIL NUMBER," a real nifty ol' *Life* cover. Good stuff inside too! Pahls says he can get dozens of these for me at 35 cents each.

Our typewriter got taken away cuz' we didn't pay up th' bill on time. Dam!

Yeh, we got *Loco* no. three, haven't seen anymore *Loco*, though. Why don't you write to Sev an' ask him about it, he ought to know if anybody does! By the way, how many letters you got from Severin?

I's is going to visit Stan Lynde (*Rick O'Shay*) over th' spring vacation. He is going to give me some tips on comic strips and give me some of his original artwork. Put that in y'pipe 'n' smoke it!

Yes, yes, I've seen *Panic*. I bought it like a sucker. Seen *Post* thing. Seen Roth's[3] articles (all of 'em) for *TV Guide*, pasted 'em in my *Almanacs*! Haven't you noticed all th' small stuff he's doing in *TV Guide*? Nifty picture of Ed Sullivan by Roth in the latest edition. Thanks for th' holiday Roth work, pasted it in with the rest.

Squatront is making a big deal in fandom, ought to be a top-quality fanzine. I can't wait to see it, with your editorial 'n' all, hah hah, ought to be a fairly enjoyable experience! I hope for your sake that that Severin cover comes out alright. Is it on a carbon or regular bristleboard? What's on it? I mean, what's the plot of th' cover? Beautiful? Choke. A year ago you thought Severin stunk!

Blackhawk, hmmm. Charles sent for *Shag* number two, so we'll be seeing th' story, so you better do a good job, heh heh!

An 1860 comic book? My gahd! I-I-I can't imagine what it could be like! Mostly writing, huh? Describe more fully, as much as you can! What's it called? All th' ECs are Charles', an' he's not willing to trade any of 'em for it, so how about selling it to me for a dollar, huh kid?

I got a brand new copy of *Pogo* no. 14, and 12. Also I got an *Animal Comics* Feb-March 1945, one story by Kelly "Albert the Whaler." It's in the annual, boy, neat cover by Kelly on it too. Th' comic's in perfect condition! I'm an *Uncle Wiggily*[4] fan, myself, so I like the *Animal Comics* for two reasons. *Uncle*

---

[3] Arnold Roth created *Poor Arnold's Almanac*, a Sunday strip which ran from 1959 to 1961. See bibliography.

[4] A gentlemanly rabbit character, created by Howard Garis for *Animal Comics*.

Wiggily used to be a comic strip during the first quarter of this century. It was drawn by a good cartoonist named Lansing Campbell back then! It was written by Howard Garris, and possibly drawn by him at the very first. Campbell sure was a good artist, though. Drew neat ol' fashion animal characters. Some of his *Uncle Wiggily* stuff is in May, 1920 *Cartoons Magazine*. Which reminds me, Pahls sold me two copies of *Cartoons* 1914 and 1917. Nift! *Uncle Wiggily* was kind of like *Pogo*... but yet like *Winnie the Pooh*, but yet... hmmm. It's different than both, I guess.

Ever hear of *Master Humphrey's Clock*? A magazine put out by Charles Dickens?

Got a mess o' old *Our Gang* and *Our Gang with Tom and Jerry* comics recently. All of 'em have Kelly work in 'em. Lessee... I got October, December 1946, June 1947, June, August, October, December 1948 and January 1949. Eight to be exact. Three have neat Kelly covers, all have stories by him, the *Our Gang with Tom and Jerry* have the *Our Gang* story by Kelly in the back (the last story). Also got an ol' *Felix* recently June-July, 1949 (WOW!). Charles got two old *Donald Duck*s, "The Pixilated Parrot" in perfect condition, ha! You can keep yours! Also *Donald Duck and the Totem Poles*, 1950 I think! Also I got the 1947 edition of *Santa Claus Funnies* with nift Kelly work!

Convention? What convention? Yer sick! No more notes! (Jus' kiddin').

Your Vigor for Life Appalls Me

DEAR BRITT:

SORRY I HAVEN'T WRITTEN IN SUCH A LONG TIME, BUT (HOO-BOY) HAVE I BEEN BUSY! I JUST MADE A COUPLE TAPES, ONE FOR MYSELF WITH ALL MY OLD RECORDS ON IT, SO AS TO PRESERVE THEM AFTER THOSE OLD RECORDS BREAK. RIGHT NOW I'M LIS-TENING TO THE TAPE I MADE FOR PAHLS, 24,00 FEET OF VARIOUS TYPES MUSIC! MOSTLY OLD STUFF, IT'S TAKEN THE WHOLE DAY TO RECORD IT! HE'S GOING TO RE-CORD SOME OF HIS RECORDS FOR ME AND SEND ME BACK Th' TAPE. CHARLES GOT JAN., '49 DISNEY COMICS AND STORIES, SAYS HE'LL TRADE IT FOR YOUR MARCH '49, HOW 'BOUT IT? SEND Π WITH YOUR NEXT LETTER IF YOU AGREE TO TRADE. JAN. '49 IS IN GOOD CONDITION,

I GOT AUGUST, 1956 "BARNEY BARKER" IN GOOD CONDITION. COMPLETELY BY SEVERIN' 'CEPT FOR ONE LI'L STORY. WHAT YOU GIVES?

BESIDES TYPING I'M FLUNKING DRIVER'S EDUCATION, BUT I HAVE LEARNED TO DRIVE ANYWAYS.

I GOT THE DEC, 1957 ISSUE OF PLAY-BOY AT CARROLL'S MARKET FOR 15 CENTS AND IN GREAT GOOD CONDITION! THAT'S THE ONE WITH THE BIG ARTICLE " THE LITTLE WORLD OF HARVEY KURTZMAN", PRETTY GOOD, TOO! YOU GOT IT YET?

LUCKY, LUCKY, YOU GOT THAT '43 DISNEY!

Robert Crumb Letters 1958–1977   17

DON'T GET TOO UPPITY 'BOUT IT THOUGH,
KID! REMEMBER, WE GOT JANUARY '42,
HAH! POOR CLOD!

WHERE YOU GITS BACK
COPIES OF HOO-HAH, COM-
RAD OL' FRIEND? HOW MANY
YOU GOTS, HAH?

BOY, THOSE KURTZMAN AND
ELDER TAPES ARE LOUSY! L
GOT GYPPED OUT OF 12 GOOD
ECs. YOU CAN'T EVEN UNDERSTAND
WHAT THEY'RE SAYING OVER THE PHONE! AND THE
TAPES ARE NO BIGGER'N THE BOTTOM OF A BEER
BOTTLE!

L WROTE TO KISCH ABOUT THOSE COMICS
WITH KELLY WORKIN 'EM. I'LL PROBBLE NEVER
EVEN HEAR FROM THE OL' GEEZER.

HOO-BOY, ARE WE GETTIN' DOUBLES O' COMICS!
GOT THREE APRIL '49 DISNEYS, THREE DECEMBER
48s, TWO JUNE '48S, THREE M. MOUSE "TOM TOM
ISLAND"

YOU GETTIN' MAD # FOUR, EH? GAG... I
FEEL SICK! & GOT EVERY ISSUE 'CEPT NO.
FOUR! IF L DO GET NO. FOUR, L GONE
GET MY MAD COMICS BOUND INTO TWO BOOKS.
THE FIRST TEN ISSUES IN ONE, THE REST IN
THE OTHER.

SEND THE 1890 COMIC AND iLL SEND YOU
ONE OF THE PICTO-FICTIONS. OKAY? SWELL!

HOW IN ALAH'S NAME DID YOU GET
ALL THE POGOS IN GOOD CONDITION?! TELL
ME SO I CAN, OKAY, KID! (I FEEL MORE
SICK NOW!) PLEASE TELL ME, KID! I WANT!
I WANT! I WANT! I WANT! (SOB)

I'M SENDING BACK PAHLS PICTURE! WHAT O'CLOD! LATEST ISSUE OF FANFARE IS GOOD, ISN'T IT? THEN LOOK AT SQUATRONT .... WELL ... I GUESS YOU KNOW.....; I'LL SAVE MY COMMENTS ON SQUATRONT 'TILL LATER

SO YOU THINK THAT THE CCA IS A GREAT AND NEEDED ORGANIZATION! HOO-BOY, I GUESS THAT WERTHAM BOOK HAS REALLY BRAIN -WASHED YOU! PROBBLE WOULD CONVINCE ME, TOO, IF I READ IT! PAHLS, IN FANFARE, MAKES THE CCA OUT TO BE A PRETTY MISERABLE ORGANIZATION (AND FLOP!) SEEMS IT'S PUTTING COMICS ON THE DOWNGRADE, DESTROYING THE INDUSTRY. EVIDENTLY YOU'VE BEEN BRAINWASHED BY OUR DEAR DR. WERTHAM.

WHAT'S THIS IDEA YOU HAVE THAT WILL CAUSE A NEW REVOLUTION IN ECDOM. NOW YOU SOUND LIKE DELAIN, (BIG ENTERPRISE MAN)

YES, I STILL HAVE THE "TOMB OF TERROR".... WHY? (MINE!)

GUESS WHAT? AT A JUNK STORE IN FREDERICA I FOUND AN ORIGINAL BY JAMES MONTGOMERY FLAGG! A FAMOUS CARTOONIST EARLY IN THE CENTURY, YOU KNOW.... THE GUY WHO DID THE "I WANT YOU" UNCLE SAM POSTER. HE'S IN THE ENCYCLOPEDIA, AND I HAVE A 1917 JUDGE WITH A COVER BY HIM. ANY-WAY, THIS ORIGINAL BY HIM IS A SKETCH OF A GIRL, AND TH' GUY ONLY WANTS 2 BUCKS FOR IT! HOO-BOY, I GET IT ONE OF THESE DAYS!

IS THE DONALD DUCK STORY IN THAT '43 DIS-
NEY DRAWN BY THE SAME GUY THAT DRAWS IT
NOW? BET HIS DRAWING LOOKS ALOT DIFFER-
ENT IN THE '43 COMICS THAN NOW. THAT WAS
17 YEARS AGO.

I GUESS YOU KNOW THAT SHAG HAS
QUIT,... NOT ENOUGH SUPPORT.... I FIGURED IT
COULDN'T LAST.... SQUAPRONT PROBABLY WON'T
LAST.... I WISH IT COULD SEE THE DAY THAT
THIS WOULDN'T BE SO, BUT ALAS.... I SEE DARK
DAYS AHEAD FOR FANDOM... EC FANDOM WILL
DIE OUT IN THE NEXT COUPLE YEARS, MOST
LIKELY.... THE DEATH OF MAD WILL KILL FAN-
DOM FOR GOOD.... THERE MAY BE AN UPRISING
INTEREST IN EC SOMETIME YEARS FROM NOW,
BUT I THINK THE PRESENT FANDOM IS SOON
TO BE DOOMED. I THINK FANFARE WILL KEEP
UP IF MARTY DOESN'T DEVOTE TOOMUCHOF THE
MAG TO EC, AND MORE TO OTHER SUBJECTS IN
THE ENTERTAINMENT FIELD AND ISSUES IN GENERAL,
HE PLANS TO SELL THE MAG TO PEOPLE IN THE
UNIVERSITY. YOU MUST ADMIT THAT EVEN NOW,
EC FANDOM ISN'T AS ENTHUSIASTIC AND FIERY
AS IT USED TO BE.... IT SEEMS FAIRLY DEAD
RIGHT NOW.... ALL THE OLDER FANS ARE GROW-
ING UP AND GOING OUT INTO THE WORLD TO
EARN A LIVING, LEAVING EC BEHIND FOR THE
TIME BEING.... ALL THESE NEW GUYS WILL
PEDER OUT SOON.... IT'S INEVITABLE,... TAKE
TEAGUE FOR INSTANCE... OH, NEMMINE.

EC FANDOM

R. CRUMB

Your Vigor for Life Appalls Me

Y'KNOW I'M STILL MAKING R. CRUMB AL-
MANAC. ALL I DO IS ▬▬▬ MAKE A REAL
NEAT COVER, AND A COUPLE REAL NEAT PAGES
INSIDE, AND THEN I JUST MESS WITH THE
REST OF THE BOOK... PASTE STUFF IN IT, DRAW,
SCRIBBLE, ANYTHIN'....

YOU STILL HAVE THAT
OLD CLODDOG NAMED BERT?
'MEMBER HE FOLLOWED ME
HOME LOTSA TIMES... COULD-
N'T SHAKE TH' CLOD NO
MATTER WHAT I DID... HE'D
HANG AROUND TILL I FED
HIM OR OUR CAT CHASED
HIM AWAY... POOR OL' CLODDOG!

WE WENT OUT TO GARY BURLINGAME'S
PLACE SUNDAY.... PLAYED MONOPOLY AND ARGUED
RELIGION WITH TH' FAMILY.... HIS MOTHER SURE
GETS SHOOK 'BOUT IT.... GETS CARRIED AWAY, Y'
KNOW... GETS HER WORDS ALL MIXED UP 'N'
FUMBLES ALL OVER... ECHHHH, WHAT A CLOD...
IT STARTED RAINING WHILE WE WERE WALKING
OUT THERE, ▬▬ WE WERE PERTY WET WHEN WE
▬▬ GOT TO HIS PLACE....

HO HUM, I'S IS TIRED, MEBBE I'LL GO
GET READY FOR BED NOW.... MEBBE I
AUGHTA FINISH THIS LETTER FIRST, I DUNNO.
I WAS GONNA GET PERRY MESSIN DONE TO-
NIGHT FOR WINTER BUT, DARN, COULDN'T GATHER
UP ENOUGH AMBITION TO START IT, ALSO I
HAVE TO GET WINNIE THE PHOO DONE FOR PAHLS,
THAT OUGHT TO BE A GOOD STORY WHEN
IJ'S DONE.

WRITE
SOOD;
R. CRUMB

P.S. IF YOU DON'T WANT TO TRADE.
POGO NO. THREE FOR POGOS 4 AND 6,
THEN HOW BOUT TRADING NO. FIVE FOR
4 AND 6 ? OKAY? AND TRADE YOUR
NO. THREE FOR THOSE TWO PICTO-FICTIONS.
MEBBE I'LL TRADE YOU 'BOUT SIX EC's
FOR IT, I DUNNO! WHAT SAY?

Y'KNOW CHARLES AND
ME WAS LYIN' 'BOUT HAVING
ALL THOSE DISNEYS.... ONLY ONES WE HAVE
ARE THE ONES THAT WE TRACED THE COVERS
OF..... ALLLL LLLLIIIII EEEES!
YOU PROBBLE DINT BELIEVE IT ANYWAYS.

WHAT A LOUSY DEAL, YOU HAVING TO GO TO FORMOSA, I HOPED TO SEE YOU THIS SUMMER. I HOPE YOU DON'T MOVE UNTIL I CAN VISIT. I'D LIKE TO SEE YOU ONE MORE TIME IN MY LIFE.... MOST LIKELY THE-LAST.

NOW, ABOUT THIS HERE SQUATRONT.... HMMM....

ANYWAY, THE COVER IS GREAT!....REALLY GOOD FOR THIS DITTO PROCESS... YOU WERE REALLY LUCKY TO GET SEVERIN TO DO IT FOR YOU.

YOUR EDITORIAL IS TYPICAL OF THE AMBITIOUS NEW COMER'S. I KNOW YOU WERE TRYING TO BE FUNNY AND ALL THAT IN IT, BUT, WELL, KID.... TWAS RATHER ON THE CORNY SIDE... BUT, AFORE YOU GET RILED UP, LET ME SAY THAT I THINK YOU WILL IMPROVE AS TIME, AND SQUATRONT, GO ON.

THE "CLASSICS ILLUSTRATED STORY" WAS GOOD, INFORMING, AND INTERESTING! BY THE WAY, THEY HAVE STACKS 'N' STACKS OF THE EARLY CLASSICS COMICS FROM THE FORTIES AN' ALL, YOU KNOW OF ANYONE I COULD SELL 'EM TO,... I CAN BUY THEM AT A NICKEL EACH (ALL IN GOOD CONDITION) AND SELL 'EM AT, SAY, TEN CENTS EACH, I NOTICED THEY HAD THE ORIGINAL OF "LES MISERABLES" (NO. 9) COPYRIGHT 1943, UP THERE.

SAY, WHERE DID YOU GET THAT LI'L PICTURE ON PAGE 17 BY THE FANFARE AD? IT LOOKS JUST LIKE OL' JOHN ZACHERLY.. PRETTY GOOD! LOOKS LIKE SEVERIN WORK!

A LITTLE PIC TO CHEER YOU UP ⇨

CARROLL'S.

BROTHER, THE WOOD INTERVIEW WAS AS DEAD AS A 200 YEAR OLD DOOR NAIL! WOOD SEEMS LIKE A PRETTY COLD CHARACTER... EITHER THAT, OR KRAVITZ DIDN'T PUT DOWN ALL THAT HE SAID... MAYBE WOOD TALKED AND JOKED ALOT MORE THAN IS EXPRESSED IN THE INTERVIEW.., PERHAPS DAVE JUST PUT DOWN THE ESSENTIAL FACTS THAT WOOD GAVE HIM, ▬ LEAVING OUT ALL THE INFORMAL TALK AND EXPRESSION, AT ANY RATE, THE WALLY WOOD INTERVIEW WAS A FAIRLY DRY ARTICLE,

THE "MAD IMITATIONS" ARTICLE WAS AVERAGE STUFF, JUST AN EXPRESSED OPINION, ABOUT THE SAME AS EVERYBODY ELSE'S, THE QUOTE FROM THE SEVERIN LETTER WAS GOOD THOUGH,

"THE INFO" DEPT., OR "A QUICK LOOK AT WHAT THE ARTIST'S ARE DOING", (FANFARE) WHAT'S TH' DIFF? TAKE YOUR PICK! I'LL TAKE "WHAT THE ARTISTS ARE DOING" MYSELF. MARTY, RIGHT NOW, IS MORE RELIABLE, AND HAS MORE INFO.

AN AD FOR FRANTIC? SOMEBODY'S SICK! GOLLIES, I DIDN'T THINK JOEL MOSER COULD GET ANOTHER ISSUE OUT SO FAST, THE LAST ISSUE WAS JUST OUT ONLY SEVEN MONTHS AGO!

ENB 'S STUFF IS REALLY GOOD! THAT BOY CAN SURE TURN OUT GOOD HUMOR

HOO BOY! THAT AD SECTION! THAT CLOD MIKE BRITT SURE SENT IN ALOT OF WANT ADS, DIDN'T HE? WILL J. THAILING DOESN'T WANT MUCH EITHER, DOES HE? I'D LIKE TO SEE ANYBODY COME UP WITH SOME OF THE STUFF HE WANTS! WALT DISNEYS COMICS 1942 AND UNDER! HAH HO! I WISH I HAD ALL THE COMICS HE ALREADY HAS, HALF OF 'EM WOULD DO FINE! WELL, I'VE COMMENTED ON EVERYTHING. ONLY 17 PAGES IN THE ISSUE ANYWAY. I HOPE TO SEE A LONGER ISSUE NEXT TIME, AND A LONGER LETTER FROM YOU NEXT TIME, TOO!

WELL, WHEN DO YOU PLAN TO GET
THE NEXT SQUATRONT OUT? YOU HAVE
ANYTHING READY FOR IT NOW? WANT A
CONTRIB OR TWO FUM ME? I GONNA
HAVE ARTICLES IN GCHHHH AND FANFARE
COME THEIR NEXTISSUES. (NEX TISSUES,
OR NEXT ISSUES)

HAH! AS PAHLS SAYS IN
FANFARE # TWO.... (THE ZINE SCENE)
FOO, STILL THE BEST (B-E-S-T)
AMATUER MAG! GET THAT? NOT
SQUATRONT, BUT FOO!

FOO IS BEST!
SQUATRONT ISN'T

HOW'S
BEAT,
CLOD?

OH, WELL... I JUST KIDDIN'! KEEP
IT UP. YOU'RE DOING A GOOD JOB, YOU'LL
GET BETTER AS TIME GOES ON!
YOU WRITE SOON, OKAY? TELL ME
HOW YOU GOT ALL THOSE POGOS, TOO!

MAKE A COVER FOR YOUR NEXT
LETTER? ● OKAY! SAME SIZE AS
THIS! I'M ALWAYS ANXIOUS TO
GET YOUR LETTERS IN MAG FORM!
A FEW COMMENTS ABOUT THIS
COVER! IT COULD TURN OUT THE
OTHER WAY AROUND SOME DAY, I
DUNNO! ALSO, I'LL PROBBLY NEVER
TAKE UP SMOKING SEEGARS, AND
FURTHERMORE POTRZEBIE BOUNCES!

Your Vigor for Life Appalls Me

[This final page of letter 7 could not be reproduced in facsimile.]

Consider yourself lucky a critic of such stature as myself takes time out to give remarks on your crummy little sheet.

I don't like the cover because I don't like Severin's style!

The editorial wasn't as funny as it tried to be! I must compliment you on one thing... You admitted it was a lousy issue!

"Classics Ill" article..........................RUBBISH!

"Have you bought *Fanfare* yet? If you haven't that's wonderful! Ya see when you buy *Fanfare* you are merely causing competition for *Squatront* and *Squatront* wants to create a monopoly"... HAW, HAW, HA, HA, HA, HA, HAW, HAW_____YIK! You're not funny Britt, you're a cornball and besides that, you're all wet, too!

Interview'n Wally Wood...................TOTALLY DISGUSTING!

MAD Imitations...............................   "   "

So who cares what Johnny Craig's doing? Who cares what Al Williams[1] is doing? Hah? Huh? Who gives a damn? WHO CARES??

Anybody who says that *Frantic* is tops in humor and artwork should not only have their head examined but their teeth kicked in!

"Scenes We Might Have Seen".............The idea is completely copied from *MAD* and goes to show you that all *Squatront* is, is a cheap *MAD* imitation and should be classified with trash like *Zany, Frenzy, Panic, Think, Nuts, Shook Up*, etc.

---

[1] Crumb means Al Williamson, whose gleaming fantasy visions made him one of the stars of the EC science-fiction line. He spent most of his post-EC career working on the *Secret Agent X-9* (*Secret Agent Corrigan*) and *Star Wars* newspaper strips, while contributing comics to Dell, Atlas/Marvel, Warren, and others. When the *Star Wars* strip ended in the '90s, he returned to comic books, predominantly as an inker.

[...]

Say, I have a *Famous Funnies*[1] 1944, in <u>excellent</u> condition with a Buck Rogers story in it (six pages). 20 cents and it's yours. Also in it are such old heroes as Invisible Scarlet O'Neil, Chief Wahoo (with Steve Roper), Dicky Dare, Scorchy Smith and others.

Also *Donald Duck in Bigtop Bedlam* in good condition. 35 cents takes it away (that's what I paid for it).

I don't know why you want Fiction House Comics, but I'll take your word

that you won't sell 'em to Thailing[2]. I'll look for 'em at Carroll's. They'll set you back 15 cents each. Speaking of Thailing, he doesn't want much, does he? Do he have anything for sale?

Just how much <u>is</u> Kisch charging for his comics? What's the highest price and the lowest price, so I can get an idea of his price range? I wrote him 'bout a week an' a half ago, probbly won't reply. Please tell me his price range.

I'll let you know when I'm coming up. Sure hope I can make it before you go to Formosa.

Nope! Haven't seen *Cracked* no. ten. The only humor mag sold in Milford anymore is *MAD*. I figger either the rest (except *Cracked*) have gone out of business, or the news dealers just aren't ordering them anymore.

You talked to Jules Feiffer? Lucky lucky! How can you remember the conversation well enough to put it in *Squatront*, or did you take notes?

Poor Arnold's Almanac starts Sunday in the *Philadelphia Inquirer.* I gonna collect it! I'll have every strip!

About the Stan Lynde article... ah... er... hmm... brrmph... I... heh... heh... seemed to have... er... made a little mistake... hih... hih, it seems I forgot I <u>offered</u> to do the article for you, and then when Marty Pahls <u>asked</u> me to do one on Lynde, giving a few helpful hints and suggestions, I told him (ulp) that I'd do it for (ulp) him! Sorry

---

[1] *Famous Funnies* is the first standard sized comic book not published as a vehicle for advertisements, developed by Max Gaines and Harry Wildenberg, published by Dell in 1934.

[2] Bill Schelly says, "One of the best-known collectors and comic book dealers of the late 1950s was Bill Thailing [...] who had begun buying comic books in the mid 1930s."

about this kid... but being as Marty <u>asked</u> me to do it, I'm doing it for *Fanfare* instead... Deepest apologies, but I don't think it'll break you not to have it! Besides, Marty sent *Fanfare* to Stan, and got a letter from him on it. Marty seems to want the article pretty much, and I think you can see my point. Okay? Mebbe I can illo a story for *Squatront* instead. Okay? (Ulp).

Looking forward to the Jules Feiffer work on *Squatront* # two's cover. What's it of?

Hmmmm, I forgot that I have to do (well, I don't <u>have</u> to but...) that English writing for you... I'll do it right now... hold on... (can I sign my name? heh heh)

Say, how cum the fancy English text lettering... you gonna have the cover offset?

Well, I just did the lettering. Boy, it sure is hard to get the thickness of each letter exact! Don't forget to thank me. I don't think it's exactly what you had in mind, but I guess you're satisfied with it. It's not <u>EXACTLY</u> old English text, but I think it looks better for a magazine title. Well, <u>TAKE</u> IT 'N' <u>LIKE</u> IT!, is what I mean to say.

Look for my work in *Fanfare* three. I did a five-page comic story: "Winnie the Phoo." In my opinion, it turned out fairly well. Pahls is going to send me a sample of it after he mimeos it... or is it ditto? I dunno... Which is which? Also look for one-picture cartoons by me and Charles in *Fanfare*.

I did a four-page comic story for *EChhhh*: "Perry Messin'"... I drew it on tracing paper, and Winter planned to go over it onto a stencil... Just between us, he will probably louse it up!

You poor CLOD!
I got *MAD* 27 and 29!
HAH HAH! You Don't!
poor
CLOD!
I got all *Pogo* books!
I got all *MAD* pocket books!
I got EC Picto-Fictions!
I got *Pogo*s 6 thru 16!
I got <u>ALL</u> *MAD*s 'cept no. four!
I got Dec. '59 *Playboy*!
I got 3 *Animal Comics*!
I got both *Trump*s!
<u>WE</u> got *Disney's*: all 1950! 11 from 48, 10 from 49!
I got *Life, Judge* mags!
I got 12 *Our Gang Comics*!
I got ALL *Humbug*s!
I got 15 dollars!

Dear Marty:

The tape you send will really be great! I only wish I owned a recorder, so that I could play it whenever I liked. Forty songs in all... and all original recordings! Gosh, I can hardly wait! Thanks for the detailed description of some of the music. It really sounds like the kind I like!

A new radio show started here recently which plays three old records a day. I've only heard it once, but they played three good jazz songs. The first was "Oh! " by some small group... I could tell it was early jazz... the real noisy kind. The second one was something I'm unfamiliar with, and I don't recall the name of it. The third was a Paul Whiteman number. Real neat! Don't recall the name of it, but I'm familiar with the song. It had that old 1920s "A-Ru-Du-Le-Du" in it, you know? The show came from Atlantic City, and the announcer noted that Whiteman used to play on Steel Pier in those days. I wish I coulda been there! Heh heh.

From the looks of the list you sent, the tape will be very entertaining and inspiring. I hope to be getting it soon! The tape will be a treasure. I may get ahold of the Whiteman and Beiderbecke albums some day, I hope. I'm glad they're mostly instrumentals, too.

I like Gibson's work alot. An issue of *American Heritage* a long time ago had an article on him about 15 pages long, all work that he did in the 1890s and early 1900s, all about the Gibson Girl, pages from magazines that he did, real good!

This month's issue of *A.H.* has a small article about him on the last page. Seen it? Tells about how he made paper cut-outs, and shows some he did when only eight years old! It's unbelievable! I can't even do <u>that</u> good now! Detailed cutting and positioning of the characters, it seems impossible that an eight year old kid could have done them!

Hope you can get more *Life*s and *Judge*s soon. I really like them, some really good artwork in them! (You know the old *Life* started in 1883 and ended in 1936.) Those two Held *Judge* covers are really good... See if you can find some earlier *Life* mags. I sure appreciate the trouble you're going to on my account. Thanks again.

I'll be going to Stan Lynde's on the 29th of this month! I'm sure anxious for the time to come. There are several reasons why. For one thing, Stan can give me lots of points for technique, using brushes, and tips on drawing in general, show me lots of originals, and possibly do me one or two.

Another reason: I'm anxious to see New York, being as I've never been to the great city before. It really ought to be quite an experience! I'm going up on the bus, which will arrive in the evening at a big terminal right in the middle of town, so there'll be lots to look at on the way, and I like to look at city scenery too! It'll really be exciting.

The third reason is, Stan told me that there are alot of second-hand magazine stores in Manhattan. (Has von B. or Ivie ever told you of any?) He says that possibly he'll take me to several of them. If not, I'll get their addresses at least, and write to them. I hope they pay off... and <u>BIG</u>!

I'm staying for three days. Stan said he might let me ink in a strip! Yerks!

I can't wait to see how "Winnie the Phoo" turned out. Sure glad you liked it! I was afraid that maybe it would get messed up in some places in the printing processes. When is *Fanfare* no. three coming out? I'm looking forward to seeing it. Doing "Winnie" had its benefits for me. Some of Shepard's techniques, for instance, I've swiped for my own use. Like the way he shades in tree trunks. I used his technique with this on that last page of the *Golden Buc* that I did. Notice?

I'll tell you why the signature didn't come out good on it... See, when I drew the splash in lightly with pencil first, I had the middle sheet in there so the sheet wouldn't get messed up in my sketching. I forgot to take it out when I started to go over it darkly, and had the whole bottom half of the panel done before I noticed my boner. The part I had done came out beautifully on the middle sheet. When I had to go over it all over again, there wasn't enough carbon left to make it very dark. Ah, well... the trials and tribulations of ditto process arting.

Say, I really don't care much about that book with the Crandall[1] pic in it, so I'll clip it out and send it to you, rather than describe it... Describing something, especially something like this, is rather awkward for me. I'm not too good at writing, let alone writing a description of something. This little book has some mighty fine work by high school students in it, especially one boy named James Russell Bingham. There are three or four pictures in here by him. I feel kind of small when I look at his work. O' course, most of these kids went to "technical" high schools and academies. I'll send you the book if you want it. I don't care too much for it, actually. Tell me if you want the whole book, or just the Crandall work, and I'll act accordingly, okay?

Yes, I have two of the Picto-Fictions. Really great stuff in ECs last days! Some of the best art in them! Too bad they didn't last. Both the ones I have have Crandall work. *Terror* no. 2, April '56 with "Horror in the Freak Tent" and *Crime Illustrated* no. two, April '56, with "Motive" by Crandall. Both are very well done. Yes, I noticed how he uses so many different techniques in one story. He must have had alot of patience!

Do you get *Poor Arnold's Almanac* out there in Ohio? I like the strip alot, myself! Roth's humor is, what you might say, <u>DIFFERENT</u>! I like every-

---

[1] Reed Crandall drew the popular military strip *Blackhawk* from 1942 to 1953, when he joined EC. During the '60s, he worked on several titles, including *Flash Gordon*, and provided classic illustrations for Edgar Rice Burroughs books.

thing about the strip, art <u>AND</u> writing. It sort of reminds me of *Humbug*. I have the first four... no. 1: "Baseball," No. 2: "Clothes," No. 3: "The History of Medicine," No. 4 (this Sunday's): "Dogs."

Since the *Inquirer* is one of the main papers in this locale, and since Roth is a native Philadelphian, *Poor Arnold's Almanac* has had alot of advertising around here... posters, ads, and everything. The bus depot owner here in town gave me a poster recently. Perty neat, done by Roth! Shows Whistler's Mother reading *Poor Arnold* and laughing. It's just in simple black and white, no shading, but it's still pretty neat. Over the picture it says, "WEW! POOR ARNOLD'S ALMANAC," under the pic: "EVERY SUNDAY, INQUIRER ROTOCOMICS."

The stuff I use to paste comic strips in books isn't exactly paste... or glue... It's called "paper cement"... It doesn't harden or stain... and if it smears on something, it can be easily rubbed off with the finger, leaving no mark. If you want to remove what you've pasted later on, you can pull it right off the paper without it tearing. Good stuff! Right now, though... I don't know what to do with these *Poor Arnold* strips. They're so big, I don't have anything big enough to paste them in, and I don't want to cut them up. I suppose I'll get a scrap book.

22 June

Received the tape today in the mail. I'll ask my father to bring the recorder home tomorrow night... I'm really anxious to hear the tape! "A Hot Afternoon" (whew... a hot afternoon is right! Tha's what it is today!)

Our school will start in early September, and if the board goes ahead with integration, there will probably be trouble a-plenty. About 90% of the kids here are negro-haters. This state passed a law recently that <u>all</u> schools in Delaware must be integrated by a certain date. I don't know when, though. Alot of the schools are definitely integrating next year. I'm not sure about here, though.

The librarian, as brilliant as she is, said she definitely believes Wertham in *Seduction of the Innocent*.[2] I told her that I remember very clearly the days of horror and crime comics, read many of them, and had many friends who had read them, and that I saw no difference in my friends who read comics heav-

---

[2] *Seduction of the Innocent*, written in 1954 by the psychiatrist Dr. Fredric Wertham, asserts that comic books are a main cause of delinquency, moral degeneracy and illiteracy among juveniles. This book helped to fuel the anti-comic book hysteria of the '50s, leading to the formation of the Comics Code Authority. Ironically, Dr. Wertham later published a very positive book about fanzines and fandom (*The World of Fanzines: A Special Form of Communication*), in which he reprinted some of Crumb's early illustrations. He praised fandom for its sense of community, spontaneity, moral integrity, creativity, and especially for existing "without any outside interference, without any control from above, without any censorship, without any supervision or manipulation."

ily (even crime and horror) than in those who didn't read any at all. I told her that Wertham grossly exaggerates many things, and that, most likely, if a kid who hangs himself didn't have the comic to look in, he probably would have killed himself some other way. Wertham had no strong argument on this point.

When I said that the child who reads crime comics may have been sadistic to begin with, I suppose I should have clarified my statement. I was thinking of the incidents which Wertham points out... little kids who stick pins in girls' eyes, and say they saw it in comics... Wertham doesn't state that kids that do these things are few, compared to the number that read crime comics, and there are just as many that do these things that DON'T read comics at all! A kid who jabs a girl in the eye couldn't have been completely influenced by a comic. Think of the thousands of other kids who probably read the same comic and didn't jab anybody in the eye. Like you say, "irrelevant 'case history'"!

I agree with you that kids on the whole read comics, crime or what have you, just to be entertained.

You can't get rid of a whole industry because of a few wrong-doers. You might as well say get rid of cars... because some people are careless drivers. Get rid of crime comics because a few kids take them wrongly.

Another thing, Wertham quotes kids when they say what they like best about comics, and all the quotes are generally the same: "I like where they shoot the girls" or "where they stab the cops" or somesuch. Sounds to me like little kids trying to be smart-alecks! Wertham takes a distorted view, it seems to me!

Anyway, the librarian told me that Wertham is a psychiatrist, has studied children, and knows alot more about it than I do. I asked her if she ever read any crime comics. She said no.

I haven't read anywhere or heard anywhere that the elimination of crime and horror comics has decreased juvenile delinquency. In fact, it's increasing. That proves how much comic books mattered! You know what they're starting to blame now? Mark Twain's *Huckleberry Finn*!!

Charles hasn't decided on what he's going to do now that he's out of school. He's thinking about a few things, but nothing definite has been decided. Right now he's just loafing around, not doing much of anything. What do you plan to do eventually? I'm not quite sure about my own future. I'm even a little baffled. There are so many indefinity things... like the future of the cartoon industry, what the public will like, what I can do best myself... All this makes the future look rather hazy... Which is best? Comic strips? Magazines? Not comic books, unless there's a great reawakening!... Possibly the animation field... hmmmm... yik.

As for the *Golden Buc*, I get sick when I think of it! We had a Christmas issue, all complete to be printed, but the printers said that some of the type was light and some dark, and that it wouldn't come out right when printed... And me with three big articles in it, and lots of cartoons... Blech! This town of Milford is fairly illiterate... Nobody wanted to join the newspaper staff at all! This year, at first, we had about twelve or thirteen on the staff, most of 'em quit, and the rest just did their studying during the period the staff was supposed to meet.

We had two typists... and one of them is a simple-minded girl who can't spell worth a penny... even with a written <u>COPY</u>. You can see that by all the penciled corrections that had to be made in the paper. The whole thing got fairly agitating at times.

The original of the page I did was 12 by 18. I've looked all over this town for artists' pens, all they have are the speedball pens, and a few oil paint brushes, no drawing brushes... Say, what is a croquille pen? What does it draw like and how can I get one?

I received *Shag* no. three recently. Your letter in it was pretty good, only I don't think you should have poured it on so strong. Remember, the new fans entered fandom under different circumstances than the older fans. I agree with you that satire mags are just a fad, but it's through *Humbug* that most of the new guys are in... Old ECs come secondarily... I don't think you should have to do things in "the prescribed manner" in fandom, being as it actually isn't an organized club. The new fans are interested in a slightly different thing than the older fans. It's mostly the humor angle that they're going all out for.

Maybe their mags aren't too funny, the art isn't any good, and so on, but at least they're learning, improving by mistakes... as I know from my own experience in this. I think as the new fans grow older, their work will mature, and they'll lean more to the serious writing, but for now, they're gaining experience, learning what's best and what isn't. I agree with you also that they overdo the Kurtzman praise to the point where it is tiring and boring, but you also must admit that *Hoohah*'s writers praised EC, sometimes to the point of corny sentimentality. Tha's my opinion, anyhow. Speaking of *Hoohah*, bwah, you know where I can get any back issues... hah? hah? hah? I'd really like to have copies of my own.

So you're going to try to get a plug in *MAD* for your checklist, yiiii!... That won't be too easy, I don't think! Those people at *MAD*, for some reason, just don't seem to want to plug fan stuff. Charles and I tried to get them to plug *Foo* three times. O' course, this is a little bit different, but still, chances look pritty slim.

I don't know if 1,000 copies will be able to be printed in offset here, but I suppose so. I'll see.

If I go to art school, I'll have to work my way while going. I don't think I'll be able to save up enough for it beforehand. Say, are correspondence schools as good as art schools, as far as you know? These over-the-mail things look doubtful, but if they are good, I'd take one of these, which is ten times more convenient and less expensive than art school. I don't know anything about the art department at Delaware University, but next year I plan to read all the college folders at school that have art departments. The school doesn't have any on art schools, so I'm sending for these myself. I know of several art schools around the country. I'll look into the School of Visual Arts in New York.

What are you majoring in in college?

Why would you pick the School of Visual Arts if you ever planned to take up art? What is there about it that makes it your favorite?

You must have had a great time at Put In Bay. It must be quite a place! I've never been in an airplane myself, and I'm not in any hurry to fly in one. I have an unfounded prejudice against airplanes. Too many of 'em crack up!

I'd liked to have been there that night just to watch all the drunks. Myself, I'm going to try to avoid drinking. It's never done anyone any good. Doesn't hurt some people, but <u>can</u> harm some... and <u>does</u> harm many... Alot of great people have been ruined by drinking. I'm going to completely stay away from liquor, not even "just a little sip"... I'm staying safe while I can... nothing stronger than Coca-Cola for me... I hope I can stick to my resolution. Same with smoking!

Yes I got the *Jack Davis Draws Cowboys* ad. Pretty neat art by Davis, who is one of my favorite cartoonists. I may send for the set one of these days. About a year ago I saw a similar ad for Davis drawings... only they were Civil War generals... five or six of 'em I think, at something like $4.50 each. Notice the address of the ad is the same as the address of *Humbug* in the last issue.

Well, I'm really looking forward to hearing the tape. Just the kind of music I've always wanted! Will send comments in my next letter.

Your Vigor for Life Appalls Me

Dear Marty:

Yes, I've played the tape you sent... I enjoyed it very much... Alot of great music on it... I only got a chance to hear it one time, but I really enjoyed it!... Thanks muchly for going to the trouble!

I liked the first side most, though. Alot of Paul Whiteman's were great!... Hmmm, actually, it's hard to say... Well, I guess it's just that the Ted Lewis numbers aren't as good as the rest... It's hard to pick favorites on side one... I guess the University Boys' number "Lovable and Sweet" is about my favorite... But then, there are so many others I liked alot... Hmmm...

Side two:

You're right about some of Whiteman's numbers being overly-sophisticated, but there are four or five that I especially liked... Mainly "That's My Weakness Now" and "Baby Won't You Please Come Home" I guess, are my top favorites... Anyway... it is generally a great tape... I hope I get a chance to hear it again soon!

Yes, H. T. Webster is one of my favorites too... The school library has a book called *The Best of H. T. Webster* (Simon and Schuster)... Really great stuff he did! I especially like "The Timid Soul."

I've heard of Harrison Cady... but as far as I can remember, I've never seen any of his work. I'll look in my old *Life* magazines and check for work by him.

Well, I've been to New York... Your letter came while I was up there. I got back on July second... It was really an interesting trip... I won't say I had a heck of a good time or a ball or anything like that because I didn't... It wasn't really fun, but was interesting... The trip up there was dull until we got near New York City (I took a bus up) where I was constantly straining my neck to see the sights. On the way up this guy, a genuine New Yorker, all complete with accent and kill or be killed attitude, chewed my ear off for a couple of hours with his life story... and made me sick to my stomach with his cigar. I can smell it yet! I learned alot about traveling on this first excursion by myself... One thing is... do what you think is best, and not what some clod you meet on the bus tells you to do... This New Yorker told me to wait in the waiting room of the terminal for them to pick me up. I thought it would be best for me to wait right at the place where I got off the bus, but like a fool, I listened to that character instead of my own judgment. When we got there, he showed me where the waiting room was in the huge terminal, which was about a quarter of a mile from where I got off the bus... but all in the same building! Well, he left me in the waiting room and said "This's all I can do for ya; if they don't find ya, ya always got anuff money ta get home"... Then he left. I never saw him again... I waited there for about an hour and began getting worried... But finally Stan Lynde and his wife found me, they said they had been waiting for me down at the unloading busses door... That's where I knew I should have waited! I guess they missed me in the crowd when I got off.

Anyway, we then left the terminal, after having Cokes, and went out to his place in his Volvo... brand new! He said his wife dented the door on the old one they had last week, so they right then and there went out and got a new one! (Ah... the life of a cartoonist!)

We went through the center of town going to his house, and I saw 42nd Street, Times Square, and Fifth Ave., all array in their nightly glitter, really a spectacular sight... All the lights of the huge ad signs and movie theaters (of which there are about ten on each side of 42nd Street... all in a row!).

Stan lives quite a ways out. We went through a tunnel to get across the East River to Long Island... Stan says as we reach the tunnel... "that takes us out of this over-sized anthill."

It took about a half an hour to get to Massapequa Park, which is a typical "suburbia," U.S.A.! Miles and miles of modern ranch style homes with neat little lawns between neat little streets, with convenient little shopping centers neatly distributed throughout. Frightfully boring set-up, although most people like it that way, men out with their power-mowers whistling as they walk them along... The wives lazily reading magazines and sipping drinks while relaxing on contour chairs, etc.... Of course, it was night time when we got to his place... but I witnessed the suburb life in the days I was there.

It was really interesting, seeing Stan's studio, and watching him work... Gosh, he sure takes alot of time with his work... I watched him ink in a strip... and he goes so very slowly... taking pains with every detail... It's amazing! Stan says, though, that many cartoonists don't spend much time with inking, and just zip right through it.

Putting out a comic strip is <u>much more complicated</u> than I thought! First, he has to type out a script, which he takes in to the syndicate editor in New York every five weeks to be checked and changes made wherever necessary. The script's layout has to be very exact... Each day's script is put on a separate sheet... and all work has to be in six weeks ahead of publication. Second, he talks over the week's layout with his assistant, who lays out the strips and does lettering. He tells his assistant about the size he wants each panel and about where he wants the lettering placed. The assistant pencils and inks the panel borders and pencils and inks in the lettering. Then Stan pencils in the characters and background of the week's strips. Stan takes alot of time with his penciling, and does a very detailed job. Here again, he said alot of cartoonists just do a sloppy job, but he likes to do a good job with penciling because then he can make any changes before inking, saving the trouble of whiting out mistakes. Finally comes the inking... which, like I said, he spends the most time on... It takes him about an hour and a half to ink in one strip. He leaves the areas he wants blackened in for his assistant... He puts a small "X" in the space he wants blackened in...

After the inking is done, the strips go back to the assistant for corrections on the lettering... and filling in the black spaces... Then Stan mails the strips in to the syndicate for the week... Then the whole routine starts over the next day... Whew! Stan says he usually works about ten hours a day... He says he sometimes envies the people who just go to work from 9 to 5 every day for 5 days a week.

While I was there I penciled several Sunday pages for him... just put in the boarders for him though. Heh heh.

Stan knows several cartoonists... and meets most of them at the cartoonists' convention... He told me an amusing story. Says one time the chairman of the convention was asking several cartoonists what they were doing to help people improve themselves and such... Kelly (Walt) stood up and said "Cut out this tripe! These guys are just trying to make money by being funny!"... Stan said he thinks Walt was a little high that night... He says Kelly is a real character! Well, I could go on about the interesting things Stan told me about cartoonists forever... but I'll tell you about his studio... It was really interesting... It's upstairs in the house, and is quite big... It has a small library in it which is really interesting... I got a chance to look over most of the stuff in the library... He's got several books on cartooning, including a few he received while taking a correspondence course... Really many helpful tips in them... This one book on how to get into cartooning was really good. I'm going to follow some of its suggestions. Stan is a big EC fan, and especially of Severin. He has many *Prize Comics Western* (real old ones) and *Two-Fisted Tales* and *Frontline Combat*s... along with all the old *MAD*s and a few other ECs... He likes Severin's work because it's so authentic, he says. He's also fond of Davis, but he likes EC art in general, although, he says, EC sometimes overdid the "blood and guts" angle.

Stan has many books on western stuff... especially ones with plenty of pictures, which sometimes help with authenticity in the strip... He says comic strip artists have huge files called "morgues" with clippings from magazines and newspapers... clippings of all sorts... of just about anything you could want to draw... The older a cartoonist gets, the larger his file gets... Some cartoonists have morgues worth thousands of dollars.

I learned about how Stan got the Chicago Tribune-New York News Syndicate to buy his strip... They were looking for a western strip, and when Ferd Johnson[1] quit his own strip to take over *Moon Mullins*, that left a space for *Rick O'Shay*. He showed me much of his work prior to *Rick O'Shay*... a strip he did while in the Navy called *Ty Foon*... a little Navy man who looked like Rick O'Shay except his nose was larger... Stan used a few EC techniques back then... and his work was really neat! *Ty Foon* and a one-panel cartoon

---

[1] Ferd Johnson drew the comedy western strip, *Texas Slim and Dirty Dalton* for 18 years, before taking over Frank Willard's *Moon Mullins* in 1958.

called *Tired O'Livin'* he did for *Our Navy* magazine at two dollars a strip… He says it wasn't the pay that counted, it was just seeing his work in print and gaining the experience that was most important… After he got out of the Navy he worked for the *Wall Street Journal*. By the way, he did *Ty Foon* for two years…

Anyway, he worked for the *Wall Street Journal* for about a year, attending the School of Visual Arts at night and working on a strip to sell on weekends… "Occasionally, I even slept!" says Stan. He showed me a strip he was working on before he turned to humor… It was a western strip on the serious side… He did about twenty strips to show to editors, but it was never accepted… And it was really beautiful work too! You don't realize how really good Stan is at serious, realistic, human-type work! Really good work. It must really be hard to sell a strip! Stan says it just takes hard work and you have to want it bad enough to not give up… He says he was lucky to get a strip in as young as he is… Of course, he says that praying also helps, and that he's been praying for it since he was twelve. By the way, the Lyndes are Catholic you know.

Stan says to get all the training you can. He says he learned many things from training that it would have taken years longer to learn on his own. "As for fine arts training, most cartoonists dislike the formality of it." He says PRACTICE all you can. Practice is the most important thing! And draw and practice what you know and what interests you most.

I looked at a few sketch books he dabbled in when he was 18 and 19. He filled one with almost nothing but one-panel jokes that he thought up on the spot… just penciled… but he sure was witty in his late teens… Some of those jokes are a scream!

On my last day there, Thursday, July 2nd, we went into the city… I wanted to go to a few back-date magazine stores and Stan had some business to attend to. Here again, I learned much. Especially about being in the New York crowds… The streets are so crowded that you have to walk fast in order to avoid being knocked down! If you slow down or stand still in a moving crowd on the sidewalks, you may wind up on your face! Either you walk straight and make them get out of your way, or they'll make you get out of their way! Yessir, it's dog eat dog in that jungle! I also learned how to use swinging doors… the hard way… I've used swinging doors before, but never like in New York. The people really make the things whirl, and you have to step lively to get in there in order to go through or… BAM… the thing hits you in the back! The automat is another thing I learned to use… That's probably what I'll be eating at while working my way to the top… You have to run to a vacant seat at a table if you see one or somebody else will beat you to it! And there's nothing wrong with four perfect strangers all sitting around the same table… It's hard enough to find a chair, without worrying who you're sitting with! Yes, you've got to learn to not let people push you around in New York… And manners there are long gone and forgotten! It's really a rough town!

Stan used to live in Greenwich Village and said that he would have taken me there but it's too hard to get through the winding streets that you have to take to get there. His wife, Jane, is a New Yorker, and knows the city pretty well. She said she knew where there were several back-date magazine places... So we parked the car and walked the streets shopping at the bookshops. The back-date magazine stores are long and narrow... and to get to the comics you have to squeeze thru kooks leaning over back-date pornographic magazines. The stacks of comics, way in the back... looked inviting and full of good items... But, to my dismay and disappointment, in about eight places we went to, I didn't fine ONE comic for my collection, not ONE in all those stacks 'n' stacks of comics I went through! I suppose I should have known that if there ever were any good comics in those places, the New York fans would get them in a hurry! All the places I went to sold comics at five cents each and such... So I guess they really wouldn't get any rare or old comics, just new ones are about all I saw, few under 1955.

Well, after that discouraging search... I said good-bye to Stan and his wife, thanked them for everything, and stood by gate 29 in the great terminal to wait for the bus... That's where they left me, at about 7:15... I was to catch a 7:30 bus home. Well, I summed up the three days while standing there... Interesting, but not especially enjoyable, though I'm really grateful to Stan for letting me come there and learn so much!

Brother, I had an awful time getting home... I didn't stop worrying till I got off that bus at Dover and saw my parents and Charles standing there waiting for me. First off... when I was about to get on the 7:30 bus that pulled in at gate 29, the driver told me I was supposed to go down and get on a bus at gate 25... Well, I stood at gate 25 for about 15 minutes, when that bus pulled in, the driver said, "Anybody going to Norfolk go down to gate 23"... Well, some people also going to Dover went down there so I followed... By this time I was worried I was going to get on the wrong bus, being as it was supposed to go to Norfolk an' all... Well, a bus came in at gate 23 that had Norfolk at the top... People started getting on, and finally there wasn't room for anybody else, so I had to wait another fifteen minutes for the next Norfolk bus... I was worrying all this time that the darn bus wouldn't go anywhere near Dover... and I didn't see anybody around anymore that was going to Dover... Finally the next bus came in, and I was the last person to get on it. Then some Navy man on the bus, I heard him say: "This bus don't stop till it gets to Norfolk," this really had me worried, and like I said, I wasn't relieved till I was standing at the Dover bus station with my suitcase. Charles was positive I'd be coming back with stacks of comics for our collections. He sure was disappointed when I shook my head! It was around midnight when I got to Dover, the darn bus, being about a 1935 model, broke down just outside the terminal, and it took 'em a half an hour to fix it, while everybody sat inside and sweltered. It was really hot in the bus while it was sitting still.

Anyway, I got home and was showered with questions from everybody, especially: "How do you like New York?"... Some things I liked about it and some I didn't... That's about all!

Now all I have left to do is write an article about Stan Lynde and the trip... This I'm worried about! I just don't know how to go about it... I should've taken down notes when I was up there... I should've had a written question sheet before I went... I should've done <u>alot</u> of things I didn't! I never was much at writing... and now it doesn't look as easy as it did a while back... Hmmm... Any suggestions from you? I need help with this thing!

Well, I didn't get to ink in a strip... But actually I never really expected Stan would let me... After watching him inking, I <u>know</u> I just would have messed it up!

Gee, Pittsburgh sure must be an interesting town, more hilly than Frisco! I've only been there once, and that was at night, but even then it was fairly interesting. I'd sure like to ride around on the trolleys up there like you did! Darn, it's been so long since I've been on a trolley car, they'll all be gone by the time I get the chance! Are there many of the old-fashioned street cars left in Pittsburgh, or are they all modern?

New York is about like Pittsburgh in the downtown section as far as buildings go... New, super-modern skyscrapers are shooting up all over, where once stood rows of old, Victorian style brownstones with fire escapes laced across them. These type buildings are fast disappearing in New York, whereas, at one time, they took up most of the city. Stan's wife was telling how the bowery is changing. It isn't so much of a slum as it used to be, and bums don't hang around there like they used to. The whole section is being modernized.

"Winnie the Phoo" only turned out fair, eh... Hmmm, oh well. I think I can figure about how it turned out... grayish, with the lines being thicker than they really are... But, that's not too bad... I'm glad you liked the art anyway.

I hope you can get *Fanfare* no. three out soon... I'm anxious to see it... Hope it's as good as number two... You know, I wish Doug Brown was a little more ambitious... I'd like to see another *Spoof* come out... He's probably got enough material by this time for <u>six</u> issues*!*

Mike Britt's stopped writing. What's the latest on *Squatront* no. two? You know? I sure hope he can keep the mag going.

No, I never <u>did</u> get the books you recommended but someday, when I have my own library, and can keep my books on shelves, where they belong... I'll probably buy all the books you recommended and any <u>like</u> them that I see. Anything I <u>don't</u> have with plenty of stuff on eras in America, I'll buy. The more I find out about the American past, the more interested I get in it... The present too, for that matter.

I'll see if I can get an extra copy of the *Inquirer* "Rotocomics" this Sunday... to send to you. How should I send it, folded all up and put in a standard envelope or what?

I'll show Miss O'Connor, our librarian, the article on Wertham's book if I ever get *Spoof* no. five... Yes, I surely will, it ought to put her in <u>doubt</u> of Wertham's philosophy, at least! If not make her reread the book and see Wertham's big mistakes!

Thanks very much for the croquille pen, I've used it and I like it very much... In fact, I've given up altogether using this plain old fountain pen for drawing. I can do so much more using the croquille, the different line thicknesses and all... Thanks alot for sending it. They don't sell even a facsimile of a croquille in this area. Stan uses just this kind of pen for his work. I'll send a sample of my croquille pen work with this letter.

Sure hope you can get the *MAD* plug for the checklist, it'll be a boon to *Fanfare* sales and a boon to fandom... Like you said, it will uncover many EC fans who have longed to meet other EC fans and find out all that there is to learn about EC by being in fandom.

The *Our Gang* no. 1 is really a collector's item, I was lucky to get it... in good condition too! The Kelly work is really beautiful! The cover shows Spanky McFarland, Buckwheat, Froggy, Janet, and Mickey all dressed up in gaily colored old fashioned clothes having their picture taken by Barney Bear with Tomcat crawling up his back after Jerry the Mouse. Real neat... white background. The letterhead is different than on the ones you sent me.

The inside cover has a photo at the top of the gang in a homemade office, supposedly where *Our Gang Comics* is made... then an introduction written kid style with backward letters and all supposedly written by Spanky, supposedly the editor... It also lists the contents, sort of like a magazine. The first story is 10 pages long. "Our Gang" illoed by Kelly... Sure is neat, a little different from his later work. The story concerns selling scrap to a junk man for ammunition during the war, giving the money to the Red Cross, and the Gas House Gang interferes and all... Typical of early forties, almost like the thirties.

The second story is "Barney Bear," drawn very weirdly. That's only three pages.

"Tom and Jerry" is next. Nine pages. The artwork isn't too hot. Next: "The Story of Johnny Mole," Text with small pictures bordering it. Six pages.

"Flip and Dip" isn't drawn as good as in '48, and is rather crude. Six pages.

"Pete Smith's 'Lions on the Loose' Retold from the Pete Smith Metro-Goldwyn-Mayer Specialty" text with a sketch of Pete Smith and a cartoon. Two pager.

"The Donkey in the Lion's Den," sloppily drawn and not much. Three pages.

Another "Barney Bear" with a subtitle: "Wants a Good Plan for Hiber-National Defense!" By Kelly. Six pages.

"The Milky Way"... about the Three Little Kittens... Seven pages.

"Jimmy Wells, Explorer" text with nine illustrations... Four pages.

"King" about a dog... Nine pages.

Photo of the Our Gang kids on the back... with Barney Bear, Tomcat, and Jerry Mouse peeking from behind it... Drawn by Kelly.

I also obtained *Our Gang*s no. 4, 10, 18, 19, 22, and 28... along with all the ones you sent... which gives me quite a collection.

Gee, a whole <u>box</u> of old records? And what records! Boy, would I like to get my hands on some of them! I hope you can get them on a tape soon. Many of them are favorites of mine!

Friday, July 10

Well, speaking of old records... I've hit upon a few myself. I got up to the Carroll's Market rummage sale early today and didn't have to dig under a bunch of boxes of junk to get to the records. They were all in boxes on a table, and I came across several albums full that I hadn't found before! In fact, I bought one whole album full... 17 records in an old Victor album with the trademark on the cover. I also bought about eight or nine others, a couple broken ones I got free. I'll list 'em. First in here is "Ave Maria," an extra large one-sider personally autographed by the singer. Another extra large Victor that sold for $1.25 when new... It's still in great shape. In fact, all the records are in perfect condition. I get 'em at 25 cents each. Anyway, this extra large Victor sounds like a recording of vaudeville acts... The ol' corn, complete with clapping and shouting audience... 'Tis called "Hans and Gretchen" by Miss Jones and Mr. Spencer with orchestra / "The Professor and the Musical Tramp" by Spencer and Hunter with orchestra... Both are comedy routines with music. No. three... a Victor... "She Gives Them All the Ha! Ha! Ha!" by Billy Murray / "Stop! Look! Listen!" by The American Quartet... The first is a comedy song, vocal with music background. The other one I like pretty much... neat band music in the background and refrains.

4. "Toddle" by the Benson Orchestra of Chicago / "Moonlight" by Paul Whiteman & His Orchestra... Both fairly good numbers.
5. "Louisiana" by the Sterling Trio / "Beautiful Anna Bella Lee"... Charles Hart and Elliot Shaw... both fair.
6. "Night" Club Royal Orchestra / "Soothing" All Star Trio & Their Orchestra — both, especially the first, are good jazz tunes.
7. "Just Like a Butterfly" Franklyn Baur / "Just Another Day Wasted Away" Johnny Marvin - Ed Smalle... These are slow numbers... nothing great.
8. "Don't You Remember the Time" Louise Terren - Charles Hart / "Down Yonder" Peerless Quartet... The first isn't much but "Down Yonder" is great! Both have a high pitched orchestra in the background... I really like the "Down Yonder" arrangement. One of my favorites. Also has banjo solo.
9. "Just a Little Love Song" Paul Whiteman / "Ty-Tee" by Whiteman. Side one has a musical saw on it. Both good jazz arrangements.
10. "Ain't We Got Fun"/"Scandinavia" by the Benson Orchestra of Chicago... "Ain't We Got Fun" has always been one of my favorites, and I've

always wanted an early version of it. Now I've got it and it's great! "Scandinavia" is good too!

11. "Oh Gee! Oh Gosh!" / "I Love You Sunday" by the Benson Orch. Both great numbers... Neat banjo plucking in the first... This has a small chip out of it and the beginning is ruined, but it's still great!

12. "Venetian Love Boat" / "Virginia Blues" by the Benson Orch. Both good, typical '20s style!

13. "California" Club Royal Orchestra / "Who Believed

[...]

Well, that's what I got up at Carroll's, quite a few good ones in this bunch. I'll get 'em on tape sometime for you in the future. Also you can put your new finds on tape for me, okay?

Hope I get *Fanfare* no. three soon! Write...

Bob Crumb

P.S. Don't forget to make th' cover
I sent... Only no hurry...

July 22, 1959
Milford, Delaware

Dear Marty!

The town library got some books in lately. I checked out *As You Pass By* and *I Remember Distinctly*... Both books are of great interest. They would also both make great reference books of people, places, and things in my drawing. *As You Pass By* is really interesting, comparing the drawings with the maps of the little areas... showing the present street boundaries and all... Really interesting... Also interesting: George Templeton's diary... old photos... good book...

Have you ever seen *I Distinctly Remember* (No, *I Remember Distinctly* is it). It has that *Life* cover you kept of the ones you sent me that you said you had in reprint for a long time... This is the second book I've seen that cover in, so could have either book... Do you have it, or have you seen it? Really good... lots of good photos... "From 1918 to Pearl Harbor."

Yes, I'd like very much to see the *Peter Rabbit* comic with reprints by Harrison Cady. I looked up work by him in the old *Life*s and found a couple pictures... I like his style... real neat. Send the *Peter Rabbit* comic when you can.

Say, can you still send me those *Felix* stories... Or don't you want to clip them out of the comics? Send them if you don't mind clipping them out. I've only got two comics with Felix strips in them.

I bought a round trip ticket from Dover to New York for about ten and a half bucks... I went by Trailways Express.

Funny... I didn't think you were oblivious to the fact that Stan does daily strips too! If I knew, I would have told you to begin with. Yes, Stan does six dailies a week... I can see where you'd be inclined to think it strange that it takes Stan so long to do just one Sunday and nothing else every week! Since I save the daily *Rick O'Shay*s, I don't have one on hand to send you now... but if I ever get an extra one I'll send it to you. I couldn't get a Sunday *Inquirer* for you this week... Nobody seems to buy it but our family... I'll try next weekend though. The daily *Rick O'Shay* has a continued story, but at the same time, each strip has a joke to it.

Ferd Johnson did a strip called *Texas Slim* before he took over *Moon Mullins*. This gave Stan room for his strip... because the editor was looking for a western strip to take the place of *Texas Slim*... and Stan came along just at this time... Of course, Stan says not to over-estimate the part luck plays in getting a strip... He says it's those who work the hardest who usually succeed in the strip business.

Yes... Stan told me some things about Harold Gray[1]... While I was there,

---

[1] Creator of *Little Orphan Annie*, which debuted in 1924. See bibliography.

The Sunday News was preparing an article on him. (It just came out this week). But anyway... when we went into the city... Stan had to stop in at the syndicate office for some reason. When he came out he said the editors were digging down into the early *Orphan Annie* strips... and when Gray got there, he was escorted by several bodyguards. Stan says that Gray is really a valuable person to the syndicate and they don't want to lose him! He also explained to me why Gray makes his characters with blank eyeballs. It helps the reader get more out of a strip like *Orphan Annie*, the adventure type, when he has to imagine part of it for himself, because he will imagine what he likes to imagine... and helps him enjoy the strip more when he uses his imagination somewhat. The reader imagines what the eye pupils should look like in each panel, and gets more out of it that way... Get it?

For the same reason, Gray never draws a dead body... He will show alot of people standing around looking at a corpse, but he never actually shows it. The reader imagines the corpse more terrible than could be drawn... This increases the mood of the story.

Say, good idea... keeping a Sears-Roebuck catalog on hand... I'm going to find ours... I knows around the house somewhere, save it.

I forgot to mention... Ferd Johnson <u>was</u> assistant to Willard, and had his own strip at the same time... *Texas Slim* was drawn just like *Moon Mullins*.

Don't recall the name of Stan's serious western strip that he was trying to sell... But I've got to ask Stan, being as I'll have to include it in the article... which, by the way, I haven't started yet!

I asked the dealers at the bookstores if they had any more comics than those that were on display and they said no... And of the ones on display, I didn't find ONE that I wanted and I didn't see a single EC...

You heard from Britt yet? Can't think why he's stopped writing.

We may have to move this August some time... My parents have picked out a nice house for rent in Dover... and they're pretty decided on moving, but not positive... Also... we're going on a trip to Philly late in August... sometime before my birthday... which is August 30th... What date do you suppose you'll be here? I hope it doesn't get mixed up in our moving plans or the Philadelphia trip... What a fix! Well, I think everything'll work out alright... I don't think I'll be able to go to Philly with you though... I'd like to, being as we both like to see the same things and all... and we could travel the city when we pleased... Not so when I'm with my family... But... my mother doesn't want me to (you know how mothers are).

If we're in Milford when you come, we'll pick you up at the Dover bus station. If we're in Dover, we'll pick you up at the DOVER BUS STATION! Heh heh. There are lots of interesting places around Milford (hah! What am I talking about!). Anyway, there's a <u>few</u> places I can show you... But we'll be walking, Charles and I don't drive. But, it's not a very big town... so it'll be easy enough. "Jimtown" ought to interest you... Tha's where all the negros live... You'll really see some colorful characters around that neighborhood.

Lessee... What else around here is interesting... Hmmm... All I do mostly is sit around the house and draw, read, write letters, or play records... or walk downtown and read magazines in the stores... I anxiously await trips out of town, to the cities... Milford's so dead, like most small towns... Nothin' but nothin' to do! The daily visit by the mailman is a big event... I wait in suspense for letters and packages.

Anyway, your visit ought to be interesting... and a change from the humdrum existence.

The *Our Gang* number one is copyrighted 1942, but has no month dated on it.

The "Oh Gee! Oh Gosh!" that I have isn't the one you think it is... The subtitle in parenthesis is "My Feet Won't Behave"... not "Oh Golly I'm in Love"... but it's still good! Send the *Raggedy Ann and Andy* when you can.

Say, did I tell you I got a pre-Trend[2] recently from a friend... *Dandy Comics* no. seven, 1948. Want it? Is in good condition.

Don't forget to send the other stuff you said you'd loan me... What is among the stuff?

Boy, you got some more grand records... I never knew so many LPs were put out with re-recordings. I'd really like to send for some of the Camden LPs you listed... They're 1.98's I suppose. Do they have covers? If so, what's on them?

I've got one of the 78s you mentioned... The Cliff Edwards "It Had to Be You" and "California." Got it from Bill Garbutt.

I saw a 1931 movie the other night... a comedy starring Marie Dressler... Really interesting. I studied every scene it showed. Some were views of streets and parts of towns. Really kept my eyes glued to the TV set.

We'll really have some tapes to send to each other! You've gotten some great stuff to put on another tape for me. And I've gotten lots of old records to record... Some of them are cracked and could break any day now... I'd like also to get them on a tape for myself. We can do some recording when you visit.

I think you're right... I did get clipped on those records... But I think someday... music lovers will pay <u>more</u> than 25 cents for alot of 'em... And after I get them all on tape, I may be able to sell them at a profit sometime in the future... I just wish I could get the same volume on tape as the records have originally... On tape the music sounds muffled or something... I'd liked to record them on LPs at a recording studio... That'd be the perfect thing!

Anyway, I got a bunch of old records again last Friday, July 17... They range from poor to very good. (I'm glad I'm getting to Carroll's early these last few weeks. There are still more where those records came from!)

---

[2] EC comics before the New Trend imprint.

Got 24 this time. I'll list them...

Large size twelve inch records:

—1. "Rambler Rose" / "Leave it to Jane" - Joseph G. Smith & His Orchestra - Victor

—2. "Possum Supper at Darktown Church" - Victor - Vaudeville Company with Orchestra / "Barn Dance Medley: 'Cuddle Up a Little Closer,' 'Starlight Maid,' 'When You Steal a Kiss or Two'" - Arthur Pryor's Band - Victor

—3. "Cuban Moon" / "Ziegfeld Folies of 1920" - Joseph G. Smith's Orchestra - Victor

—4. "Allah's Land" / "Tulip Time" (from "Follies of 1919") - Sherbo's Orchestra - Columbia

Regular size records:

—5. "Laughs You Have Met" (vocal) - Evans, Moule, Augarde, Farkda and Shepard / "Ticklish Reuben" - Carl Stewart with orchestra (comedy songs) - Victor

[...]

alot of good ones among these... I'll include them with the other ones I got on a future tape.

You're right about having to play records three or four times to appreciate them... Just about all the ones I got July 10th are growing on me, after several playings... And some of this latest find are too... Well... this's brief... I'm gettin' down to the library tonight...

INK BLOT TEST

BOB CRUMB

September 2, 1959
Milford, Delaware

[...]

BE IN GOOD CONDITION, OR I DON'T WANT
IT! I'LL SEND TH' TWENTY CENTS WITH THIS, ALONG
WITH 25 FOR SQUATRONT... SEND BACK THE
20 IF TH' FELIX IS IN BAD SHAPE. I'LL
GIVE YOU 15 CENTS FOR POGO PARADE,
BEING AS I'VE ALREADY GOT IT, BUT I'D LIKE
TO HAVE IT IN BETTER CONDITION. TAKE
IT OR LEAVE IT. I'LL SEND 15 WITH THIS
TOO!
    i GOTS POGOS 1, 3, 4, ■ 6, 7, 8, 9, 10, 11, 12,
13, 14, AND 15..... ALL IN EXCELLENT CONDITION,
'CEPT NO. 1 GOT NO COVER.
    I CAN GET ALL ANIMAL COMICS FROM 45
THRU '48, AND WILL GET 'EM SOONS I GET
THE MONEY,
    CHARLES HAS GOT ALL DISNEYS NOVEMBER
'47 THROUGH DECEMBER '52, ALL IN GOOD
CONDITION.
    KEEP YOUR EYE OUT FOR LULUS 1950 'N'
UNDER.
    WE GOT LOTSA COMICS, BUT I DON'T
FEEL LIKE GOIN' THROUGH RIGHT NOW....
CHARLES GOT A STACK OF 45 'N 46 DISNEYS
TODAY... PLUS "THE THREE CABALLEROS" COM-
PLETELY BY KELLY.... BEAUTIFUL WORK! (49 & 45)
SOME OF KELLY'S BEST WORK, FROM FRONT
TO BACK COVER COMPLETELY BY KELLY!

(JEWELS)

WELL, ANYWAY....
WE WALKED OUR
FEET OFF AT
PHILLY 'N' ONLY
GOT A FEW ECs....
ABOUT 10. ALL
PERFECT CONDITION
15 CENTS EACH.

AFTER THREE UNCERTAIN YEARS IN
DEAR OL' MILFORD, DEL.... WE FINALLY ARE
LEAVING.... I HOLD NO REGRETS, FOR
MYSELF.... MILFORD NEVER GAVE ME
ANYTHING TO BE THANKFUL FOR, AND GAVE
ME ALOT TO HATE IT FOR... I'LL BE GLAD
TO LEAVE MILFORD AND ALL ITS IGNORANCE
AND PREJUDICE.... DOVER, WHERE OUR NEW
HOUSE IS... IS AT LEAST AN IMPROVEMENT
OVER MILFORD... WITH A GOOD SIZE LIBRARY
AND TWO COLLEGES. MAYBE I'LL FIND SOME
ONE WITH MY INTERESTS IN DOVER!

LIVING IN MILFORD HAS BEEN A HINDER TO ME AND NOT ONE BIT OF A HELP! GOOD RIDDANCE TO TH' TOWN AND MOST OF THE PEOPLE IN IT!

A FEW THINGS I DON'T LIKE ABOUT GOING TO DOVER:

1. ADJUSTING TO A NEW SCHOOL. THIS IS MY BIGGEST WORRY.

2. WE ARE LIVING OUT IN THE STICKS NO NEARER THAN A MILE FROM ANY PLACE IMPORTANT. (THE CLOSEST BEING CARROLL'S MARKET)

3. I'M WORRIED ABOUT SOME OF MY STUFF GETTING DAMAGED IN THE PROCESS OF MOVING.

BUT ON THE WHOLE, IT'LL BE A LOT BETTER THAN STAYING HERE IN MILFORD!

OUR ADDRESS ARE SEPTEMBER TWELVETH WILL BE ROUTE ONE, OAK DRIVE, DOVER DELAWAR'

GET'NA BOX!   ERF!

WELL I BEEN SICK.

THAT CHARACATURE OF YOU THAT JULES FIEFFER DID AIN'T SO HOT! I CAN DO A BETTER ONE MYSELF!

SAY..... YOU KNOW I BEEN TO SEE STAN LYNDE. (PRONOUNCED "LINED") MEBBE PAHLS SHOWED YOU THAT LONG STORY OF TH' TRIP I WROTE TO HIM... IT TELLS ABOUT TH' WHOLE THING. YOU STILL WANT THAT ARTICLE?

HMMM

SO I HEAR YOU'RE NOT GOING TO
FORMOSA, EY? SO MAYBE I COME UP
AND VISIT YOU DURING CHRISTMAS
VACATION, EY? SO MAYBE? HUH? WE
TALK 'BOUT OL' TIMES 'N' STUFF? DRAW
PICTURES 'N' THINGS? HUH? HUH? 'N'
THEN WE HAVE AN ARGUEMENT 'N' I
LEAVE? (HEH HEH)

ME 'N' YOU..... BITTER ⬛ ENEMIES TO
TH' END... EEEYAAAH!

R. CRUMB
TH' TEENAGELESS
TEENAGER.....
(MY GLASSES ARE BROKEN)

Dear Marty:

Got a little item at Carroll's market yesterday that you might be interested in... *Heroic Comics* November 1945... nearly perfect condition... I'll list th' contents...

Cover is a painting by Harvey Fuller (?)
First story (4 p.) by Alexander Toth[1]
Second story (4 p.) by Harvey Fuller
Third story (2 p.) no name signed
Fourth story (3 p.) by Toth
Fifth story (4 p.) by "C. B."
1 pager (1 p.) Toth
6th story (6 p.) Woody Gelman
7th story (6 p.) C. W. Winter

You interested maybe? If not, you know anyone who might be?
Picked up some other interesting items yesterday:
A little set of paperback storybooks by Frank King (really illustrated by him... it says so on the first page of each...)
Skeezix and Uncle Walt © 1924
Skeezix and Pal © 1925
Skeezix at the Circus © 1926
Skeezix out West © 1928
Boy, sure is neat artwork! Perfect condition!
Pogo Possum no. two.
Say, you left some clothes here... We will send 'em to you. Also I'll send th' stuff you left behind in the envelope... Don't forget to send those two records... in exchange for the one I gave you... I'm gonna write to that one bookstore where we got the ECs... I bet they have everything for comic and magazine collectors there! (For a price). Eeyaah!
Say... I found *Famous Funnies*, no. one, 1934, perfect condition an'... an'... an'... LIES!
Keep yer eyes peeled for *Little Lulu*, 1950 'n' under and *Felix* 1946 'n' under. Will appreciate it.

---

[1] Alex Toth, an "artist's artist" renowned for his elegantly designed, minimalist artwork, began his career as an artist for Eastman Color / Famous Funnies and moved on to work for National, Dell, Warren, and other publishers. Most of the latter part of his career, beginning in 1960, was spent creating designs for Saturday morning cartoons.

I must go down to the sea again and see the communists. The communists sit on the beaches and mend lobster pots. J. Carroll Nash is their leader. Paul Robison is a commie too, according to Marty Schnieder. Me, I'm a clod. As a conformist, so am I. The floor looks like a mirror with basketball tickets on it. Crumb's a bum. So's Britt. (It must be glands). I once had the "GIs"... not only once but many a time. He is a GI; it runs (ick) in the family. The crumbs on the chair raise my hair. Britt Michaels is cracking up. There's alot of trash in hash. The red and blue color birds of the misty mornings among popcorn and old transfer stubs in the public square of childhood mornings. If heat keeps rising, what will become of Hell? Cable Mable a sable, Abel? Coffee in a cup; eyes in a head; water in the brook; Pahls on the walls. Crosslegged reading wild Basil Wolverton halfway up skyscrapers in dusty halls of adolescence. Marty Pahls is sick! So's Britt. I give up!

Your Vigor for Life Appalls Me

Dear Marty:

We'll send your clothes off to you soon, sometime this week...

Perty good work in th' comic section of your last letter...

I got a kick out of the picture of the segregationists in action and the sign ENTERING MILFORD, A FRIENDLY CITY... Well, they started some negros in the first grade at the white school... Opening day there was a reporter with a camera waiting around to see if there would be trouble 'n' get in on the scene for his paper, but the day passed with no trouble and the reporter went home disappointed... There was alot of griping and grumbling about it...but nobody roused the "nigger-haters" to the point of a mob. If there had been one fiery enough in the school to rouse hatred, you can bet there would have been plenty trouble!

Boy, I'd like to have some o' those records you got recently... "Me and My Shadow"... "Hallelujah!"...by The Astorites, sounds good...

"Charleston," by Whiteman... Lucky little nobody, you!

"Mountain Greenery"... "Sleepy Time Gal"... All favorites of mine! Just send them with your next letter, okay? (joke, heh, heh, sob)

I haven't gotten the list of X label records for you yet, but I will soon... possibly tomorrow, 'tis raining today... There's alot of other re-recordings of jazz too, one called *Blackbirds of 1928* I think is a "repressing"...

I recall one or two Riverside LPs, also...

Say, send a few *Life* mags 'n' *Judge* mags for the *Heroic Comics* (good condition) and the Dandy Comics.

I like those *Skeezix* books quite a bit myself. Me thinks I'll keep 'em...

Yes, I have the address of Reedmor Bookstore. It's 607 Market Street Philly, of course... Speaking of Reedmor, my mother took Charles and I to Philly a couple of weeks ago. The guy that was supposed to be "sick" last time we went was there at the bookstore when we went... We didn't get over twenty comics but it was a pretty good bunch, the ones we did get... rare ones, like I got three '46 *Little Lulus*... *Albert and Pogo* '46... Charles got the original *Snow White* comic, 1944... with a cover by Kelly... *Bambi's Children*, 1943, sixty-eight pages... *Bambi* 1948... We paid plenty for these though... Also Charles got several *Disney's* and a couple *Donald Duck* comics... While in Philly Charles got some original soundtracks from Disney's full-length cartoons *Snow White*, *Pinocchio*, *Bambi*, *Sleeping Beauty*, *Cinderella*, and *Song of the South*... Most of them are pretty good.

I got *Only Yesterday* from the town library... 'S a good book, just what the worshipper of the past ordered... 'S really interesting, informative, and colorful... I'd like to do a sort of a comic strip on events and people of America's past, or even a magazine about America's people and events of the past and present.

Goshes, when is *Fanfare* no. three gonna come out?... If you don't get it out soon, they'll only be three issues out this year! Shocking, my boy... shocking indeed!... But mainly, I wanna see "Winnie the Phoo"! (Sob)

Say, you heard from Doug Brown recently?... "We're going to have some fun with the new *Spoof*!"... That's what the clod said in *Spoof* number four... It wasn't too much fun waiting for "the new *Spoof*" and it never showed up anyway!

I don't know about getting the *Animal Town Comics* thing photostated. I have to find out about it somewhere here in Dover.

I'm looking forward to getting those records you're sending... I've just about worn out all the ones I have...

I have a good art class here at Dover... It's an extra long period, and the art teacher does a very meticulous job at teaching art... almost as good as art at college, from what I know about it... Of course, it seems a little bit over-serious to me but I s'pose I'll get over that... He goes into the subject of painting very deeply... and it is quite a change over the liberal method of teaching at Milford, and the puny art department and lack of art interest there. There are at least a few kids interested in art here...

All in all I have a fairly easy school day, two study halls a day, history, which I enjoy (U.S. history it is), English, in which I also have an interest, typing and math, I don't like at all. For these subjects I have the same teacher, the only woman teacher I have, and an obnoxious human besides... I'd like to have sketching two hours five days a week. I'll bet that's enjoyable... Is the teacher strict or liberal, does he give the kids much freedom to sketch what they want?

Say, you still have that letter I wrote you describing the Stan Lynde visit. If you do I'd like to borrow it for a while... I want to use it for the article on Stan Lynde for Britt... There's alot of stuff in that letter that is good info for the article but I've forgotten it myself now, so, okay?

LATER I got downtown today 'n' got a list of the remaining jazz records I thought you'd be interested in at that place... Some of them were gone, much to my surprise... but I'll list the ones I could find...

Great Jazz Brass — This isn't X but I thought you might be interested in it anyway. Most of these aren't X, but anyways... This one has King Oliver... Louis Armstrong, Jack Teagarden, Wingy Manone, 'n' others...

Jazz Digest on the Period label...

Blackbirds of 1928 Duke Ellington, Ethel Waters, Mills Brothers 'n' others — Review

Fats Waller *Ain't Misbehavin'* — RCA. This is definitely rerecordings

Riverside Dixieland Sampler... one song from each of the Riverside LPs...

A *String of Swingin' Pearls* — In this one are Frank Trumbauer, Eddie Condon, Bud Freeman, 'n' others.

At the Jazz Band Ball with the Dukes of Dixieland — X

Piano Jazz — Jelly Roll Morton, Alex Hill, Mary Lou Williams, J. J. Johnson, Frank Melrose — Brunswick

Well, that's all I could dig out now, I didn't have much time to look. You probably not innerested in any of these cause me, noodnik that I am, don't know much about jazz LPs like you do.

23 October 1959

Today I went to Carroll's Market...th' ol' Protestant minister who sells junk at atrocious prices had a bunch o' new stuff in this week including a coupla stacks of records, which I immediately went through and picked out the following

1. Little Dutch Mill
   "Riptide" — Guy Lombardo, Oriole — early '30s
2. "You Know You Belong to Somebody Else" /
   "Love Sends a Little Gift of Roses"
   —The Bar Harbor Society Orchestra Vocalion 1921
3. "Someone Is Thinking of You" /
   "The Sorrow of Pierrot" — Max Dolin's Orchestra
   — Vocalion 1921
4. "Fair One" /"I'd Love to Fall Asleep and Wake Up in My Mammy's Arms"
   — Benson Orchestra — Victor

5. "Buddha (My Own)" — Van Eps Quartet / "Afghanistan"
   — Selvin's Novelty Orchestra — Okeh
6. "The Road to Bally Rae" — Reed Miller /"The Minstrel Boy"
   — Charles Hart — Vocalion 1921
7. "The Cup of Forgiveness" / "Olimpica" — Max Dolin's Orchestra
   — Vocalion 1921
8. "Oh!" / "Mystery!" — Paul Biese and His etc. — Victor
9. "On Miami Shores" / "Now I Know" — Joseph Knecht's Waldorf Astoria
   Dance Orchestra — Okeh
10. "The Buffalo Rag" — Vess L. Ossman with Orchestra
    — Victor (one sided)
11. "'Somebody's Sweetheart' and 'Good Morning, Judge': Medley One-Step"
    — Joseph G. Smith / "'Oh My Dear!': Medley Fox Trot" — Victor
12. "Carolina Sunshine" / "Oh What a Pal was Mary!" — Prince's Orchestra
    — Columbia
13. "The Lovelight in Your Eyes" / "Down in Maryland" — The Boardwalk
    Orchestra — Vocalion 1921.
    (You have this one on your list)
14. "By A Waterfall" / "True" — Guy Lombardo — Okeh, early 30s
15. "Lola Lo" / "Three O'clock in the Morning" — Joseph G. Smith's
    Orchestra — Victor
16. "When Hearts are Young" / "Journey's End" — The Bar Harbor Society
    Orch. — Vocalion, 1921.

I managed to bring the price down to ten cents apiece for these after arguing with the miserly ol' preacher for ten minutes... That pious (supposedly) ol' bird charged a lady a dollar fifty for a beat-up ol' birdcage ... 'n' charged a coupla poor negros four dollars for some rags... The husband was disgusted with the price but the wife bought 'em 'n' handed over th' money... for a few dirty ol' RAGS!!! God, what a robber!

Our record player is being fixed right now... I haven't had a chance to play any o' these yet... Alot of 'em had cases, the Guy Lombardo cases had little NRA emblems on 'em... That's how I figured they're early '30s... sometime before 1935, when th' NRA died.

Britt wants me to visit him this Christmas... I'd shore like to see th' clod again after over a year of not seein' him... Mebbe if I save my money... 'course I'm not working now so it'll be sort of a Christmas present, I guess... I'll go after Christmas, which will allow me about five days to visit... I'll visit you come next summer, 'n' Britt again, too...

About the magazine... it seems Charles has lost enthusiasm and is backing down, which means that he won't be doing any work in it, an' won't be putting in any of the cost... Me, not being able to work now cuz of school... looks like we'll have to cancel our plans... at least till I can possibly talk Charles into coming back into it... He's spending money on records and is saving for a hi-fi, so... looks like our magazine plans are out the window for the time being, and maybe for quite a long time... I'd like to go into a magazine again, but there's the age-old problem of money...

When you go to Cleveland next 'n' get some *Life* mags for me (I hope) get a couple of the earliest you can find an' a couple of the newest, up to 1936, when *Life* died... I'd like to see some of the older and newer ones... Also a few in-between of course... I sure have alot of stuff I can thank you for... Yes, quite alot, an' I hope to have more, records, comics, *Life*, *Judge*, *Vanity Fair*, *Puck*... What am I saying!!!

Say,... are there any *Vanity Fair* or such at that place... I'll pay a fair price for any you find...

Well, guess tha's about all I can say this time... No much this time... I must close now and go pay homages at Yimmy's grave... Gubbye...

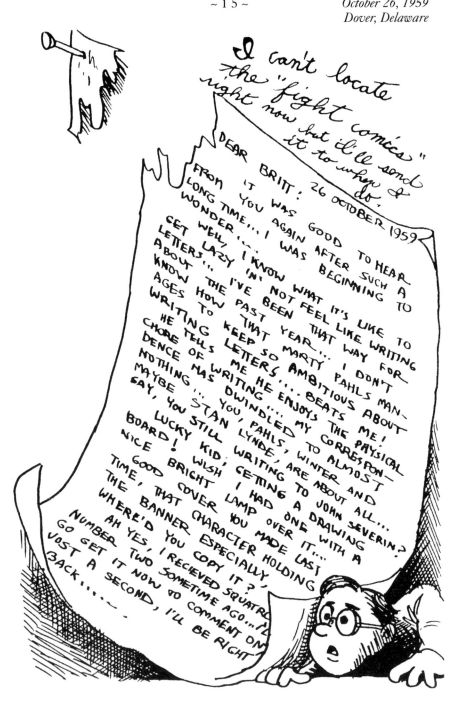

I can't locate the "fight comics" right now but it'll send it to when I do.

DEAR BRITT: 26 OCTOBER 1959

IT WAS GOOD TO HEAR FROM YOU AGAIN AFTER SUCH A LONG TIME... I WAS BEGINNING TO WONDER... WELL, I KNOW WHAT IT'S LIKE TO GET LAZY 'N' NOT FEEL LIKE WRITING LETTERS... I'VE BEEN THAT WAY FOR ABOUT THE PAST YEAR... I DON'T KNOW HOW TO KEEP SO AMBITIOUS ABOUT WRITING THAT MARTY PAHLS MAN-- HE TELLS ME HE ENJOYS THE CHORE OF WRITING LETTERS... BEATS ME! DENCE OF MY CORRESPON-- NOTHING HAS DWINDLED TO ALMOST MAYBE... YOU, PAHLS, WINTER AND SAY, YOU STAN LYNDE, ARE ABOUT ALL... LUCKY KID, WRITING TO JOHN SEVERIN? BOARD! I WISH I HAD ONE STILL GETTING A DRAWING NICE BRIGHT LAMP OVER IT... GOOD COVER YOU MADE LAST TIME, THAT CHARACTER HOLDING THE BANNER ESPECIALLY WHERE'D YOU COPY IT? AH YES, I RECIEVED SQUATRO NUMBER TWO SOMETIME AGO...I GO GET IT NOW TO COMMENT ON VOST A SECOND, I'LL BE RIGHT BACK...

I'll start at the proper place, the cover... The caricature of Mike Britt by Jules Feiffer just doesn't look like the Mike Britt I once knew... I never cared much for Feiffer myself, but you're doing good, my boy... at least you're getting BIG NAMES... That's what counts, isn't it?

Your letter and layout, I notice, are getting more professional...

"Book Review" was good, keep it up. Maybe you'll come up with a book that I might be interested in.

The caricature on page seven looked a little more like you than the one on the cover... But if it didn't say that it was Mike Britt in the text, I never would have known... Know what I mean?

Your little story "Talking with Jules Fieffer" (Feiffer) was amusing and entertaining... I think you're developing into a fairly good writer, with a pretty easy style that isn't hard to read... Keep it up!

Page ten and eleven didn't interest me too much... How do you reproduce the drawings by Feiffer in ditto?... Looks like it'd be a pretty painstaking job. Well, anyway, those two pages might be prized by Feiffer bugs, which I am not... To me it seemed a waste of space...

I'm glad to see Kravitz has regained his good name by making up for that lowly article in number one by doing a fairly good job this time... The Kurtzman interview was a little more lively and interesting.

By the way, have you seen *Kurtzman's Jungle Book*?[1] 'Tis a good collection of stories it is... really good, in fact... There's wit, and plenty of human interest in Kurtzman's comical style... I really like the li'l book... If you haven't seen it, you ought to soon as you can... While I think of it, have you seen any new *Pogo* books since *G. O. Fizzickle*? If you have, please let me know...

I haven't read *Free Lancers for EC* yet, and probably never will. I looked over the artist's signatures to the side of the page and didn't find anybody I was particularly interested in, but, for most fans, I imagine it's good and informative.

Say, I'll break away from this again for a minute to tell you while it's in my mind that I have a copy of *Heroic Comics* with Alexander Toth, a couple stories, in fact... mint condition, November 19...45... "Truly a prize" as Marty says... What you gives?

Now back to *Squatront*... No wait... I got a *Prize Comics Western* at Carroll's Market recently, mint condition... July-August 1952... cover by Severin, Elder... first story by Severin, Elder... second story by Severin and Elder, third story is by some unknown noodnik... You want? If so, what you gives?

Now back to *Squatront*... I skipped over "Info"... By the by, Davis did a cute little caricature of Wally Cox (Mr. Peepers) recently... nifty, boy... I past-

---

[1] A collection of four satirical "graphic novellas" by Kurtzman, published as an original paperback. An improved edition (shot from the original artwork) was released in 1986 by Kitchen Sink Press.

ed it in one of my *Almanac*s. It was in the *Philadelphia Inquirer* a while back... I'll show it to ya when I visit (we'll talk about that later).

I enthusiastically looked over "The Collector's Corner" hoping to find something I need, but all I find is a big fat column o' stuff that I collect that you called "Wanted by Mike Britt"... (blurch, I feel sick) an' a bunch o' lists of ECs... I'm collecting 'em now you know 'n' got a fairly good stack at the present time... Up in Philly I got alot... an' when I got that 1950 *Weird Fantasy* no. 16 in mint condition and two of the special Civil War *Two Fisted Tales* at five cents each at Carroll's, I was persuaded to collect all ECs... I'm not going to be an addict about it, but just take 'em as I find 'em and save them all... I have every issue of *MAD* in good condition now. I replaced quite a few *MAD* mags with ones in better shape... Sure is a good feeling to know I have 'em all... When I think of that *MAD* rampage we went on in 9th grad, <u>WIS</u>!!

NOW BACK TO *SQUATRONT*...

The letter column of any fanzine is always good... and sometimes the best part of a mag (not in *Squatront*, though you do a fairly good job on the rest of the "zine").

I always enjoy the letters... Severin's was a scream... really a zany bit... That one from R. Crumb was my favorite, though.

Putting a surplus first issue cover on the back was unnecessary but it did make the issue a little thicker, I guess.

Well, so much for *Squatront*... All 'round it was about the same as number one, with only a slight improvement.

I don't think you should go half size... You say things are gonna be different next time... in the next issue... Just how are things gonna be different, huh? huh?

Say, send me about ten carbon sheets and I'll do a bunch o' stuff for *Squatront*, mebbe a cover 'n' a story 'n' stuff... Charles thanks you for sendin' the Robert Newton stuff 'n' says that if you ever find any more similar material to send it to him, okay? He isn't going to do a Long John Silver story because he doesn't think you'll ever get another issue of *Squatront* out... and he docsn't want to waste his time doing a story that will never be printed. Tha's what he says, besides, he's lazy.

I just hope you get a third issue out a little sooner than you got this issue out... I think that would be an improvement itself, don't you? I'm gettin' tired of waiting six months for fanzines that are s'posed to be out in "a month or so" as they all say.

Say, give me a definite statement on whether the next issue is gonna be large or half size, so I know what size to make the stuff if you send carbons, okay?

Thanks for the *Felix*, it filled in the gap between Aug.Sept. 1949 and Dec.Jan. 1950... It's not in such hot shape but good enough for now.

Thanks for offering the March '49 *Disney*, but Charles already has it.

He has the complete years of '48, '49, and '50 and '51 and only needs 3 from '46 and is getting Dec. '46 soon, only needs November of '52 and needs Feb., March, May, June and July to complete '47 and has four from '45 and two from '44 and Jan. '42. All the ones he has are in good shape, too. An' he also has a fabulous *Donald Duck* collection, by the way... Recently Charles got the musical soundtracks from several of the Disney full-length cartoons... *Snow White, Pinocchio, Bambi, Dumbo, Song of the South, Cinderella, Peter Pan* and *Sleeping Beauty*, boy, they sure sound good... These are the original soundtracks, y' know... Get that straight!

If you have access to a tape-recorder me 'n' Charles'll make a tape for you 'n' send up... We can borrow one from Latex and we have several tapes 'n' we could lend you one 'n' if it's possible you could record some of your gab 'n' send it back, hokey? Be sure to let us know.

I'll try to get up to visit you this Christmas vacation... I hope ours is as long as yours... I sure hope I can make it... We sure have alot to talk about... I'll bring along some of our old stuff... the *Almanac*s, school logue, little note-books 'n' stuff. I think I'll be able to make it... Th' paying of traveling expenses will be a Christmas present from my parents (I hope) being as since school started, I had to quit working.

I'll enclose the *Fight Comics* here. I wrote it down here so's I don't forget. Don't forget to send the 35 cents next time... I'm hard up for every cent I can get... Maybe I oughta get out 'n' sell some surplus *Foo* mags (only a few hundred left). That'd get me some cash.

Well, there's not much to tell about Marty's visit... We showed him all around that cruddy little town of Milford... had lots of long discussions about everything, including you and your ways. We took him up to Carroll's Market 'n' made a big strike that day... He was kind of disgusted with the whole set-tup and the place in general of Carroll's Market... Can't say I blame him... We had a good pillow fight 'n' Charles 'n' I turned the whole mattress of Charles' bed over on him... What o' laugh that was... Yimmy, one of our cats died on my birthday, 'n' Marty was here for the birthday... We all ran out the first night he was here to a car smash-up, some drunks pushed another car up into the Coscerrelli's front porch... One night the power went out 'n' we

CLICK

fooled around with candles for about two hours...

We had the tape recorder 'n' messed around with all the time till we got sick of it... We went up to Philly the last day he was here but didn't get much even if we did walk our feet off from 13th to 6th street... Canvassing the blocks, snooping in all the bookstores... My mother took Charles 'n' me up to Philly just recently 'n' we made quite a haul at one bookstore. (My source!)

We got quite a bit... I got three '46 *Little Lulu*s in mint condition, *Albert and Pogo* '46... Charles got the original *Snow White* (with a cover by Kelly) a bunch o' *Disney's* an' two '47 *Donald Duck*s plus two old *Bambi* comics...

We is gonna write to 'em one of these days 'n' get some more comics.

You wanted me to list all my comics with Kelly work in 'em... Hmmmm... Here goes...

Pogo - 1, 2, 3, 4, 6, 7, 8, 9, 10, 11, 12, 13, 14, 15, and 16
Animal Comics - 7, 13, 29
Our Gang - 1, 4, 10, 18, 19, 22, 26, 27, 28, 29, 35, 38, 47, 49, 50, 51, 53, 54
Santa Claus Funnies 1944, 1946, 1947, 1950...
Christmas with Mother Goose - '47
Raggedy Ann no. 3 and 4
Fairy Tale Parade 1946
Pinocchio

Well, that's all... Actually, it isn't as much as you seemed to have thought.

Charles got the soundtrack of *Blackbeard the Pirate* on tape recently when it was on TV... Now he can practice imitating Newton from first hand sound of Newton's voice... Not just from memory...

I've got a pretty good collection of 78 records now... About 75, I guess... ranging from turn of the century ragtime to early thirties orchestras... fox trots, jazz 'n' lots stuff... Pahls is gonna send some soon...

Say you know those hardcover Disney books like *Mickey Never Fails*... We have four of 'em beautifully illustrated like Disney cartoons... *Little Pigs' Picnic and Other Stories*... *Water Babies' Circus and Other Stories*... *Pinocchio* ... *Here They Are*... These books sure have neat illustrations... We also got recently *Pinocchio*, a large book with original scenes 'n' sketches by the Disney artists... Boy, 'tis beautiful... Also got *Mr. Toad* a big book with beautiful illos... All these we got at Carroll's for about two cents each... What luck! They're in good shape too!

Charles will trade March '46 and June '49 *Disneys* (good condition) for July '56 and January '57 if you have them in good condition... What say... God, Charles has got two stacks of *Walt Disney's Comics and Stories*, each a foot high... Hoo Boy!

He's got a stack of doubles almost a foot high...

Wattaya gonna do with all those Big Little Books... Use 'em for a bonfire 'n' toast marshmallows... Tha's th' best thing... The new house here in Dover is about the same as the one we lived in when we first came to Delaware... You remember it? It's like that only made out of brick and is on the outskirts of town... out in the woods... Whadda lousy setup... so far from town every time we want to go to town we have to wait till my mother goes shopping...

Haven't made any friends in school... There isn't anybody interested in cartoons... The art teacher sure is different from Kunkle... real serious about painting 'n' real precise about everything...

I haven't got my report card yet, but I think I did good in everything but typing, which I hate as much as ever... I have it pretty easy in this school...

First period... history (U.S.) easy

Second period... study hall

Third... typing... blech

Fourth... math... blech

Fifth... art... okay, but hard.

In between fifth and sixth I have lunch, which isn't counted as a period

Sixth... English... not too hard...

Seventh... study hall... That's the whole school day... It sure seems to go fast... especially after lunch... I got out of phys. ed... I hated it... Sure is a relief not to have it... Playin' football with a buncha noodniks... Phooey on gym!

We were thinking of going into another magazine and even had it all planned out with Marty 'n' we were going to have you in it and all but it just petered out... I'll explain in my next letter if I remember.

Gosh, you haven't got many ECs as I thought you had... Well looks like I'm running out of room so I'll just say so long and write soon and YOW!

Drear (Drear??)
Try again!
DEAR Britt:

Wowee... I'm glad I'm collectin' ECs now... Got two at Carroll's Market... *Crime Patrol* no. 16, February-March 1950, and *Tales from the Crypt* no. 37, August-Sept, 1953... Both in good condish... Hooboy... I was about to send you all my ECs when I got 'em...

I'm sorry I didn't mention it, but I already had the *Felix* 3-D... Thanks for the *Tom 'n' Jerry* though.

I'm saving the *Heroic Comics* and the *Prize Comics Western* for you... I'll send the *Heroic Comics* for the 1949 *Felix* if I can't find the *Fight Comics*...

Boy, those photos you sent... 'specially you and Delain 'n' Pahls... what a bunch o' clods! Delain looks like Stayton... kinda! Sure is a big clod... just like Stayton... Photos of people posing like that are obnoxious... You clods take the cake! As you can see... this cover is taken from that one o' you in th' car... People are noodniks... 'n' especially in posed photos. You haven't changed at all since the days before you left Milford! I'll send a school photo of myself when I gets 'em so's you can look at my obnoxious pan.

You were lucky to get the 1941 *Disney's*! Recently I got *Animal Comics* number 17... Kelly did the whole comic except the *Uncle Wiggily* story. The cover is a Kelly masterpiece. The cover has a maroon colored border around it. The stories he did inside were "Albert and Pogo," "Hector the Henpecked Rooster," "Cilly Goose," "Blacky the Lamb," and the one panel jokes... It's a 36-page comic but a prize... The stories by Kelly are typical of his nonsense.

Boy, am I being kept busy these days! Lottsa letters been coming in lately... I've been given several art jobs at school. The art teacher here is a good one... lot better'n Kunkle! He is educating the art class, not just telling them to do the projects. He's taken particular interest in me cuz I'm the only kid in the class who wants to make a career of art.

Right now I've got the job of designing the school emblem to go on the school jackets, got two Christmas posters to do, and a lady wants a painting done (a Christmas painting) which she will PAY ($$$) me for!! I just finished doing a painting for a high school play and caricatures of the three football coaches for some dance at school... So you can see I have my hands full these days.

I've seen *Twilight Zone*... I don't think it's so hot... It's good, I guess, but not THAT good!

Enclosed are some traced things... The *Disney* cover is August '45... honest, no lie... All the small tracings are from Kelly's *Three Caballeros*... You can tell Kelly worked for Disney... His animated style looks like scenes from cartoons, doesn't it?

Wowee! Gee! Can I have your autograph, Mr. Britt? I saw your name on the inside front cover of *Cracked* number twelve and I'm gonna start a Mike Britt fan club! All kidding aside, I think the cover of the latest *Cracked* is the worst thing Davis has ever done.

Thanks for the old car material... Appreciate you sending it as it will be popped into my reference files immediately.

I'm now (finally) in the process of doing the Stan Lynde article for you. You'll have to type it out on the masters yourself... I'll do a couple pictures on regular paper 'n' you can trace them onto the carbons. I'll probble have it ready by my next letter.

That Feiffer drawing of Ely doesn't look much like him... Evidently you didn't do too good a job of explaining Ely to him.

You... got... *Songs of Pogo*... you... lucky... lucky... no good... meek... cruddy... little nobody... I'm looking forward to seeing this on my visit.

February '47 *Disney* looks like a pretty neat cover... Describe the colors.

Hmmm... Davis's "Wacky Placs" are perty mizzuble... Davis must really be hard up for cash.

Recently we got a bunch of St. John three-D comics at Carroll's... All in perfect condition, the glasses were never even used... Lessee, there's five of 'em... Two *Mighty Mouse* comics, *Whack*, *Three Stooges*, and *Tor*... All the illustration in these is good. Better even than ordinary comics... They took special pains with these to give them a more powerful 3-D effect.

It wasn't Pahls who persuaded me to collect ECs... as I had told him in many letters previous to his visit, I'd collect ECs if I ever made a big strike, and got a whole bunch (cheap) at one time... Well, it just so happened that I did get a whole bunch cheap at the bookstore in Philly, while Pahls was visiting here... Actually, we didn't talk much EC while he was here... except about those Williamson originals he got in New York... I must admit they were good!

Yes, Marty is really a gabber... The minute he got off the bus he started in, and I didn't get a word in edgewise, hardly.

I'm glad you're not going to make *Squatront* small-size... If we'd have wanted to make *Foo* full-sized it would have cost exactly twice as much as it did!

[...]

'n' all the *Almanac*s 'n' little note books about getting the *MAD* mags 'n' stuff. I'll bring all 31 issues of *Almanac*... so you can see what we've been doing since you left last year.

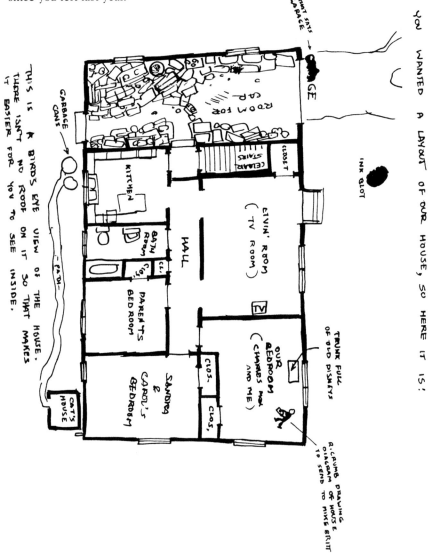

We've got *Donald Duck*, "Land of the Totem Poles" (good condition) for sale or trade if you want it. It's February 1950 and all 52 pages are illoed by the good *Donald Duck* artist (guy that draws *Scrooge* comics)[1].

I like the idea of doing a big scene of bristle board with tempera paints... That ought to be fun... I've been working alot in tempera lately, and this idea of yours is a good one... In fact, maybe I'll do something like this on my own right here at home (if I can swipe the 'quipments from school).

Yeah, our visit this Christmas should be quite enjoyable... We can get in a nice bitter argument over some trivial 'n' not speak to each other for 'bout a day an'... an'... an'... we can read the school logue and our faces turn red, 'n' talk about kids in Milford 'n' fandom 'n' Pahls 'n' Stayton 'n' cartoons 'n' people 'n' life an'... an'... an'...

I ain't comin'! (ha ha joke)

You're right! I don't never do no homework! (My English proves it) What little homework I do get I do in one study hall. I only get homework in two subjects... math and English... The other three are all non-homework classes... Glad I don't have to go to some rough school like you! Har!

Almanac number 31 is the last issue. I'm changing the title to *Arcade*, which I think is better. *Almanac* is too dull.

Did I tell you Charles bought a hi-fi-stereo recently. Records sure sound good on it!

HMM, SO WHAT ELSE IS NEW? Except that Charles and I are leaving the Catholic Church. We've discovered some facts which pretty well prove it (the Church) to be wrong in many things. I won't go into these facts here. They're much too deep to go into.

..........................Well, at any rate..
hmmm..
I seem to be running out of things to say...

You got many friends out there? Know anybody who's interested in cartoons in your school? Nobody except me who's interested in cartoons in Dover High School. Ah, the cartoonist is indeed a rare breed.

You still in contact with Jerry Keating?

Got a galfriend?

I don't.

---

[1] Carl Barks, the highly acclaimed Donald Duck artist and creator of Uncle Scrooge, wrote and drew original Donald Duck stories for Dell's *Walt Disney's Comics & Stories* for 22 years, from 1943 until his retirement in 1965.

Your Vigor for Life Appalls Me

Dear Marty:

That cover on your last letter was neat... Except for the sloppiness, the coloring was good... I think it was the combinations... The cover has an attractive appearance... good lettering.

Thanks for compliments on the "Hey Dinkle Book" and "The Brombos"... You shure poured 'em on thick! Kind of surprised me that you thought they were so good... I didn't know they were so wonderful until you told me...

Yes, the "Hey Diddle" is copied from Kelly's system in his books... Actually, we got the idea from the *Pogo* books. I've just taken up the book-reading habit about this past year... I've read some of Dickens' (*Tale of Two Cities, Pickwick Papers, Christmas Carol*). I like his stuff, but I think my favorite writer is Mark Twain... His work holds a charm and color for me. He puts it down simply and clearly, yet in a pleasant way that I like.

Anyway... I'm glad you liked our stuff so much, it certainly makes me proud to know that you and your friends there enjoyed it. Of course, I hope to improve 100 percent before I start my professional career... About schooling... I'm yet undecided... I know I need it, but I'm so discustingly lazy, I probably won't have enough money when the time comes, nor the ambition to work my way through... I hope I get up enough ambition in the next few years, but I doubt it.

Right now I'm listening to an LP I got yesterday. It's called *Quarterlodeons*... recordings of nickelodeons, eleven different ones... They're all owned by a guy in California who charges a quarter to play 'em (thus the title).

These nickelodeons are comprised of pianos, mandolins, drums, triangles and everything else under the sun... The way they sound is uniquely mechanical... sometimes grotesque and weird... I don't think too many people appreciate the way they sound nowadays... (they were popular in the 1880s and '90s) but I like them... (typical of my obscure tastes) I don't know if you'd like the record or not... Mebbe I'll put one tune from the record on a future tape when I send one.

Did I tell you about the book I got at the state library called *Cartoon Cavalcade* by Thomas Craven... comprised in 1944... Ever seen it?.. It's a history of cartoons from the 1880s to 1944... The format is this... He has a few pages of text before each chapter telling about the famous cartoonists from each era... and about the attitudes and philosophies of that time. The chapters then have about a hundred pages of reprints of the best cartoons of the era... The names of the chapters are:

1883-1916 American Humor and the New Century
1916-1932 World War One and the Impudent Decade
1933-1943 The New Deal

'Tis really a good book, giving a pretty clear picture of the cartoon history of 1883 to 1943 (alot has happened since then that could take up a whole book!... Thomas Craven has nothing about comic books, they were still too young then, I suppose). Anyway... the reprints are from all the famous cartoon magazines... *Life, Judge, Vanity Fair...* also the famous comic strips, newspaper one-panel cartoons... books by cartoonists... several of the magazine cartoons are in some of the *Life*s and *Judge*s you sent me! This book even has scenes from Disney cartoons in it! It doesn't go into animated cartoons much though.

Things are sure piling up on you, aren't they. I guess college is pressuring you into dropping your fandom activities pretty much... I think you'll probably drop out entirely by your senior year, having only a few correspondents left, tha's what I'd venture to say.

I like your idea of us all getting together in New York next summer... You've got alot of initiative that I wish I had... I'd of never been brave enough to think of something like this... but I like the idea... I'm all for it, myself... I just hope I'll have the money... I think I will... I'll probably have a job at Latex waiting for me when school lets out (fortunately) and after working a couple weeks, I'll have more than enough money for the excursion. It's going to take some planning to get us all to New York and get us together there. I guess Ivie (ol' bwah) could meet us as we come... Does he know his way around New York very well? That's something I hope to be able to do in about fifteen years.

You know the cartoon you made of me is really funny! It looks like me, in a cloddy way that's effective... It gave me quite a good laugh... So did that "deadline"... 36 Nov. 1928... You is just picky on me!

Blackbirds of 1928 is 3.98... You gonna send money for it... If you do... send it with, please, a list of instructions called "How to Wrap and Mail LPs"... I'm afraid somepin' might happen to it through the mail.

This integration society you joined sounds interesting... Who knows, it may cause enough commotion to become a national event... like the Dayton trial in 1924 over evolution (Clarence Darrow vs. W.J. Bryan)

You know, one o' those type events... caused by experiments in a national problem... like what your society is doing... Those little experiments you're carrying out sound both interesting and amusing... It seems it would bring out into the open the phoniness of alot of people. You know, some bartender, real swell guy to everybody, then you find out he snubs certain people. Well, when you get right down to it, it's nobody's fault if they're prejudiced. After all... if they were bought up in a family of "nigger-haters"... then it's not their fault if it's been molded into them... and it'll take a mighty lot of influences to change what's been molded into a person... So, you really can't be disgusted with prejudiced people, I suppose... They can't change their way of thinking...

Matter of fact, when you think about it, there's no such thing as sin, or evil. Nobody is responsible for their actions... Their way of thinking is formed by their environment and every influence throughout their life... Think about this! If this theory, which when you think about it... seems to be more fact than philosophy... if this theory is right... then the whole Catholic philosophy of Hell and the Devil seems ridiculous... Eternal punishment in a hell for "sins" that you weren't responsible for committing... This is wrong... Could a just and merciful God be so cruel?... It makes the Church's theories seem medieval, out of date... Do you see the point? Man does anything to please himself... Everything he does is to satisfy that inner spirit... whether it be right or wrong... and his way of thinking, his ideas which his environment and influences (and heredity, to some extent) have formed, determine what will please his inner spirit, the inner master, most of all. Catch on? This makes the "free will" theory wrong... Man has no free will... He is merely a product of his environment and influences... He does what they lead him to do... not what he chooses to do, but what will please his inner master the most... And you can only do what will please your inner master... according to your way of thinking... be it right or wrong... To prove this... if you have free will, go right now and smash all your old records! You can't... because it wouldn't please your inner master. Catch on?

What do you think of this theory?

You know that bunch of records I got that I tole you about? Well, there's only a few good ones in the bunch. The "Buffalo Rag" is good... one of the best... It's just what you'd expect an old ragtime recording to sound like... I think you'd like it. On all the Vocalion records it says "copyright 1921 by the Aeolian Company"... I took this to mean that the records were made in 1921... am I wrong?

I wanted to see *The Five Pennies* but I didn't get a chance to... It hadn't yet come to Milford yet when we left there, but it had already been to the Dover theater... An unfortunate circumstance for me.

You're right! Reedmor charged plenty for the comics, they old hyster! From 75 cents to two dollars... 'Course, he didn't get away with it entirely... Charles saw an ol' *Disney* laying out that he didn't buy (too much) and while nobody was looking, he sorta.. heh heh... slipped it in with the stuff we bought... That guy at Reedmor deserved it... He's a robber his own self!

I've finished reading *Only Yesterday*... Good book... Just the kind of history book I like, sort of informal, putting in small things that aren't too important but help portray the times... I'm gonna write to Harper 'n' Brudders to find out if the book is still available to purchasers.

I've got two Currier & Ives books... One that's about the size and thickness of a large encyclopedia... The other is real big and wide, with a light brown cover, called *Currier and Ives' America*... The first one is older and has alot that's in the second one but much more besides... It contains lots political and other kinds cartoons... I bought this one at Carroll's Market, in good condition, for four and half dollars.

The other I got through the Readers' Guild for three ninety-eight... Real big, sort thin book... Did I show it to you when you were here... This one isn't as good as the older one.

— Please you Sir, if thou wouldst but tax thy memory this time, to send the letter of which I had given a lengthy and detailed description of my journey and stay at the generous invitation of the famous Stan Lynde... I would be grateful to you, kind Sir... If thou dost still possess the letter which I am wont of, to deliver in into my possession with your next letter... Do please try to keep this in your mind until such time as you desire to next correspond... In other words... send that letter about Stan Lynde trip that I wrote to ya, okay, bud?

The Sunday *Philadelphia Inquirer* "Rotocomics" (comic section) always has a full page on the back called "The World We Live In"... It always has colored photographs of a particular subject, with a brief story of the subject and captions under each photo... The Sunday of November first's "The World We Live In" was called "Trolly Cars of Yesterday"... Perfect for a trolley photo collection... Seven big full color photos of trolleys! Sure is neat! "Truly a prize!" (to quote Marty Pahls) I'll send it next time I send a large package of stuff... I don't want to fold it up too much... No, wait! I'll cut it up and send it with this... Of course, send it back when you's through...

By the way, I forgot to mention something... I'll send you back that letter after I get what information out of it that I need, okay?

I haven't got any records from you yet... Have you sent them? I hope so, I'm really anxious to get 'em! I'll try... really, I meanit! I'll try desperately to get your clothes off this week! (mainly cuz yos said you'd paid for the postage with a few items of interest to me... heh heh)

This is my second year of typing but I've never had much luck with it... Failed last year, and have this year so far too... I dunno... I git discouraged! I allus makin' errors... Either I try too hard not to, or I just don't try at all... I discusted! It amazes me... You enjoy writing you say!... That I can't understand... but it's evident enough... Your letters are always nice and long! I've put all your letters into stapled books of approximately twenty pages each! This isn't hard to do since all your letters are approximately the same size... I've got six books so far... Keep sending your letters all the same size... as I plan to keep making books... They're quite a collection, I might add... You're a good writer and getting better! Your writing is like reading a newspaper sometimes... This will get you places! Just exactly what do you plan to do after college... Do you have anything definite in mind at all? I don't. I may end up being a philosophical bum... even (horror of horrors!) a white collar accountant... (choke!) How could anybody stand such a job... I dread the thought... but that's life... cold, harsh life... looking at it realistically...

I hope you get the "*MAD* Checklist" plugged and successful... It'll be a revolution in fandom... more Tom Teagues, Ron Hesses, Jim Belchers, R. Crumbs, Sig Cases... and maybe one or two Marty Pahlses! (Your type are a rare breed, I think)

Have you ever seen any of the *Art Seminars* books... My art teacher says they're good for anyone who wants to understand painting (fine art). If you do, I recommend it! Our art teacher has them... They're kinda deep but you'd understand what they say with some thinking... They're to help people appreciate painting (high class painting). I've seen them and read parts of 'em... Good books... For further details you can look in the latest *Esquire* (the one with the neat Kurtzman article in it). I wish I could subscribe to this *Art Seminars* myself but I'm flat broke... It costs $3.75 a month and you get a book with twelve color plates of famous paintings every thirty days for twelve months... The books go deep into painting... realism, expressionism, abstraction 'n' all that stuff... In the books they show close ups of details on each painting 'n' all... Real good...

The school here has found out that I can draw... and, like at every other school I've gone to, they've flooded me with stuff they want done... bulletin board stuff, posters, paintings, drawings... After this goes on for a while, they start thinking you're a drawing machine, and can turn out stuff like a printing press turns out newspapers or somepin'... A thankless job, 'tis, but good experience... Right now I've got three jobs to do... and I'm painting a portrait of Mr. Dowd and Harvey for the play *Harvey*... which is being put on by the drama club... This is an enjoyable job and doubtless beneficial experience. I'm doing it in tempera and Mr. Dowd has to look like some kid who's in the play... Drawing his face was hard (I had only a photo to go by). The art teacher helped me... I drew Harvey (the rabbit) like Yimmy (pause while we remove our hats in reverence of the deceased just mentioned).

By the time the trip to Britt's is over I'll probably be fairly used to traveling by myself on a bus... This is a good thing, too... as it's part of taking care of myself... of which I've got alot to learn about yet... Anyway, I'm anxious to visit you 'n' Britt... I've lost my fear of going out abroad on my own... The trip to Lynde's pretty well cured that!

I could probably spend a week just poring over your collections 'n' listening to your records... Yes, we must go to Cleveland and Akron... I hope to have plenty of money to spend there... from my summer job. Yes, also I want to explore the university library you've spoken of so often... If you be coming back east with me as you said you were, that's good too... I'll have company while traveling... and you can make sure I don't get lost or take the wrong bus... you being somewhat braver in such matters than I...

My ghod... Charles bought a seventy-dollar stereo set recently (paid full with cash) and it's blasting in my ear drums right now... God... I'm going mad... such tone, such volume!... Whew, it's over... "The Sea" by the Boston Symphony was playing... Now *Peer Gynt* is blasting away!!!!

About the magazine... this is a rather touchy subject... I wouldn't want you paying more than your share for the enterprise, that wouldn't be fair... Beside... the little money I do get these days is spent on tempting luxuries and magazines that I just can't resist... I even wish I had a few dollars now...

There's a few records and magazines I wish I could buy, but not enough money... I had a hard decision just as to what I should spend my last five bucks on just last week... Finally I bought an LP and *Esquire*... giving up the beautiful Roth work in *Playboy*... some *Animal Comics* that I possibly could have gotten from Kisch, and a few other things I'd like to have... Oh well, can't have yer cake 'n' eat it too... as they say... I oughta be lucky I have so much now... Darn, wish I was still working at Latex! Then I could have all these things and print a magazine besides! As of now... I couldn't even put two cents into a magazine... unless I try 'n' sell some copies of *Foo* door to door like we did last year... By George, maybe I will!!!! Not just for the money, but also for the satisfaction of having gotten rid of a few more copies of the accursed things!

I do want work of mine in print though, and will do a story for *Fanfare* (any future issue) if it's okay by you... You can tell me how many pages 'n' whether or not I write it myself or you write it...

I really wish I could print another mag... Everybody in fandom is all for it... and it is very valuable experience and keeps life from getting too dull and inactive... I know I should be going into all kinds of ambitious adventures and enterprises... I only wish I had the initiative and aggressiveness it takes... like you have... lucky clod! Laziness is a bad habit... I'm a day dreamer instead of a doer... 'n' I wish I was both! I'm afraid of hard work and people... That's my trouble!

Yes... there was a sketch by Williamson on that *Three Caballeros* comic by Kelly... I only wish Al would have put it somewhere else than right smack in the middle of the cover!

Very true... that about *MAD* magazine... Trouble is it's going teenage... Kurtzman's *MAD* was of exceedingly higher quality to the present publication of that name! *MAD* is now made to suit the average teenage tastes... It's funny but... well, something about Kurtzman's humor that's much funnier. It doesn't make you laugh out loud like *MAD* does, you get a deep inner enjoyment... like I found in *Kurtzman's Jungle Book*... 'Tis a gem... that'n is!

That *Jazz Digest* is all modern jazz stuff... don' think you'd be too interested.

I don't think I'll ever take a liking to small-band Dixieland jazz... but I do like the big band jazz... Your Fletcher Henderson record entices me... and I like Jean Goldkette (how lucky you were to get the Goldkette on X... and FREE yet! I feel sick). I really like "The Lovelight in Your Eyes"... That Boardwalk Orchestra is my favorite type twenties music... Charlie Frye's Pier Orchestra, Hotel Roosevelt Orchestra... These type are the ones from the twenties I'm craziest about (also Whiteman). I which I could get more records of this type... You have any of this type you'd care to part with... ah... er... heh heh...

Last night on *I've Got a Secret*... there was a guy on who collected old records, and he had 50,000 records... largest collection in the world, he also has some of the rarest ones. They played several... one by Teddy Roosevelt... one by Sara Bernhardt... Lillian Russel... and a couple good ones from the twenties... Too bad didn't get to hear much of 'em.

Do you have Fred von Bernewitz's address... We want to write to him... 'Tis important so please don't forget!

Original of "Second Hand Rose" eh? Hmm... How 'bout that! Blue label Victor!? Tha's strange. You'd think it'd be black label... I must take a closer look at all the blue label Victors at Carroll's!

BLEEB:

—R. Crumb

Detail from the cover of letter. June 20, 1959

Your Vigor for Life Appalls Me

18

DEAR(?) BRITT

I STAYED HOME FROM SCHOOL TODAY
WITH A COLD (MISSABLE EXCUSE)
IT'S ONE O'CLOCK ABOUT NOW ... ECHHH,
WHAT A DULL DAY, I'VE JUST BEEN
OUT TO THE MAILBOX, DARN! NO MAIL!
I'VE BEEN EXPECTING A STACK O' OLD
RECORDS FROM MARTY FOR TWO-THREE
WEEKS NOW! GOT YOUR LETTER
YESTERDAY!

EMPTY

R. CRUMB

GOOD COVER YOU MADE THERE! HOW DID YOU
EVER MANAGE TO MAKE THE TEXT LETTERING
SO GOOD!! (ZIF I DIDN'T KNOW!)

YES, I'LL CALL YOU AFTER SIX ON THE
23RD UND GIVE YOU THE INFORMATION ON
MY ARRIVAL THERE. I'LL MOST LIKELY
GET THERE ON THE 27TH OF DECEMBER,
AND I'LL HAVE TO BE BACK BY THE 4RTH
OF JANUARY THE DAY I GO BACK TO SCHOOL,
SO I'LL LEAVE ON THE 3RD. OKAY?
DARN, WE GOT A SHORT CHRISTMAS
VACATION. WE DON'T GET OUT TILL THE

23RD! CHEAP DEAL! WHEN DO YOU GET OUT?

WHEN I CALL YOU, I'LL ONLY BE ABLE TO GIVE YOU THE INFORMATION! I'D LIKE TO TALK AWHILE, BUT THAT'LL HAVE TO WAIT TILL I GET TO MASSECHUSETTS, CAN'T AFFORD TO TALK LONG!

BOY! "TEN EVER-LOVIN'' YEARS OF POGO"! WOWEE! ME GOTTA GET THAT! SLURP DROOL... IS IT PUBLISHED BY SIMON AND SCHUSTER? IT BETTER BE, CUZ I'M SENDIN' FOR IT TODAY TO SIMON AND SCHUSTER! GLAD I SAVED MY MONEY!

IS "SONGS OF POGO" A RECORD ALBUM OR WHAT? DO YOU THINK I COULD SEND FOR IT?

WHEN I GO TO YOUR PLACE, I'M ANXIOUS TO VISIT ALL THE BOOKSTORES! YOU SHORE HAVE GOTTEN LOTTA GOOD STUFF AT THEM, FOR INSTANCE, ● "O giese Kinder!"... HOW DID YOU FIND OUT WHAT THIS MEANT?.. DID PAHLS TELL YOU? HE KNOWS GERMAN, I THINK. I'M ANXIOUS TO SEE THIS BOOK. FUNNY, THERE AREN'T ANY BOOKSTORES HERE EXCEPT IN CARROLL'S MARKET, WHICH ONLY SELLS OLD BOOKS AND MAGAZINES... NEVER NEW ONES.

YEAH, I'LL HAVE TO LOOK THROUGH THE OL' RECORDS IN THE "U-SAVE" SHOP ,, PROBBLE FIND SOME FOR MY COLLECTION.. I KNOW ABOUT THE ONES MARTY GOT, HE TOLD ME ABOUT THEM... I'LL PROBABLY FIND SOME THAT HE DIDN'T WANT, BUT THAT I WOULD LIKE. YES, I'LL HAVE TO LOOK THROUGH THE SHEET MUSIC TOO! SOME OF THE OLD SHEET MUSIC HAVE WORK BY FAMOUS CARTOONISTS AND ILLUSTRATORS.

ACTUALLY, I SHOULD INVESTIGATE THE ANTIQUE SHOPS AROUND HERE, BUT THEY'RE SO SCATTERED AROUND THE COUNTRY SIDE... NON OF 'EM ARE IN TOWN.

WOWEE! KELLY COMICS! GEE! SPEAKING OF "FAIRLY TALE PARADE" (FAIRLY?) UP IN THE BOOKSTORE IN PHILLY, I SAW A 1942 FAIRY TALE PARADE WITH A BEAUTIFUL PAINTED COVER BY KELLY! THE BRIGHT COLORS AN' THE DRAWING... I DIDN'T BUY IT CUZ THE KOOK WANTED TWO DOLLARS FOR IT.

NEITHER OF THOSE TWO YOU GOT WERE OF KELLY'S BEST COMICS.

I GOT RAGGEDY ANN NUMBER THREE AND FOUR... WHAT KELLY DID IN THEM IS GOOD, BUT HE DID VERY LITTLE WORK IN THEM.

OKAY, OKAY! I'LL SEND YOU BACK YORE DAMN JANUARY '57 DISNEY! SEND BACK MAY '58, IF YOU WANT IT. I FOUND IT (JAN. '57) IN CHARLES' SCRAP BOOK ABOUT A WEEK AGO. WHAT WILL YOU DO IF I DON'T SEND JANUARY '57, TELL YOUR MOMMY? OKAY! I'LL SEND IT! CHARLES GOT ONE IN PERFECT CONDITION JUST BEFORE YOU SENT THAT ONE... I THOUGHT MAYBE YOU DIDN'T WANT IT BACK THAT MUCH FOR ME TO BOTHER ABOUT IT, BUT IF YOU DO, OKAY, THA'S YOUR BUSINESS. BUT SEND BACK THE MAY '58!

YEEP! ARE YOU GOING TO WRITE ANOTHER LETTER TO PAHLS, A LONGER ONE? OR JUST LET IT GO WITH THREE FOURTHS OF A PAGE? HOW **COME** PAHLS SENT YOU FIFTEEN DOLLARS, WAS IT TO PRINT FANFARE? HOW COME, ALSO, ARE YOU SENDING BACK THE MONEY? AREN'T YOU GOING TO PRINT IT FOR HIM? **IF NOT,** WHY NOT? HOW DO YOU EXPLAIN THE FACT THAT POTRZEBIE BOUNCES?

FAIRY TALE
PARADE

PAINTING OF ELVES DOING SOMETHING DON'T RE- MEMBER EXACTLY.

GOLD
BOARDER

1942

YEAH, I'LL BRING THE STAN LYNDE ARTICLE UP WHEN I VISIT. I'VE GOT IT WRITTEN, BUT IN A SLOPPY FORM, I'VE GOT TO WRITE IT IN A NEAT FORM.

YEAH, THAT GET-TOGETHER IN NEW YORK WILL PROBABLY PETER OUT ENTIRELY. YOU'RE RIGHT, THERE. BESIDES, I DON'T THINK I'D BE WILLING TO PUT OUT THE MONEY FOR IT. YOU HAD SNOW IN MASS' YET? WISH IT WOULD SNOW HERE, DARN... SURE IS DREARY LOOKING IN WINTER WITH NO **SNOW!** TOBAGGANIN' FUN, I BETCHA... YEAH, WE'LL GO TOBBOGGIN COASTING AND TALKING ABOUT COMICS AND PHILOSOPHY WHILE WE'RE AT IT, HEH HEH!

I HAD A HARD TIME CONVINCING MY
MOTHER THAT I WAS CAPABLE OF GOING
TO NEW YORK BY MYSELF, IT WASN'T
HARD TO PERSUADE THEM TO LET ME
VISIT YOU, THOUGH. THE ONLY THING THAT
WORRIES ME IS CHANGING BUSES IN
NEW YORK. I HOPE I DON'T GET MIXED
UP 'N' GET ON THE WRONG BUS OR
SOMETHIN'! WISH I HAD MARTY'S CON-
FIDENCE.

VILLA DE
SAN PASSOS, MEXICO

I'M NOT TOO CAPABLE OF TAKING CARE
OF MYSELF, ACTUALLY. I CAN'T COOK, CAN'T
PRESS MY OWN CLOTHES (HORRORS OF HORRORS)
YOU CAN THOUGH, GEE YOU'RE WONDERFUL,
MARTY WAS TELLING ME HOW YOU CONDEMNED
HIM BECAUSE HE COULDN'T PRESS HIS OWN
CLOTHES.... I CAN'T EITHER... SO, TOO BAD, WHEN
I VISIT, MAYBE I'LL MAKE MY BED, MAYBE I
WON'T... YUK YUK.
      YOU'RE RIGHT ABOUT TRAILWAYS HAVING
CHEAP BUSES, THE BUS I GOT ON TO COME
BACK FROM NEW YORK ▪ WAS A BROKEN
DOWN   TRAILWAYS JUNK-HEAP. IT BROKE

DOWN AFTER IT WAS TEN FEET FROM THE
TERMINAL AND IT TOOK 'EM A HALF AN
HOUR TO FIX THE THING.
   WHEN I GET MY TICKET AT THE BUS
DEPOT, I'LL MAKE SURE I GET THE CHEAPEST
AND THE SIMPLEST WAY THERE THAT I CAN,
YOU WANNA SEE ALL YOUR LETTERS TO
ME, EH? WELL, I GUESS I'LL BRING THEM.
THEY'RE A PRETTY MOTLEY GROUP, THE
ONES YOU MADE LIKE THIS ARE ALL
DIFFERENT TITLES... LIES, PAF, GLOOM,
SPAFOON, SPAFON, MERRY CHRISTMAS, AND
SO ON.
   THAT ANIMAL COMICS 29 YOU'RE GETTING
FROM HOOVER IS PROBABLY THE SAME ONE
HE SENT TO ME FOR TRADE, BUT I ALREADY
HAD IT SO I SENT IT BACK.. TIS IN
FAIRLY GOOD CONDITION. WOWEE, GOT
FIVE (5) EFF-EYE-VEE-EEH, FIVE ANIMAL
COMICS NOW.., ALL WITH KELLY WORK...GEE!
THAT NUMBER SEVENTEEN IS THE BEST ONE...
COMPLETELY BY KELLY EXCEPT ■■ THE "UNCLE
WIGGELY" STORY! MINE!
   HAVEN'T GOT ANYTHING FOR MY
COLLECTION LATELY, 'CEPT A 1935 "LITTLE ORPHAN
ANNIE" STORY BOOK, DRAWN BY HEROLD GRAY,
TOO! THE BOOK HAS THREE POP-UP CARTOONS
IN IT, REAL NEAT! IN COLOR...
   DID I EVER MENTION TO YOU ABOUT
THOSE "SKEEZIX" STORY BOOKS I FOUND IN A
BUNCH OF JUNK AT CARROLL'S MARKET?
FOUR OF 'EM, PERFECT CONDITION (SO IS THE
"LITTLE ORPHAN ANNIE AT THE CIRCUS" I JUST MEN-
TIONED... FOUND THIS AT CARROLL'S ALSO)
   THEY ARE :
      " SKEEZIX AND UNCLE WALT" 1924
      " SKEEZIX AND PAL"   1925
      " SKEEZIX AT THE CIRCUS"   1926
      " SKEEZIX OUT WEST"   1928
   ALL THESE ARE ORIGINALLY DRAWN BY
FRANK KING, AND A FEW OF THE PICTURES

ARE FROM THE STRIP. THE BOOKS ARE KINDA LIKE COMICS, EXCEPT THERE'S ONLY ONE OR TWO OR THREE PICTURES PER PAGE. THE COVERS ARE IN COLOR... NEAT!

I DON'T HAVE "R. CRUMB JOURNAL" ANYMORE... I TORE IT UP IN DISGUST ABOUT SIX MONTHS AGO, BURNED IT, AND BURIED THE ASHES.

I'LL BRING ALL THE ALMANACS THOUGH! CHARLES HAS BEEN DOING SOME LATELY. WE'VE BEEN PUTTING ONE OUT EVERY TWO WEEKS UP TO DECEMBER 15TH. NOW WE'RE DOING "ARCADE" (MONTHLY) AND QUIT ALMANAC.

BY THE WAY, STARTING WITH MY WORDS "THAT NUMBER SEVENTEEN...." I'M WRITING THIS ON A COLD, ▄▄▄ RAINY DECEMBER THE EIGHTEENTH. WE GOT A CAR TODAY. (GEEEE!) OUR OLD ONE ▄▄▄ BEGAN TO TURN INTO AN OLD JUNK HEAP.

I'M POSITIVE EVANS DID "WHEN WORLD'S COLLIDE"... I COMPARED IT WITH "ACES HIGH" AND SOME OTHERS ... EXACTLY THE SAME, YOU CLOD! THE COMIC ISN'T "DELL", IT'S A FAWCETT PUBLICATION. MAYBE YOU THOUGHT IT WAS DELL.

WOULD A 1941 "SUPERMAN" BE VALUABLE? I HAN'T GOT DE "IMPACT" YET... WHA'S THE HOLD UP?

SPEAKING OF "CLASSICS ILLUSTRATED", I BOUGHT AN OLD "OLIVER TWIST" AT CARROLL'S LAST WEEK, I GOT HALFWAY THROUGH ▄▄ READING IT, BUT IT MADE ME SO SICK I THREW IT AT THE TRASH CAN. MY AIM WAS GOOD TOO, AS IT LANDED IN THE CAN. IT CERTAINLY DIDN'T DO JUSTICE TO DICKENS, THE WAY THEY WENT ABOUT BRIEFING THE STORY COMPLETELY RUINED IT, AND LOST ALL THE CHARM AND

QUALITIES OF DICKENS WORKS. I KINDA
THINK MAKING COMIC BOOKS OUT OF CLASSIC
LITERATURE IS A BAD IDEA TO BEGIN WITH...
COMICS ARE FOR WALT KELLY AND HARVEY
KURTZMAN, WHO APPLY THEIR GENIUS TO THIS
FIELD. DICKENS AND THE OTHER GREAT AUTHORS
APPLIED THEIR GENIUS TO THE FIELD OF WORDS,
WITHOUT ■■■ PICTURES, AND THEIR ACCOMPLISHMENTS JUST
AREN'T MEANT FOR COMICS,
     IT'S AN AWFUL LOT OF BOTHER TO
GET ALL THOSE CLASSICS COMICS FOR YOU,
CAN'T YOU GET THEM AT YOUR PLACE? IF NOT,
I'LL DO IT. I'LL TAKE THE LETTER IN WHICH
YOU LISTED THE ONES YOU HAVE ALREADY. YOU
SAY THEY DON'T HAVE TO BE ORIGINAL
EDITIONS? THE ONLY WAY YOU'RE GONNA
GET ME TO DO THIS, I'M AFRAID, IS TO SEND
MONEY, THEN I'LL HAVE TO GET 'EM FOR
YOU, OTHERWIZE, I'LL PROBABLY NEVER GET
AROUND TO IT. SEND TEN CENTS FOR
EACH ONE, FIVE CENTS FOR THE PURCHASE
AND FIVE FOR THE ■■■ POSTAGE, SOMETIMES
THEY GET STACKS OF THEM, SOMETIMES
THEY DON'T GET ANY SO YOU MAY HAVE TO
WAIT AWHILE. ANYWAY, I'LL SEND YOU ONES
ONLY IN PERFECT OR AT LEAST NEAR PERFECT
CONDITION, UNLESS IT'S AN ORIGINAL PRINTING.
     WE DON'T HAVE THE PROBLEM YOU DO
OF GETTING OVER CROWDED WITH COMICS, YOU
SEE, WE HAVE THREE TRUNKS, TWO BIG ONES,
AND ONE REAL BIG ONE, WE KEEP OUR
BEST COMICS IN THE TWO FORMER ONES
IN OUR ROOM, THE REST WE KEEP IT THE
BIG ONE DOWN IN THE BASEMENT, THE
BIG ONE HAS ■■■■ ENOUGH ROOM IN IT FOR
ABOUT A THOUSAND MORE COMICS, WE'VE
ALREADY GOT ABOUT THREE HUNDRED COMICS
IN IT NOW.

ACTUALLY, THE REASON I STAYED HOME WED-
NESDAY IS CUZ MY PARENTS HAD A BIG
FIGHT (LITERALLY) TUESDAY NIGHT AND WEDNESDAY
MORNING AND I WAS JUST TOO DAMNED
TIRED TO GET UP IN THE MORNING. I WAS AWAKE
ALL NIGHT!

    I GOT A TALL LINEN CLOSET AT ▬▬▬▬
WILLKIE'S (THAT JIP-JOINT IN MILFERD)
THAT I KEEP MOST OF MY STUFF IN. (MY
COMICS ARE ALL IN ▬▬ A TRUNK, LIKE I SAID
EARLIER) ON THE FIRST SHELF ARE ALL THE
ALMANACS AND POGO BOOKS, PLUS THOSE LITTLE
NOTE BOOKS WE WROTE IN IN ▮ NINTH GRADE,
I'LL BRING 'EM WHEN I VISITS.

    SECOND SHELF IS BOOKS, ALL KINDS
BOOKS. THIRD SHELF IS ALL BOOKS. FOURTH
SHELF FANZINES, LETTERS FROM MARTY STAPLED
INTO BOOKS OF ABOUT TWENTY PAGES EACH,
SEVEN OF THESE ... COLORED PENCILS, BOOKS, JUNK.
              FIFTH SHELF ▬▬▬▬ I

KEEP A BIG BOX
▬▬ OF LETTERS,
A SKETCHBOOK. I
ON THE BOTTOM, THE
▬▬▬ SIXTH SHELF
IS ALOT OF JUNK.
PAPER, PASTE, AND
MAGAZINE CLIPPINGS,
ETC, AD INFINITUM.
THIS CABINET IS
SO CRAMMED
WITH STUFF
YOU COULDN'T
EVEN LIFT IT
IF YOU TRIED.
    GOSHES, YOU
ARE GROWING!
    I'M NOT GROW-
ING AS FAST AS

, WAS A COUPLE YEARS AGO, I'M 'BOUT AS TALL AS MARTY.

CHARLES AND I HAVE OFFICIALLY WITHDRAWN OURSELVES FROM THE CHURCH. WE'VE BEEN WORKING ON THIS PROBLEM TOGETHER FOR THE LAST FEW MONTHS. WE ARE STILL MADE TO GO TO CHURCH, THOUGH I DON'T MIND THIS TOO MUCH, AS IT GIVES ME TIME TO PONDER CERTAIN QUESTIONS. WE USED TO BE ZEALOUS CATHOLICS DURING LAST SCHOOL YEAR, BUT FACTS CAME TO LIGHT THAT MAKE THE CHURCH'S DOCTRINES ON THE SAME LEVEL AS GREEK MYTHES. I'M LOOKING FORWARD TO YOUR REACTION WHEN I EXPLAIN THE WHOLE THING TO YOU ON MY VISIT. HERE ARE A FEW THINGS FOR YOU TO THINK ABOUT:

THERE IS NO SUCH THING AS FREE WILL,

PEOPLE AREN'T RESPONSIBLE FOR THEIR ACTIONS,

THERE IS NO SUCH THING AS SIN, MAN IS MERELY A PRODUCT OF HIS EN— VIRONMENT AND INFLUENCES, HE ORIG— INATES NOTHING.

DOES IT MAKE SENSE? IT WILL. HEH HEH.

IT CERTAINLY IS DIFFICULT TO BREAK THE BINDS OF ▬ TRAINING AND BRAINWASHING FROM THE CHURCH, IN FACT, I HAVEN'T BEEN ABLE TO COMPLETELY DO IT YET. I STILL WEAR A SCAPULOR 'ROUND MY NECK! EVER SINCE I CAN REMEMBER THE TEACHINGS OF THE CHURCH HAVE BEEN DRILLED INTO ME, AND NOW I'M TRYING TO BREAK AWAY, WHEN I'VE BEEN TOLD THAT THIS IS A TERRIBLE WRONG. IT CERTAINLY ISNT EASY. IT CERTAINLY IS HARD TO CONVINCE OTHER PEOPLE OF IT, TOO. BUT IT'S SO SIMPLE AND ELEMENTARY ONCE YOU CAN SEE IT, BUT TO SEE IT TAKES CONSIDERABLE PONDERING AND THINKING.

YOU'LL GET THE "PRIZE COMICS WESTERN" AS SOON AS YOU COME UP WITH SOMETHING GOOD IN TRADE. DON'T WORRY, I WON'T GIVE IT TO ANYBODY ELSE. I'M TAKING A GAMBLE THAT YOU MIGHT ~~GET IT~~ FROM SOMEBODY ELSE, BUT THAT'S A RISK I'LL HAVE TO TAKE, I DON'T HANDLE IT, AND IT STAYS NICE AND FLAT AND IN GOOD CONDITION AT THE BOTTOM OF A STACK, SO IT WON'T DETERIORATE.

I GAVE THE DANDY COMICS TO PAHLS FOR A BUNCH OF OLD RECORDS.... NO, NO.. WAIT.... I GAVE HIM THAT JAZZ RECORD FOR THOSE... HE GAVE ME A DOLLAR FOR THE "DANDY COMICS". "PRE-TRENDS" ARE PRETTY JUNKY... I DUNNO WHY YOU GUYS WANT 'EM SO BAD.. JES' CUZ THEIR EC'S... THA'S DUMB. I'D TRADE THAT "CRIME PATROL" FOR A GOOD '52 OR '53 EC... (NOT FOR A NEW DIRECTION THOUGH)

"PSYCHOANALYSIS NUMBER FOUR...BLURCH!

KAMEN.... BLECH! NOT A VERY HIGH QUALITY EC, WAS IT.

I AN'T SENDIN' "WHEN WORLDS COLLIDE".. THE STORY IS LOUSY ANYWAYS.. YOU DON'T WANNA READ IT, DO YOU?

WAL, I'M REALLY LOOKING FORWARD TO ~~my~~ MY VISIT..... HOPE IT SNOWS WHEN I'M THERE?.... I NEVER BEEN TO NEW ENGLAND AFORES... BET IT'S COLD UP THERE.....

OPPS! NO MORE ROOM!

and now

INTRODUCING A NEW FEATURE TO FARB:

A BENEFICIAL
WRITING
a brief
artical
I MEAN (HEH HEH)....
ARTICLE!

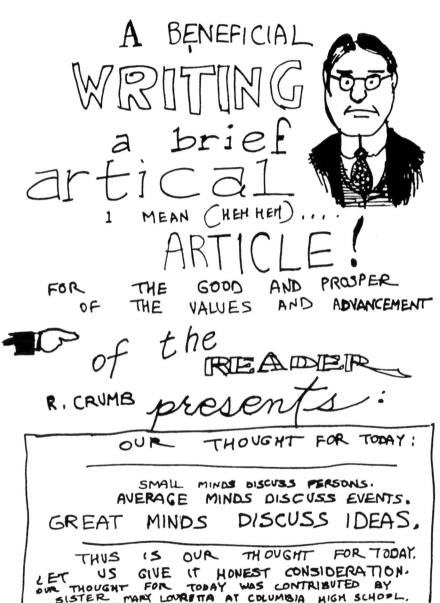

FOR THE GOOD AND PROSPER
OF THE VALUES AND ADVANCEMENT

of the READER

R. CRUMB presents:

OUR THOUGHT FOR TODAY:

SMALL MINDS DISCUSS PERSONS.
AVERAGE MINDS DISCUSS EVENTS.
GREAT MINDS DISCUSS IDEAS.

THUS IS OUR THOUGHT FOR TODAY.
LET US GIVE IT HONEST CONSIDERATION.
OUR THOUGHT FOR TODAY WAS CONTRIBUTED BY
SISTER MARY LOURETTA AT COLUMBIA HIGH SCHOOL.

Robert Crumb Letters 1958-1977

Christmas Greetings and a HAPPY NEW YEAR in 1960

SAME OLD B,M,
YEAR AFTER YEAR....
CHRISTMAS... BAH... HUMBUG!

WHAT'S CHRISTMAS BUT A TIME FOR
PAYING YOUR BILLS WITHOUT MONEY... A
TIME FOR FEELING A YEAR OLDER AND
NOW AN HOUR RICHER... CHRISTMAS...
POOH.. IF I COULD WORK MY WILL EVERY
IDIOT WHO GOES ABOUT WITH "MERRY
CHRISTMAS" ON HIS LIPS WOULD BE
BOILED IN HIS OWN PUDDING AND BURRIED
WITH A STAKE OF HOLLY THROUGH HIS HEART
HE WOULD !

Your Vigor for Life Appalls Me

19

Dear Britt:

Lousy cover this time, the idea is merely meant in good fun... though it expresses my true feelings on the matter. (heh-heh)

Clever cover you made there, perty good satire on the hero comics... I chuckle every time I look at it.

Well, thanks for letting me come and visit you... It was all in all an enjoyable week. I got home alright, but there were the usual confusions... For one thing, the Greyhound bus station wasn't "right across the street" from the "Peter Pan" place like you said it was, it was a block away, and it seemed like miles carrying those heavy suitcases... Thought I'd never make it... The 3:15 bus for New York arrived at 4:15, so I was in Springfield for 'bout two and a half hours. The station in New York was so crowded that I pushed down old ladies and little children to get through the mob. It seemed like everybody in the mass hysteria was sneering at me for my rudeness... It's lucky for me that there was another person there who was going to Dover, an Air Force guy. Other wize I would have been completely lost in the confusion. I was really relieved when I got on the bus, which was empty, so I grabbed a front seat, and didn't have to lug the suitcases through the aisle, hitting everybody in the face with them like I did in Springfield. There I sat, relaxed in the quiet bus, looking out the window at the mob of confused travelers, feeling much relieved that I was safely on the bus.

Got home around four in the morning, spent the next day, which was Sunday, taping up the *Puck*s, and getting things in order. Monday, back to the drudgery of school, which I wasn't exactly in the mood for facing after my holidays of being out on my own. My father had to go to the hospital with a ruptured appendix that day or Tuesday, he's still in the hospital, just getting over it now.

Oboy! Thanks for getting the *Puck*!!!! (slurp, drool) A few things I want to mention about this deal...

First I'll say in my letter to Marty I told him we got that stuff (*Pucks* and newspapers) at the U Save Shop at five cents each... You will verify the story, of course...

Second, when you get more (and please do!) look for one from 1898... any from that year or 1899 or 1900 or anywhere thereabouts. The more recent, the better coloring they had... Also, see if you can get the first issue, if you can, I've decided that it would be good to have it. If you can't get the first issue, get the earliest one you can manage to...

I'm sending out the *Prize Western* and the Frank King[1] books... Can't find

---

[1] Frank King, staff cartoonist for the *Chicago Tribune*, began drawing *Gasoline Alley* in 1918. The founding premise of the strip was to offer car care advice to the increasing population of middle class car owners. In 1921, the strip's appeal was broadened with the introduction of a new character, Skeezix — an abandoned infant — adding a focus on traditional small-town values.

When Worlds Collide, but I'll put something in place of it. After looking at those *Skeezix* books again, I'd say they're worth three or four *Puck*s... Two is the least, they're four of them, I think you should send me at least two *Puck*s for them... if not three... You don't like the *Puck*s but I like these, so... two at least.

Have you gotten anymore old Sunday comic sections?

If the *Puck*s aren't the originals, then how come they're all folded down the middle? Besides, the old *Life*s and *Judge*s I have are the same kind of paper.

I've played just about all the records I bought at the U Save Shop. Alot of good ones in the stack, and of course, there are a few lemons. By the way, none of 'em got damaged on the way home. Some of the tunes have caught on to us already... Others will too, as we play them more.

I'll send one of the loose-leaf folders with the stuff... I'd put some of the Latex three-holed blank paper in it, but that would mean quite a bit on the postage.

Glad to see you got some rubber cement. You don't have to spread it on thick, you know... Cheez, you shure used alot of the Skymasters.

I'll send some library tape to you soon as I can get an extra roll.

Yeh, I'll look out for comics for you... at Carroll's... I got one King Features Syndicate *Katzenjammer Kids*[2] for you... It was kinda beat up, so I taped it up with the mending tape. It had been there at Carroll's for a couple o' months.

[...]

---

[2] *The Katzenjammer Kids* was created by Rudolph Dirks in 1897 for the *New York Journal.* When Dirks left the paper, the strip was drawn successively by Harold Knerr, Doc Winner and, finally, Joe Musial.

~ 2 0 ~   *January 30, 1960*
                                          Dover, Delaware

Dear Marty:

Well, 'nother long letter from you... Ten pages this time! Hoo boy! Very effective cover of Bix... Really good! 'Bout the best work I've seen by you... Real neat technique with the brown felt-tip marker... The money for my trip to Britt's was a Christmas present, the sole Christmas gift I got from my parents. Actually, I got the bus ticket and nine dollars as the gift.

Gads... I'm crossing out words all over the place!

Yes, writers are a dime a dozen, but it seems to me that the fields of literature, art (cartooning included), acting and music are all getting over-crowded nowadays... You've really got to be one-hundred percent these days to get to the top... Sixty or seventy years ago, all these fields were just growing... but now, they've reached the overflowing point... Artists and musicians and actors are a dime a dozen too... Even <u>good</u> ones are plentiful, it seems... We got a letter recently from my uncle Bob who is trying to make an acting career for himself out in Hollywood... It always seems like he's going to get a big break and get into the big-time, but, he's thirty now and not very far along... Yes, it's all very discouraging...

But, they say positive thinking, determination, hard work, etc, and you'll reach the goal you set for yourself...

I see what you mean about having some ideas about life and society as the inspiration to base your writing on, your work should express your views of life and people... This is what I'm trying to straighten out for my cartoons. I want my work to have meaning in it... As long as we're thinking about it, we'll attain it through the years... I think I will reach the point I'm trying to get by time I'm in my forties or fifties... If I try hard enough (which I doubt) I may reach it earlier than that.

Yes, as long as you're trying to become a creative and skilled author, and keep trying, you someday will be, I don't doubt that.

When you said you crossed the threshold into a clearer and more vivid life, you gave me something to look forward to. I'm anxious to pass through that period where all the people and things around me become clearer and have more depth and more understandable... I think I understand what it is because I went through it about the time I turned nine years old... It was a very abrupt and sudden change in my thinking, making things more clear and distinct in my mind... Right now I seem to be half asleep about everything... I look forward to going through the mental advancement again.

I know what it is to have your secure foundation for existence pulled out from under you when you figure out that a religion is all objectively wrong. You're left with nothing to grasp onto for awhile. Sometimes I feel that with all the theories, religions and philosophies floating around, life is pretty much of a big confused mess, and that it's better to just observe society and study the outward results of the philosophies, that is, folklore, Americana, etc.

Most middle-aged people tell me that lots of kids our age go through this stage when we study life and try to find all the answers, but we'll get over it when we get out on our own and learn to accept things the way they are. I've presented our theories to my parents, but they are firmly against it, believe that people not being responsible for their actions is utterly ridiculous and we'll come to our senses when we're out working. It's impossible to convince them of our theories. We have to go to church until we're eighteen, my father says. Thing I don't like is, they don't go themselves.

I decided to reject conforming when society rejected me about three years back. I know I just don't fit, don't belong. I tried, but it didn't work.

The nuns mean well when they think that by teaching small children the Church is true and that they must save their souls. They think they are gathering more souls for Christ. But when I think of the Apostles Creed being drummed into me in second grade, it seems that it shouldn't be that way, telling innocent little kids that they believe in the Holy Ghost, the Holy Catholic Church, etc. But, take away religious education, and what kind of moral and ethical education do you replace it with?

I hate TV programs that have a hero who is completely perfect and straightens out everybody else or kills them... Alot of westerns, *Johnny Yuma* in particular, have this in them. Johnny Yuma has straightened whole towns in his time, the public goes for this garbage too. The program I just mentioned is the top new program of the season.

The teenage fad is really reaching extremes... Songs like "Teen Angel" (bruther), the magazines going completely sick over Fabian, Frankie Avalon and the rest of these puppets... "I have a deep and sincere love for Fabian" says this girl in *16* magazine. "Would he ever date anyone who was not famous and who he never heard of?" It's so stupid it's funny... When the teenage stars go out of style, magazines like *16* will go out with them...

Television commercials ruin everything by commercializing it to sell their product...

Hmmm... life isn't all bad, though. You can walk through the woods or get a boat and let it drift along in a stream, out in nature, and the world seems beautiful... There you're free from the standards of society...

You've got to remember that religions do accomplish some good... Nuns care for the sick in countries where these people wouldn't be cared for by anyone else... They give food and clothing to the poor... People like Bishop Sheen who try to help people better their lives...

Yes, I've decided to make my own life, and not let society make it for me, though it's not gaining me friends in school... (sometimes I think it's a psychiatrist I need). I may someday enjoy poking fun at the whole mess of society in my cartoons, I dunno.

Well, I read your essay, very good, very good... Especially since I've traveled and know just what you described, in a very good way... because it happened to me, and I felt pretty much the same as you wrote that you felt... I thought it was really good, and like the teacher's comment said, "You have the idea"... But there were some flaws... I'll list them paragraph by paragraph, I'll send back the essay along with this for you to refer to my comments with... If you don't want it, please send it back.

Paragraph one: Your beginning fell in line with the stuff you read in mediocre short stories... "The snow began... as I etc...." It kind of took a while to catch the meaning of the second sentence. The third sentence was really vague... What's it mean... oh, I see... the kid was giving the lady a rough time and... "intoned"?

Paragraph two was good, I might add here that all paragraph one did was tell you what was going on. Yes, the second paragraph was good... bringing to mind something we've all experienced but never thought about much...

Your Vigor for Life Appalls Me

When a writer can do this, he's got something on the ball... "Esprit de corps"... are you showing off knowledge here? I always thought these foreign phrases were obnoxious.

Paragraph three: Here again, the reading got confusing. As you advanced inward the wording became a tangled undergrowth, until you figured out that it was the kid-language of Billy (or Bobby or Tommy). It would have been better for you to have put the part said by the kid in quotation marks...

Paragraph four: Okay, except you didn't clarify how the kid got to his mother... "Over the top of the seat"... takes a while to catch on...

Paragraph four: "conversational prestige" is kind of a tangled thing... wording could be simpler... The rest of this paragraph is okay...

Paragraph five: This one is full of confusing phrases and wording... especially that one underlined in red by the prof... "At length I was able to engage their attention." All through the writing I find this overly fancy wording... You should use more plain and simple language, like you do in your letters...

Paragraph six: Good, but for the fancy wording...

Paragraph seven: Good, and simple as far as wording.

On the whole, you got your ideas across and show "keen perception," as you say... But you aught (ought?) to simplify your wording. In your letters you're not trying to show off, you're sincere and concise. That's the way you should be in all your writing... Hmm... I dunno, maybe I'm wrong...

Hope you can get the records off to me soon... All the ones I have now I've pretty well worn out... Right now I figure I've got 'bout three or four dollars worth coming... including all the comics I've sent you.

Since I've gotten quite a few late twenties orchestra records, I'm more and more rejecting the dull sound of the early twenties. The Joseph G. Smith Orchestra is the very essence of the dull sound. Actually, there were two kinds of orchestras in this period, the old-time bands, like the background music in *Second Hand Rose*, and the imitation jazz of Paul Whiteman and the Benson Orchestra. The former isn't too bad, but the imitation jazz is rather poor... though the songs they played make up for the arrangements... (yeek, what a way to divide a word).[1] Yes, I've been able to figure it out that around '25 and '26, just before Victor changed its black label, that the bands began to get the great sound they had in the late twenties... Glad you filled me in on why it happened... I'd been wondering about it... I have some of Whiteman's later records on Victor from around '26 or '27, I'd say from the sound, and they're really good, but I don't have any by him with the scroll label... When did he go over to Columbia? How come his Columbia records are so rare? Is it because of the famous jazzmen that played with him then?

What kind of records are you sending me? I hope you could spare some of your late twenties. Yes, even the smaller companies turned out some good stuff. Not so today. The big companies grab all the quality singers and musicians.

---

[1] In Crumb's original letter, the word "arrangements" is hyphenated as it appears here.

Among my favorite orchestras during the late twenties are George Olsen's (I should say the early thirties too) and Sam Lanin's Dance Orchestra. Banner, who recorded for this one, must have been a pretty cheap company. All the Banner records I have are in pretty poor condition. That is, the sound is fading and blurred.

Sure I'll trade the Frank Crumit records for some of yours... Make the ones you give me late twenties if you can. I'll list all th' Frank Crumit ones I have:

1. "I Married the Bootlegger's Daughter" - Frank Crumit / "How's Your Folks and My Folks" - The Happiness Boys (old label) - Victor
2. "Palesteena" - Frank Crumit / "I Wish That I'd Been Born in Borneo" - Frank Crumit - Columbia
3. "Abdul Abulbul Amir" / "Frankie and Johnnie" - Frank Crumit - (scroll label) Victor
4. "Donald the Dub" / "And Then He Took Up Golf" - Frank Crumit - (scroll label) Victor

This's all I could find... I had a couple more but I threw 'em out to make room for more records... I don't like Frank too much as a singer. How come you're collecting 'em?

I don't think you owe me a tape... Yes, I'd really like to hear some o' the records you have... Can't afford buying a tape right now... Couldn't you buy one, record your best records 'n' lend it to me... Then I could send it back and you'd have it to keep for yourself, with the records preserved on tape. If not, I'll have to wait till I can get into some money. Of the ones you listed on the last page of your letter, I'll list the numbers I'd like to hear:

"Carolina in the Morning"
"Charleston"
"Chicago"
"Collegiate"
"Hindustan"
"Hot Lips"
"He's Our Al" (is this a campaign song?)
"If You Knew Suzie"
"I'm Just Wild about Harry"
"Last Night on the Back Porch"
"Louise"
"Me and My Shadow"
"Oh Gee, Oh Gosh, Oh Golly I'm in Love"
"Show Me the Way to Go Home"
"Sidewalks of New York"
"Sleepy Time Gal"

"Somebody Loves Me"
"Who's Sorry Now"
"The World Is Waiting the Sunrise"
"You've Gotta See Mama Every Night"
"Who?"
"Blue Skies"
"The Girl Friend"
"Where's That Rainbow?"
"At Sundown"

You probably wouldn't have room on a tape for all of these... And I just wrote down the numbers I'm familiar with... There are lots of these on your list that I've never heard of, but I know I'd like if I did hear... At the end of this letter I'll list the rest of the records I got in Northampton.

Hmmm... a rare Fats Waller record worth over five bucks... Are all Gennett records rare? Don't believe I've ever seen one.

When we sold the hundred *Foo* number threes door to door, we actually did use a little underhanded play... We said we printed the magazine as an art project for the school... That's the only reason most of the people bought it, I fear... because it was supposed to be for the school. (Wot a fraud)

Britt got the old Sunday comics at the U Save Shop we found these and the *Puck*s in with an old stack of sheet music... I don't know what Britt's going to do with those Sunday supplements... They were crumbling to bits like old dried leaves... But they sure were neat... Each strip was a full page...

Yes, I'd like to have *Slavery as a Cause of the Civil War*... I'll pay the postage when you send it. Also, *Causes of the Revolutionary War*.

Is *Comics and Their Creators* out of print? Whot year was it copyrighted? Color? How many pages? Size?

Yes, we have one of those Big Little Books that was in the photo. One of Mickey Mouse in the foreign legion I think.

Charles and I have talked to Sandra 'bout floating with the herd and conforming, and thinking for one's self, but it doesn't do any good, she's been pulled in too much, she's beyond help. She says "Some people like to conform and some don't. If I wanna conform, it's my business"... Yes, girls do fall in line a little more than most boys, 'specially in their early teens... Just watch *Dick Clark Show* sometime... The audience is practically all girls... (the singers are practically all boys). They all wear a label that says "IFIC" and they all clap their hands to the music... and all are chewing spearmint gum... This scene brings out their lives in general... Po' souls.

So you may go to California this summer... You'd like the west coast alot, I think... Charles is going out to visit his friend Jack Binkinz this summer. He plans to stay there for three months. He was invited and they said he could stay as long as he wanted. The Binkinz family lives in southern California and they own one of the biggest trailer parks in the area. They're pretty wealthy.

Jack gets the whole business when his father retires. They have big parties and are part of the Encinitas high class society. Charles is pretty lucky to be going there. He'll be able to spend whole days at Disneyland, go to summer college with Jack and take free art and drama courses. He plans to visit Kisch in Santa Barbara, and generally he should have a good time out there... I bet he'll be a changed man when he comes home. He plans to go out by plane (jet). Only five and a half hours.

Britt's cousin Marylyn was only 'bout eight or nine, so...

Yes, Kelly seems to be pretty much of a nut... I saw him on TV in '56 when his record came out, it was a program about cartoons... He really acted crazy, singing and talking, I think the host of the show was embarrassed. Kelly is really an eccentric character, he acts like his cartoons.

Never told you before that I got the Camden LP *Dixieland and New Orleans Jazz* for Christmas from Carol, my sister... My favorite number on it is "West End Blues." Next would be "San"... You have this LP, don't you?

Well, last time I said I'd list the rest of my records I got at Britt's, so here they are.
1. "Sing Song Girl" - Chester Leighton & His Sophomores / "After All My Dreams" - Jack Whitney & His Orchestra - Clarion
2. "Happy Days Are Here Again" (from *Chasing Rainbows*) / "I'm Following You" (from *It's a Great*

[...]

14. "Linger Awhile" - Paul Whiteman / "Hollywood" - Joe Raymond - Victor
15. "Rose of Washington Square" / "You Ain't Heard Nothing Yet" - All Star Trio - Victor
16. "Fate" / "Lady of the Evening" (from *Music Box Review*) - Paul Whiteman - Victor
17. "Morning Will Come" (from *Bombo*) - Zez Confrey & His Orchestra / "Yes! We Have No Bananas" - The Great White Way Orchestra - Victor
18. "My Mom" / "Too Many Tears" - Ben Selvin Orchestra - early thirties Columbia
19. "Charlie, My Boy" - vocal by Billy Murray / "A New Kind of Man" - Aileen Stanley - Victor
20. "Ah-Ha!" / "Just a Little Drink" - Paul Whiteman - Victor
21. "Valencia" / "No More Worryin'" - Paul Whiteman - Victor
22. "Swingin' Down the Lane" / "Beside a Babbling Brook" - The Great White Way Orchestra - Victor
23. "Desert Isle (from the musical farce *My Girl*) / "I Like Pie, I Like Cake, but I Like You Best of All" - Edwin J. McEnelly's Orchestra - Victor
24. "Just Around the Corner" - Art Landry & His Orchestra / "Smile A Little Bit" - Ted Weems Orch. - Victor

25. "Toodle-oo" (from the musical comedy *Mary Jane McKane*)
    - The Manhattan Merrymakers / "Why Should I Weep about One
    Sweetie" - Brook John's Orchestra - Victor

Whew! Just got the last one in

~ 2 1 ~   *March 10, 1960*
                                          Dover, Delaware

Dear Britt:
    Things are fine in Mount Idy. I stayed home from school today, mainly
cause the school is closed. It's cause of the blizzard. Had quite a long vacation
due to the blizzards. It started last Wednesday and has snowed several times
since. All the roads are closed 'n' everything.
    Boy, you poor clod, living up there in Duluth... haw haw... poor clod!
    Carroll's Market has been quite productive lately, more about this later.
    Boy, you are a nice guy! You didn't even particularly care to have the *When
Worlds Collide*. You didn't believe that it was done by Evens (Evans that is). I
had to practically persuade you to take it, then Marty writes and says he wants
it alot! So I thought he'd appreciate it alot more'n you! But just to show you
I'm a good sport, and mainly I want the *Puck*s, I'll send you something else in
its place... By ghod, you better send those *Puck*s! Take care to keep 'em in
good condition!
    Tell me all about your visit with Marty. Did you tell him we stole all the
stuff? Did you show him the Frank King books?
    Your opinion of modern art is all washed up. You proved one thing to me:
you don't know much about modern art! To be sure, there are quacks who are
phony! But true abstract, cubism, impressionism, etc. are deep and complex.
I suggest you read a few books on the subject before you go around voicing
opinions about it. It is a good cover though! I hope you stick to the name *Mike
Britt's Magazine*.
    My cover on this is what I'd love my life to be, but of course, it's impossi-
ble, so I draw it and dream about it. I'm supposed to be a traveling philosophical bum, resting by a stream eating watermelons from a nearby field...
it's a warm summer morning.
    Have you seen the series in *Post* about Norman Rockwell? It's a book of
his broken up into eight parts for *Post*. I'm collecting the articles. It's inspiring to me, reading his life story. You oughta read it.
    Any prospects of comics up there in Minnesota? Hardly likely!
Eeeyaah!...
    Charles got some more old *Disney's* at Carroll's Market recently. Also a dou-

ble of *Donald Duck,* "Ghost of the Grotto" in fair condition. You wants it? What you gives?

Disney's Charles got at Carroll's:

Nov. '45

Jan. '48 in perfect condition

Donald Duck in Voodoo Hoodoo... Also, quite a few doubles. I got a few items I think you'll want:

Captain Easy[1], April 1956, number one (Argo)

Mary Worth[2], March 1956, number one (Argo)

I think maybe you have these.

Buster Brown Comic Book:[3]

numbers 29, 40, 41, and 43...

These have work by Krigstein and Crandall and some that looks something like Williamson or Frazetta or one of those guys.

Tip Top Comics, January 1946, number 114 (United Features Syndicate)

Stories: "Li'l Abner"	five pages
"Curly Kayoe"[4]	five pages
"Nancy"[5] (all half pages jokes)	five pages
"Jim Hardy" by Dick Moores[6]	five pages
"The Captain and the Kids"[7] (one page jokes)	five pages
"Ella Cinders"[8]	five pages
"The Triple Terror"	five pages
"Bill Bumlin"	five pages
"Strange as it Seems"	one page

Also, *Famous Funnies* December '52, number 203

Contains: "Tom Terrace, the Vagabond Adventurer"

    (not strips)   eight pages

---

[1] Easy first appeared in Roy Crane's strip *Wash Tubbs* (1924), as Wash's pal. He became so popular that Crane created the Sunday strip *Captain Easy* in 1933.

[2] Created by Mary Orr in 1932, *Mary Worth* started as a popular strip called *Apple Mary.*

[3] R. F. Outcault (*The Yellow Kid*) created *Buster Brown* in 1902 for the color section of the *New York Herald.* See bibliography.

[4] *Joe's Car,* later titled *Joe Jinks,* was created by Vic Forsythe in 1918 for the *New York World.* It passed through a long succession of artists, until Sam Leff introduced the popular character Curly Kayoe, after whom the strip was renamed.

[5] Ernie Bushmiller's creation, *Nancy,* became a regular feature in 1940, before which the character, *Nancy,* played a supporting role in his comic strip, *Fritzi Ritz.* See bibliography.

[6] While assisting Chester Gould with *Dick Tracy,* Moores conceived his strip *Jim Hardy,* which first appeared in 1936 and lasted only a few years.

[7] When Rudolph Dirks left the *New York Journal* in 1912, he had to leave behind the rights to the title *The Katzenjammer Kids.* He was, however, allowed to keep the rights to his characters, which he revived for the *New York World* under the title *Hans and Fritz,* changing it again to *The Captain and the Kids* in order to deflect the anti-German sentiment of the day.

[8] By Bill Conselman and Charlie Plumb, *Ella Cinders* started in 1925 and became popular for its artistry and publicity stunts.

"Scorchy Smith"[9]   six pages
"Dickie Dare"[10]   five pages
The rest is advertisements.

All these are in good condition! I'll trade you *Tip Top* and *Famous Funnies* for one *Puck*. The two *Argos* (if you don't have them already) and the four *Buster Brown Comics* for two more... But cripes! You want six comics for one *Puck*. It's not the 30 cents I paid for them that counts. Hell! For that matter, the *Puck*s didn't cost you anything! So, it's not the money that's important, it's how much a person values the stuff. The great Keifer did the cover of the *Famous Funnies*! Remember, I still have the *Sparkle* comics, too!

I got those Classics Illustrated binders. Two of 'em. They're really neat. You say they're soft, flexible plastic, you're wrong, bhuddy! They're hard cardboard, jes' like book covers! I got all twenty three of my *MAD* comics in one... They fit perfectly! I have my *Pogo*s in the other one. Speaking of *Pogo* comics, it stands to reason that if you got a copy of *Pogo* number five in real good condition, you'd keep it and send me your old beat up copy. And I already have one myself in poor condition... Got it at Carroll's Market a while back. I have all the *Pogo*s now, only numbers one, two and five are in poor condition.

I have all the Jack Davis Valentine cards now except seven, and most of the Monster Cards. Boy, those Monster Cards are neat! I found the *Fight Comics*, I'll send it to you to make up for the *When Worlds Collide*, along with the *Dick Tracy* book of strips and the black folder. And if that doesn't satisfy you, I don't know what will, ya petty kook.

I'll also cut out a comics page or two from the *Inquirer* and send 'em along, but you're gonna pay postage!

Thanks for returning the *Arcade* book. I like the back cover you did. Quite a laugh.

Couldn't get any library tape. Sorry!

I lent the double of *MAD* number one to a kid in school and got it back a total wreck. The *Dick Tracy* book makes up for it, okay?

List the dates of the ten *Puck*s you got. Hope you were able to get some of the later ones.

Charles is expecting a big load of *Disney's* in the mail. The dates range from 1945 to 1956... none for over fifty cents... all in good condition. When Charles gets these, he'll have every *Disney* from the fifties... Ha! Jellies! Also, he'll have every issue from March '47 on up! JELLIES!

---

[9] Created by John Terry for the Associated Press, *Scorchy Smith* was eventually propelled into popularity by Noel Sickles (written by Milton Caniff) and later by Frank Robbins.
[10] Milton Caniff's Associated Press adventure strip, *Dickie Dare*, started in 1933. When Caniff left to create *Terry and the Pirates* for the Chicago Tribune - New York News Syndicate in 1934, Coulton Waugh took over the strip, followed by Mabel Odin Burvik. The strip was discontinued in the late '50s. See bibliography.

Thanks for sending the tracings! You were lucky to get the 1942 *Disney's*. You spent alot of time for nothing tracing June 1945. Charles already has it in perfect condition! Say, I betcha... Lies! Forget it!

Y'know, Britt, you oughta practice sketching people, realistically... Sketch interesting faces, hands, bodies, wrinkles in cloth... This will be of great benefit to you... I know, cuz I've tried it! You have got to learn to be more versatile if you want to be a cartoonist or illustrator... You've got to know how to draw more than just simple cartoon characters. You can be a higher quality cartoonist if you know how to draw people... and can draw them well! Take my advice! This is important... Everybody in the know has told me so!

Funny... I haven't heard from Marty for a coupla months, you have any idea of what could be holding him up, being as you visited him just recently.

What all did you get in Ohio!? Anything good?

I got on the staff of the Dover school newspaper. Actually, I was asked to do art for it. It's called the *Ecolian* (eeh-cole-ian), whatever that means. Anyway, once on the staff, I took a vote with myself and decided to do the whole front page myself as a magazine cover. I'll send you a copy when it comes out with my cover. I also suggested that every issue have a cover like that, which they have now decided to do.

It's done with offset process. I consider myself pretty lucky to get this chance. I'll see my work in print, and know that about four hundred other people are seeing it too.

My marks in school weren't so good last time... I flunked two subjects, English and typing... Sheees! I've lost all ambition for school, except for history and the *Ecolian*. I won an American Legion award or some kind of award for history... I dunno just exactly what, nobody would tell me!

Friday afternoon, 11 March 1960

Have just been to Carroll's Market, the stinking place... The smell of it makes me sick... gag... Anyway, there were a few comics there that we wanted... eleven, to be exact... three that you may want...

So I leave you with our thought for today... Get lost!

No, all kidding aside... our thought for today...

Quit running yourself down!

By the way, I've started selling *Foo* in school... have done pretty good, it made a big hit in Dover, not like in that cruddy Milford! I've sold quite alot of 'em here... There's this kid, Ernie Lenhart, a junior, wants to do a magazine with me, like *Foo*. I don't care much for the idea, but I'll go along with it... I'll send you a copy, though I'll probably be ashamed of it. We decided to call it *Arcade*...

What's your plans for *Squatront*?

Don't tell Marty about this magazine I'm going into, please! I'm too ashamed of it to tell him about it... The only reason I'm doing it is to get my work in print, express my ideas to a large number of people. You savvy? Write soon!

Say hello to Hal for me! Heh heh... gulp.

Father Corrigan gave a sermon over the radio this morning... haw haw! "On this particler occasion... ahemmmmh!..."

WIS was here!

St. Patrick's Day,
                                                          March 17 1960
                                                          Dover, Delaware

Dear Marty:

Whe-e-ew! At last... I was about to write your parents and ask them when the funeral was going to be, or maybe my sympathies to them on your elopement or something! Sheeeh!

Well... thanks, thanks, and thanks again for the Paul Whiteman discography! This is what I've been waiting to see for a long time... I had started determining the approximate dates of my Victor records by the numbers on them, but now with this... Hmm, bwah!

I'll really treasure it! I've got eighteen Whiteman records, seven or eight of them are from '22, though. And only two are from the quality era ('25 and up).

Hmmm, there's so much to tell, I'll probably forget half of it before I'm finished with this letter.

My "Valencia" is on the plain label, and it's my latest Whiteman record. Wish I had some of his scroll label and Columbia records. Maybe someday I'll make a big strike... Ha!

I'll begin by telling you about some records I just got recently... An old lady gave me some, others I bought (ten cents each, I don't get hooked anymore).

Here they are:

1. "Kentucky Babe" / "Chicory Chick" - George Olsen & His Orchestra (late thirties) - Majestic

[...]

I don't know exactly how much you owe me in old records, I've lost track... But I did give you a buck, *Dandy Comics*, *Crime Patrol*, and *When Worlds Collide*. How much postage will this cover... Oh, by the way, don't send any pre-1925 records unless they're old standards (which I don't think you'd part with). Hmm, for that matter, do you have any over 1925 that you don't want?

Read *archie and mehitabel* by Don Marquis (cartoons by George Herriman[1]). I think you'd like it!

I'll send you the Frank Crumit records, only something bad has happened... Your favorite one, "Abdul Abulbul Amir" has broken! Very sorry about this. It's got a chip about an inch and a half out of it... Do you still want it? I don't know how it happened, I was just going through the records a while back and there twas, broken. The others are okay though.

---

[1] In 1910, George Herriman created *Krazy Kat* for Hearst's *New York Journal* as something of an after-thought. The Kat's antics appeared in miniature, just below Herriman's main strip, *The Family Upstairs*. The Kat's popularity allowed Herriman to turn *Krazy Kat* into a regular feature in 1913, and the timeless, visionary strip ran for 30 years, until Herriman's death in 1944.

I've been hearing alot of Al Jolson lately, and they played a bunch of his old records on the radio a while ago... I've grown to like his singing! Especially the older records. I have an old Jolson Columbia record (blue label). You want it? (free)

Haw haw! Toobad Dave Ski beat you to the Whiteman twelve incher, poor clod. I bet that was an aggravating incident... To me, getting any of those kind of records is only wishful thinking. Do these record places you visit have lots of late twenties dance numbers?

What did Britt get while in Ohio? I suppose he told you where and how we got the *Puck*s and comic pages... I lied to you in my last letter cuz Britt said something about you being disdainful of thieves. Before you get mad, remember I'm not responsible for my actions! Heh heh.

The cover on your letter is pretty good... pretty funny.

Talking about teenagers, there's a good article in the March issue of *Esquire* called "Teenage Heroes: Mirrors of Muddled Youth," by Thomas B. Morgan. Really a good article, alot of the stuff you've said in it. Also in this issue is a neat cartoon by D. Levine, full page and in color. It looks just like the old *Puck* cartoons, and done in the same method (litho-crayon). The only thing wrong with it is that it doesn't fit in the 1960s... It doesn't bring out the era, and it looks rather English.

Have you seen *Shock*, the new pocket size magazine, cover and inside work by Davis, and short stories by famous horror and science fiction writers. Some are old stories, but a couple are brand new.

I got an old book called *You Have Seen Their Faces* (1937). It's about poor people in the South. Ghod, I didn't realize how extreme things were then, about like France before the Revolution, that's what the South was in the thirties. I wonder if things are much better now.

The tenant farmers and share croppers literally lived in bondage! They had to work on plantations for 180 dollars a year and if they tried to leave they would be beaten or the plantation owner would get a sheriff (elected by him) to arrest the poor slob. Each year the soil got worse and they had to work harder to get cotton out of the farmed-out soil. It was pretty pitiful. Shows photographs of the people, the farmers, who didn't know what a good meal was (they eat cornmeal and molasses and use snuff), who couldn't read, who never had electricity, they take out their bitterness toward the landlords by lynching niggers and going to church every Sunday and going through frantic spasmodic gyrations because they know when they die they'll go to Heaven and won't have to work or go hungry anymore. The politicians, who thrive on the ignorance and prejudices of the people, and the landlords, who said they knew how to handle the niggers if they didn't keep in their place and no nosy northerners better go around saying that niggers got rights to have this and that... All in all things were miserable then, and probably aren't much better now. It's hard to believe that such a class of peasants exists in America!

They papered their walls with magazine pages. I notice some old (neat)

Post covers in one photo here. Being as they didn't care about morals, they just kept having more and more children "like watermelons in the summertime." This made matters worse and worse, along with the decline of the fertility of the soil.

Have you seen the series of articles in *Post* from Norman Rockwell's autobiography? I'm reading and saving them. It's inspiring, reading about his career and working his way up. It was simpler in those days. If you had exceptional ability and ambition you were in. Not so now. He did his first *Post* cover in 1916... I have a *Judge* cover from 1917 by him... He has something most illustrators just don't have, though I can't exactly pinpoint it. Can you get old *Post* mags out there?

I've been practicing faces lately, and cloth wrinkles (a science in itself) and hands. How you likes th' cover on this? Paul Whiteman should be fatter. He was in the movie *King of Jazz*, I copied the photo out of Charles's book, *Pictorial History of the Talkies* by Daniel Blum. Really a great work, that book. It starts with *The Jazz Singer* and goes up to 1958.

Speaking of books by Daniel Blum, Charles also recently got *Pictorial History of Television* in the mail... Some of those shows really bring back memories. The thing about this that I like is that I myself have lived through and seen most of it. It doesn't go by years like Blum's other books, but program by program.

What surprised me most was that there was broadcasting in New York as early as 1930! And there was regular daily programs in New York area all through the thirties and the war time, though the number of TV sets stayed at 7,000 all during this period, up until 1947, when the first national network came on.

Thanks for the book *The American Revolution Considered as a Social Movement*. Do you want this back? It's really interesting and brings out good points. I'm only about halfway through it now, though.

I'll look for the *Catcher in the Rye*. You usually pretty well know what kind of stuff I like... I sent for the fifty-cent *Only Yesterday* recently.

Your English class doodles show that your faces are looking freer, and less awkward. By the way, how you doing in your studies these days?

Concerning the early work you sent me... the artwork is good for kids your age, but more than that, it shows you had a great love to write, which makes for great authors, and you have the perseverance and will that it takes, you're not lazy, and you're not afraid to set out on your own. From what I gather of an article called "Wishing Won't Make It So," (*Writer's Digest*) you show all the qualities of being a writer, if not a top writer. It says that although writers are "a dime a dozen" as you put it, they're not all diligent and persevering, which I think you are.

Your brother Norman did a good job illustrating "The Cricket on the Hearth." If he had only kept up his art, he'd be a good illustrator by now. His work seems to improve through the comic. How long did he work on this?

Odd the way he made everybody with their eyes closed there for awhile.

You certainly must have read alot of books then, unusual for a kid your age... I was still reading comic books about this time, and didn't take up regular books till I was fifteen. Wot o' clod, me!

Yes, I have Britt's address, now, in case you don't have it yet, hartiz...

2773 Miller Trunk Highway

Duluth II, Minnesota

I pity Britt, isolated up there, o' course, he may find a few second hand stores, mebbe. You're lucky in that you live right in the center of the old comic, old record belt, which seems to be the middle Atlantic states (not counting Delaware), Ohio, Indiana and Wisconsin. This is also where most colleges and cultures are, adding New England.

I bet Britt's sore cuz I gave you th' *When Worlds Collide*, but after all, he didn't seem to want it very much, whereas you did, so I thought you'd be alot happier to get it than him.

Yes, yes, and yes... do send a tape of your best records! Make it one o' the permanent kind, then I'll buy one and record some of mine and send it to you. I don't have enough good records to fill up a whole tape like you (jellies), so you can use it for your own purposes.

Do you think it is any use to try to get old records off an antique dealer cheap? I've been to one place, the old geezer has piles of old records, good ones too, but when I wanted to buy some he was just leaving and said to come back later. I had picked out about thirty records, doggone it, I'm goin' back there, but I don't want to pay atrocious prices for records. How much did Dave Ski pay for the Paul Whiteman scroll label twelve inch number?

I know a lady who has a pile of old sheet music, she let me look through it one time, but she wants to keep 'em, darn it... Old Vallee, Cantor, Jolson covers from the twenties, also alot with the famous orchestras from the twenties on the covers. Real neat covers on alot of 'em!

What kind of records did you look for at the U Save Shop? Would you have gotten any of the ones I listed that I got there if you had seen them? Or did you see them all and pass them up?

Were the 10 inch Paul Whiteman Columbia records black labeled like the others, or were they special labels like the 12 inchers, do you know? Are these scarce (10 inchers)? I imagine they are, since you don't have any.

What were some of the other, if any, great orchestras from the twenties? Was Whiteman's the only big-time famous orchestra?

Your facts about religion and society are good, really good points there... It gives a person a whole new look on the world. Now you can look at the whole picture, not just one little part of it... Get what I mean?

Do you believe that Christ existed? If so, he performed miracles, proving he was God, and God wouldn't lie, therefore there has to be a Hell. This is what Christians say. I've read that responsible scholars now except (accept) the fact that Christ existed. (This is not a Catholic writing.) But some believe that it was actually Saint Paul who started the religion as we know it. What have you to say about this? You know anything about this?

You know, the more I read and study, the more I can tell if a writer knows what he's talking about or not, and I'm surprised at how many phonies I run across!

Another thing, the more I study society and the nature of man, the more ridiculous some of the doctrines of the Church seem to be, and so superstitious, and people think they're living in a modern age... They haven't seen anything! Christianity may be dead in five-hundred years.

But, there must be a reason why intelligent men, who study theology for years, believe in their religions...

Why are you becoming convinced that you're never going to reach the point you're striving for? Not a defeatist attitude, it isn't like you!

During my religious period, when I was trying to be a fervent Catholic, when I look back, I see that I had to keep convincing myself that I truly believed and loved the religion, though it was a false front, deep down there was nothing 99 percent of the time. I couldn't see how the saints could be so sincere and strong in their faith, and why couldn't I, if I had free will? But now, this theory that I believe in is something you don't have to convince yourself of. It's just cold facts and there's no getting away from it!

Your paragraphs on the conditions of society have broadened my understanding of the world considerably, along with what you've told me about the theories of the make-up of man's nature, which I've heard something of before, but which are generally not publicized much. Mark Twain, who believed in these theories, is called a crackpot by the Church (naturally).

Wasn't Freud's theory turned into a popular fad during the twenties among the "Lost Generation"?

I'd like to find a copy of Menken's *The American Mercury* magazine. (It was popular among the "Lost Generation.")

There's one theory that all man's drives are sex motives, or something like that. Do you know anything about this theory?

Some of the English comics that Alan Dodd sent Britt are really neat, not like that stuff you sent me. Over there they take *Uncle Scrooge* comics, by that greatest of all regular Disney artists[1], and make Sunday strips out of it, putting good coloring on it and all, and it makes pretty neat strips too! *Camber*, while I'm talking about Dodd, is a great fanzine... Dodd is really a good writer, and prints plenty of great art, really tops for mimeograph!

Wish I had a typewriting machine! It sure would help on these letters... Maybe I'll buy that old 1905 job at Carroll's Market, that damn repulsive place! (If you hang around there long enough, the air begins to make you sick. If it wasn't for the old comics, I'd never go near the place!)

---

[1] Carl Barks

Speaking of comics, Charles has every issue of *Walt Disney's Comics* from June, '45 on up to the present. (Ha! Don't cover it up, youse is jellies!)

I got a couple of those Classics Illustrated binders recently. Neat! Hard covers and all for only a buck apiece. Do you have any? I got all 23 of my *MAD* comics in one (and I'm proud of the little book!). And my *Pogo* comics in the other. The only trouble with putting Dell comics in them is that they're a little wider than the Classics Illustrated, and they kinda stick out of the side, but still, they're better off in a bound book.

For some ridiculous reason (probably cause I had nothing better to do) I've copied down the titles, labels, and serial numbers of all my records on to index cards. You know, about half of all my records are from 1921, '22 and '23... what a collection of lemons...

You took alot of time and patience to preserve the old Sunday comic pages, but then, I can see why, the old paper is as brittle as ashes... But what about the strips on the opposite side? Weren't they any good?

Do you keep all your old records in cases and albums, or just in a couple of big stacks? Mine are all in albums, the better ones, the rest are in old paper cases (which I found about a hundred of at Carroll's Market) in a box. Do any of yours ever break? The only one of mine that ever broke was the Frank Crumit one, and just the one you wanted too, of all accursed luck!

WELL, WRITE SOON, AND SEND
ME SOME RECORDS!
—R. CRUMB

April 4, 1960
Dover, Delaware

Dear Marty

Well, good day, Sir... Here I go again... First off, I'm glad you liked that cover... I was kinda proud of it myself...

Yes, the "Paul Whiteman Discography" is quite a thing... I've marked with a red "X" all the records I have... Really a painstaking accomplishment, compiling it, I imagine... I'm really grateful for you sending it to me. Gollies! Hope you hear from ol' Paul Whiteman hisself about it! How old is he now? You know? No, wait... I have it right here in a book... Just looked it up, he's seventy this year... Perty old... I have this book *Panorama of American Popular Music*... It has a good but brief history of jazz... divided into two chapters "Ragtime, Blues, Jazz" and "Jazz Becomes a Sophisticated Lady"... in the ladder chapter, the author thinks Whiteman's early records, with orchestrations by Grofé, were pretty great because Whiteman and Grofé started a new kind of orchestra music in 1919... I'll have to play some of those old Whiteman records again and listen to them with a new point of view... Hmm.

Another unique kind of cover you made there, and with a good point to it... Very good point! Very attractive coloring, really neat! Keep it up...

Did you get any of those records from Sam Hannan? Toobad he has a stubborn father, but that's typical! I'd really like to have those records! I don't have many scroll label Victors myself... and none with Roger Wolfe Kahn. I have only one with Nat Shilkret, Leo Reisman is on the other side... It's one of my favorite records... Wish I could get some more. If you got ahold of alot of this kind (like from Sam Hannan) could you send me a couple, or mebbe just one? Hope you were able to get the Jelly Roll Morton and Jean Goldkette records from him... You lucky kid... How did you happen to meet Sam Hannan? I'd like to know so's I can try it too! Heh heh.

Say, I heard the songs from *Sunny Side Up* on TV last night on a special doing songs from movies... Put the records you have of those songs on the tape if you can... I like them! I have one record with two of the songs they played... "Forty-Second Street" and "Shuffle Off to Buffalo" (Hal Kemp Orch. - Brunswick) from the early thirties.

How far back does Bluebird label date? Wasn't it a branch of Victor? I remember down in Milford seeing a stack of Bluebird records with jazz, but that was before I became interested in the stuff. They were in an old furniture store. I went back to buy them later but they were gone. My luck!

Speaking of my luck, I went to that antique shop to trade my records that I don't want for all the ones I had picked out a couple months ago, but when I got there the place was empty... And I mean empty... Not a stick of furniture left in the place! A sign on the front window said, "THIS BUILDING TO BE USED FOR JEHOVAH'S WITNESSES MEETING HOUSE." I felt sick...

Hmmm... Interesting account of that place you went to call your father, something like some of the dumps I've seen around here.

Yes, Cole Porter sings himself on the record, with piano accompaniment. Tis in perfect condition too! One of the Edison records is black label, the others are white and black. They're one-fourth of an inch thick, so I guess that means "hill-and-dale" groove... The Edisons are in excellent shape, like new... The old lady who gave 'em to me had a whole cabinet full, but I only took those few as samples... I'll look for those two Edison reissues you mentioned.

Yes, yes... save any for me that you don't want that you think I might like... I'll send a dollar with this letter, I want I want I want I want...

Wha-a- alternate master?

You lucky lucky... Places all over to get old records where you are... I hope we can get to some of them when I visit. I may even get a few that you missed. Eeyaah!

Does Dave Ski have a big collection? Does he ever pay large sums for a record? Seems every place around here has been thoroughly cleaned out of records of any great value... I'm gonna hunt through Wilmington this weekend. My mother said she'd try to take me. Any good ones I get here are cracked or something!

Yes, I'll say picture label Columbias are scarcer than scroll label Victors. I've never even seen one.

Thanks for the list of orchestras... That guy at the antique shop had a stack of Perfect records with Sam Lanin Orch... Whenever I think... Also there was a bunch of Whitemans from '25 just before they changed the label... I'll look for *The Story of Jazz*... Something I'd really like to read!

I met an old jazzman recently name o' Ted Scudder. He was born in one of those small towns around Chicago. He started out by playing in a high school jazz band, and played trombone in a jazz band from 1914 to the early thirties. The band played in Chicago clubs and parties. He remembers his days during the jazz age well. One of these days I'm going to get him to talk more about the twenties, his own experiences and people he knew. He says he used to know Bix well, and alot of the famous jazz musicians. Says Bix "didn't know Christmas from Easter most of the time..." He has eight-thousand jazz records. He bought 'em when they came out since jazz was first recorded up to progressive, now. He has lots of rare ones, including King Oliver Gennetts and others. He had one King Oliver on Gennett that was worth <u>8,000</u> dollars! Reason: only two copies existed. I don't know why or how this happened. But he had it in a shed with some others and a fire destroyed it... Now there's only one of that record left... It must be priceless! He says he'll show me his records sometime, but he doesn't have access to them now... He lives in Smyrna, and his records are with his wife in Lewes (they're separated). He says as soon as him and his wife come to terms he'll get the records and show 'em to me... He found one he had laying around the house... "Margie," (medley introducing "Singin' the Blues") / "Palesteena" by the Original Dixieland Jazz Band (Victor - 18717, 1920). He gave it to me... I figure when he shows me the rest of his records I'll probably find some more that he doesn't want. Ted gave it to me cuz he thinks it's kind o' corny. He never cared for the big bands. When I asked him if he had any Whiteman records he said he thought Whiteman played "ricky-ticky music" or something like that... He says Bix was frustrated when he played for Whiteman 'cause he couldn't let go and play as much as he wanted to. The same with alot of other jazz men who played with big orchestras. Ted liked mostly the small bands, but I'll bet anything he has at least a few Jean Goldkettes, Red Nichols and such... He says he has some Wolverine recordings! Ted tells me about the same stuff I read in your letters, but mainly I want to see his records! He's inclining more toward progressive jazz now.

I'll send you the Original Dixieland Jazz Band record with the Frank Crumits... to replace the one that broke, okay? Mebbe you'll be a little more ambitious about sendin' me some then. I'm "jacking you up to send records" as Britt put it... And it's a dirty rotten thing to do, especially sending that *When Worlds Collide* to do it!!

I got most of my good records at the U Save Shop...

Hoo boy... a Salvation Army warehouse full of records... What a story Dave Ski told you! Such things are beyond my reach I suppose... things like thousands of records...

Charles wants you to "keep your eyes peeled" (eeyaah!) for photos, scenes, pictures of Robert Newton as Long John or Blackbeard or any scenes from Disney's *Treasure Island*. If you do find any, he'd appreciate it if you sent 'em. By the way, Charles has every *Disney* now from June '45 to the present. Wowee! Jellies!

Catcher in the Rye isn't in either of the libraries (school, town) in this town, doggonit! I'll have to look in the state library when I get the chance this summer. From what you say about it, I'm anxious to read it.

Send me a sample of the results of the style you used to do the *archie and mehitabel* comic page. I'm curious as to the general effect it gives. I've only read the one book of the series. In fact, I didn't even know there was a series till you told me... I really like the li'l book. Literature <u>and</u> art-wise, it's great! Colorful and warm!

Hmmm... I wish you lucky with your book! You'll get a tremendous amount of writing experience while doing it, and by the time you reach the end you'll probably notice a gradual improvement all through it. You've got a good topic, and I hope that along with criticizing our society (and it needs it!) you'll put some color and warmth into it. Try to bring out the fifties, capture it as an eyewitness, and also put some human warmth and folkishness into it. Oh well, it's your book, you know what's best for it!

True about our political system has become stagnant and stale. It's very noticeable looking at history of the U.S. Campaigns are more tradition now and have less really full meaning. There are no definite differences between the parties and, as you say, they've become institutionalized. It seems that the old donkey and elephant are just laying around because they're too old to move, but they're no longer of any use and might as well be shot and buried. Our history teacher, an old historian, spent a whole period ranting about those "idiots" down in Washington and the absurdity of the recent political game. Has your society (the one opposing segregation) done any lunch counter sit downs?... Oughta try it... heh heh... Of course, that business has kinda gone out of proportion... But, as Mr. Hynbach, the history teacher, put it, when a class of people has been stepped on for centuries, they reach the point where they feel they have the right to do some stepping on. Consequently, the sit downs in lunch counters fad.

Thanks for letting me keep *The American Revolution as a Social Movement*. No, you didn't send the one on slavery, send it if you can find it in your heaps of stuff... I'll enclose one or two of our older "two-man" comics, as we call 'em... I think you said you wanted older ones... We first started doing comics together in '55, I believe.

Sculpturing, you'll find, will help your art alot, and lettering is good to have, as you can paint signs as a sideline while working your way up... if you're lucky enough to get a job at it... You were wise to take those two courses... FENCING?? Ho ho!

Me and Charles cooperate? Tha's a laugh! We're always having arguments about something in one of the "two-mans"... (Wotta corny phrase, now that I think of it!) We're always resolving never to make another one, but we always do, they're enjoyable and do us both alot of good in creating schemes and situations, though now we're getting rather technical about it...

I agree with you on Christ. He revised the Jewish religion, but his followers after his death became radical, legends evolved, a few nuts claimed he performed miracles, etc.

Christians base their beliefs on what they believe to be historical facts. What Christ taught is beyond comprehension, they say, but you have to believe it because Christ said it was so and Christ is God... Our theories of man are based on fact, not history, as Christianity is. Now you know and I know that history can get confused. Just look at the greatest works of literature, plays by somebody back in the sixteenth century, and there's controversy over who wrote the stuff. You ask a Christian to prove our theory wrong and he says, "Christ was God and He taught differently, therefore your theory is wrong!"... But I say you can't base a theory on historical evidence... It doesn't hold up because you're merely taking somebody else's word for it when you believe history, and that person could have been lying or mistaken or mixed up. Our theories are universal and don't need history to back them up.

You could argue all your life about certain historical statements on Christ and the apostles and not get anywhere. You couldn't prove that he was God, but you couldn't prove that he wasn't, either!

One thing, how do you account for miracles, such as pictures of Mary that shed tears? A priest who has the wounds supposedly had by Christ? How do you explain this?

Very interesting, that about the place where the natives think of food as we do of sex... Very interesting, and fascinating! Actually, our moral codes concerning sex have evolved, though people think they exist as actual facts. They change all the time and probably will gradually fade, as they have been doing for a while now.

You're working on *Fanfare* three? *Fanfare*? What's that? I've forgotten, though the name sticks. What is it? A new kind of rocket? A new brand of cigarettes with mentholated, air softened, perforated, duel filtered, frazzniged knogged cigarette reverette breed?

Remember the days of fanzines? Ah memories!

Now to your stories and essays: Eduard Manet and Hogarth[1], both good essays... You're great at this type of work. I've seen a few cartoons by Hogarth, I wish I could see more! I like his work alot... It's colorful, and has more bounce and flexibility than most of his crude contemporaries...

"Me in the Boy Scouts"... this was the best of the stories, the little boy wording was hilarious, it's so typical, the incidents and the way you described them. And the people, too, were real... Did all that really happen, or is it fiction? Tha's a great story!

"Found" was good, but kind of windy... Sorta like *Dondi*[2], but the mechanics of it are alright.

"Emotional Experience" is very good! Alot of suspense built up there at the end! It made you feel you were living the story with the characters...

"Brady Lake" is also very good, especially to me personally, I guess, because it had information in it that I'm interested in, I got alot out of it. These kind of descriptions and tales of past glory of a place fascinate me... I liked it for my own interests.

The one where you talk about yourself is good... rather blunt and sarcastic, in a way... You talk to the reader, the prof, in a frank way... rather confusing.

[...]

---

[1] William Hogarth (1697-1764), English artist often considered to be the first cartoonist.

[2] Created by Gus Edson and Irwin Hansen for the Chicago Tribune-New York News Syndicate, *Dondi* won the NCS Best Story Strip Award in 1961 and 1962 (when it was also made into a movie). First appearing in 1955, *Dondi* chronicles the immigration / adoption troubles of an Italian-American war orphan.

[...]

Funny, I found that Bubber Miley record up in Northampton... Toobad you missed it when you went through the stacks... Eeyaah!

When I send records to you, I'll enclose something that's insured, so that they'll be careful with the package... I'll also put the records in an album when I send 'em... See if you can do the same...

I don't know whether I'll be able to visit you this summer... I may not have enough money, work at Latex is slacking off. I just hope it picks up this summer! I really want to get out there 'n' visit ya!

I haven't heard from Britt in a couple o' months... Can't understand it... I don't know his new address...

Yeh, I don't go in much for the modern *Post* style cartoons myself... I hope I never get that style in my work!

Have you seen the *Funnies Annual* put out by the King Features Syndicate? It's number one, costs a buck, has a small history of cartoons at the beginning, and is all reprints of strips from the syndicate... Toobad the other syndicates don't do it... But, anyway, it's a collector's item...

No, I don't have *Image*... I'll send to Benson for it...

Ecolian?... I haven't the slightest idea what the word means... I'll send you the graduation number when it comes out early this June. Another cover by me... I can't do my best when I'm under pressure for something... It's always in my head that I have to suit somebody when I do it, and the ideas don't flow freely, generally. It's a mediocre cover...

Say, do you know where I can write, that is, the address of the School of Visual Arts?... In New York... I want to write and find out what their standards are on grades... At least, that's what the guidance teacher said I ought to do... heh heh...

Gee, did you get the records from that girl yet? If you got what you expected to get (Paramounts, Ma Raineys) you sure are lucky! Y'know, boogie woogie Paramount records are rare 'n' valuable... If you got them, please list them in your next letter... Any you'd care to trade?

I'm more and more tempted to go door to door for records... In fact, tomorrow after school I probably will. Dover has a pretty large negro section, and I figure that somewhere in there, there's at least one pile of good hot records!

The only thing that holds me back is shyness, the same trouble you have, but with somebody along with me, I figure I'll have more gumption... Charles has agreed to go with me.

I want to get all the good records I have on tape, which will include the ones I trade with you, so I'll send them to you after I tape 'em, hokey?

I'm reading *The Jungle* by Upton Sinclair. Good book, but very depressing. It's full of implications that man is not responsible for his actions.

Yeh, Roth holds nothing sacred... It's one of his best qualities. He brought it out most in *Humbug*... In the *Poor Arnold's Almanac* it is subdued quite a bit, but still it shows... I'd like to see the strip on Lincoln. Heh, I just happened to think... I once had a history teacher who was going on about Lincoln... He showed us a picture of Christ and said the ol' Abe looked like him, Christ. Ghod, Lincoln will be 75 percent legend in 500 years... just like Christ... heh heh. People like to believe something just because it is beautiful...

Cardinal Richelieu, who left the church, called Christianity a "charming myth."

Don't send George Olsen, as they're pretty abundant, comparatively, and I have alot of them. What I want are the good bands that are scarce. You have lots of 'em, they may be common where you live, but I don't find 'em around here. (except for those Victors in Smyrna).

I have a Sam Lanin record backed by the Roseland Dance Orchestra. Do you know if it's the same orchestra?

Hmm, alot of famous jazzmen on that Ben Pollack record. Thanks for looking it up for me. Yaz, I'll be sure to look for Ben Pollack records next time I visit that place.

Just what is a washboard band?... Saw a Bluebird record with one of those bands at this new place I've found. Would you want it? I'll get it if you do. This place is only open on Thursday and Friday and closes at three o'clock, so I don't get much chance to get to it, but I doubt if anybody else will get to the records.

Include that Goldkette's Book-Cadillac record you have a double of in the ones for trade.

Tell about your visit with Delain... or his visit with you I should say...

What does *Jazz* by Whiteman include?

Do you know if the Hot Record Society still exists? Or the Hot Record Exchange? Back in the late thirties when *Jazzmen* was written, it seems they thought that hot record collecting would grow and become an established institution, almost like stamp collecting or something. What happened? It seems to me that it never came over. The war?

My sister Sandra, thirteen years old, has a teenage complex something awful. She wants to date seventeen year old boys cuz one of her friends is (luckily my mother just laughs at the whole thing)... Anyway, she's got tons of those teen magazines, which I look through. They kill me... the stuff... those boys in New York really know how to get the most out of the teenage bit... What psychology! Actually they oughta be ashamed... I'll quote from one article that really gave me a laugh...

"Why Do They Knock Me?" <u>supposedly</u> written by Fabian... concerning what the critics say about him. Listen to this:

"I think the public is hard to fool. Most people know what they like and don't pay much attention to those who try to tell them what is good and bad. I've learned that fans are fans not because of what they read, but because of what kind of job a performer does. That's true of my fans, anyway. For, if they had listened to my critics, I would never have sold another record."

How true, how true!... that last statement.

Yes, I'd like to see some of your mags and books on jazz... Send anything you think I'd be interested in or increase my knowledge of the subject. Are you getting any more interested in progressive jazz? Scudder is now a progressive fiend.

Speaking of Scudder, I haven't had much chance to talk to him lately. I'm not actually in the Theatre Guild, I just sorta hang around. Charles is in it, and I just go with him to some of the meetings and rehearsals. I dunno about Scudder, Mart, he seems to not give much of a damn about his past or his records... He seems to try to avoid talking about it much... I dunno, maybe it's my shyness... Anyways, he's more wrapped up in horse shows 'n' stuff now, and doesn't care to talk about his past... I've called up where he lives but he's never home, but still, I'll get him on the phone one of these days and talk... I can talk better over the phone anyway, when I don't have to look at the person I'm talking to.

Y'know, it was the people who made the *Jazzmen* book, who started the search for Willie "Bunk" Johnson, and found him. Before that time, he had existed only in legend.

I've made this index of all my records (on index cards). It seems like a waste of time and effort, but nothin' else to do.

I got a good laugh out of those fake labels you made... Clever of you... Then I played them out of curiosity... GAG!

Monday, 16 May, 1960

Well, I never did go door to door... I wanted Charles to go with me but he backed down... So I tried to go myself but just couldn't get up enough gumption... Dammit!

Garbutt was down (or up) again yesterday (lucky kid, he was rejected from the service). We went to an antique shop he knew of. I had been there once but there weren't no good records. This time there was a big box full of 'em! Good ones too! I got a small stack, about ten, out of the box (the best ones, I only had a little money), but the old lady wanted fifty cents each for them and they weren't in real good shape, so I put them back and walked out... after trying to bring down the price, to no avail. Garbutt came out shortly after with three records he bought. When we got home I traded him three old Guy Lombardo records for them... They weren't the best of the lot (at the antique place there were a few jazz items, on Emerson, Harmony labels) but they're good anyways. We played them at the shop on an old Sonora machine, that steel needle probably ruined 'em... I haven't used my needle on them yet, I still need a new one...

"Let's Talk about My Sweetie" / "Thanks for the Buggy Ride" - Paul Ash & His Orchestra - black label Columbia
"Give Me Today" / "School Day Sweetheart" - Colonial Club Orchestra - scroll label Brunswick
"Show Me the Way to Go Home" / "I'd Rather Be Alone in the South" - Singing Sophomores - black label Columbia

Well, all for this time. Write soon and let me know on the trading...

R. Crumb

P.S. Enclosed a few items for your amusement (or disgust)...Don't forget to send the Paul Whiteman and Arnold Roth letters.
    No need to return newspapers.

GAK!

~ 2 5 ~   *September 17, 1960*
                           Dover, Delaware

Dear Marty:
    The first letter after a visit is allus a hard one to write. You say it all in person and there ain't much left to say afterward in a letter.
    Got some records in Wilmington, though... And, oh yeah, Hurricane Donna came ripping through here last Monday... Ten or 'leven trees are down, a little flooding, but that's about the extent of the damage. Guess I shoulda wrote sooner, but there just hasn't been anything to say, and besides, I've been swamped with homework since school started... Ghod! I've never done so much homework in my life!
    I guess you're home now, by the time this letter reaches Ohio. How was it at Carol's place, ya lucky clod? What did you do in New York? Have o' good time? Did you talk to Kurtzman? What did Ivie think of the *Arcade* issues? Tell me all! Everything!   ...Yea'm.
    Send me a list of the records you got from me, will ya? Then I'll send back a list of those I want ya ta tape. Also, send a list of some of your records that you think I'd want taped, I'll appreciate it. Did you get any records in Philly or New York? Hope you can get the records you're gonna send me off soon, so I'll quit regretting all those ones I gave you... I'll help pay for the postage...

half the cost... Ya see, I'm near broke as it is, so that's 'bout all I can afford to contribute.

Charles would like to borrow that issue of *Chuck Crumb's Funnies* that he sent you... the one that had Fauntleroy spelled ten different ways in it. There's something he wants to check in it. Also don't fergit you owe me some old *Life*s and *Judge*s... Also, be sure ta send back the three issues of *Arcade*. Sheey! You're gonna have quite a bit of postage on your hands!

Say, were you in New York when the hurricane hit there?

Mmmm... Pahls, when are you gonna wise up!

I might as well list all the records I got 'n' then come back to the letter:

Damn, I was a soft-hearted fool to give up that Bennie Moten record that you had agreed to give me... Damn it... Oh well, I'm still gettin' the Williams' Cotton Club Orch., which is really a good'un. Did you find anything about that orch.?

Well, here's the list:

Victor 21219	"After My Laughter Came Tears" - VR / "In the Sing Song Sycamore Tree" - VR - Virginians
Victor 19676	"Mamie" - VR / "Montmartre Rose" - VR - Jan Garber & His Orch.
Perfect 14923	"Somebody Lied about Me" - VR - Sam Lanin Orch. / "My Ohio Home" - VR - Deep River Orch.
Victor 18680	"Slow and Easy (an Indigo Fantasy)" / "Whatcha Gonna Do When There Ain't No Jazz?" - Esther Walker
Velvet Tone 1878	"Button up Your Overcoat" / "I Wanna Be Bad" - Patsy Young - orch. accomp. Real good muted trumpet accompaniment and solos
Vocalion 14644	"Oh Gee! Oh Gosh! Oh Golly! I'm in Love" / "Maggie (Yes Ma'am)" - Billy Jones and Ernest Hare
Harmony 323	"Climbing up the Ladder of Love" - VR - Lou Gold Orch. "There's a Little White House" - VR - Bar Harbor Society Orch.
Cameo 742	"Got No Time" / "All Aboard for Heaven" - The Blue Dandies (Vocal)

Victor   "Want a Little Lovin'" - Fred Hamm & His Orch. - VR /
19915 "Tie Me to Your Apron Strings Again" - Jack Chapman's Orch.

Gennett   "Just for You" /
7119   "I'm Going to Live My Life Alone" - 5 Red Caps (black label) good
                        piano and guitar solos... negro vocal group

Oriole   "I'm Blue over Two Blue Eyes" - Billy James Dance Orch.
950   "Mine" - Majestic Dance Orch.

Velvet Tone   "I'd Love to Call You My Sweetheart" /
1300   "How I Love You" - Jane Grey - piano accomp.

Harmony   "Say It Again" - VR /
127   "Drifty and Dreaming" - Harmonians - VR

Cameo   "That's a Good Girl" - Seven Little Polar Bears - VR /
1018   "Lonely Nights" - Bob Haring & His Orch. - VR

Clarion   "Sentimental Baby" - Conrad Grey & His Mariners - VR /
5107   "Sweet Jennie Lee" - Wally Edwards & His Orch. - VR

Victor   "The Blue Room" /
20082   "Valencia" - The Revelers

I'll do that "Hey Ol' Cat" picture for you soon as I can. I enjoy doing anything in the field of art that I know will be appreciated. I just have to find the time.

Say, when ya send th' records send those ones you forgot to bring with you... "99 Out of a Hundred" by Sam Lanin (Oriole), "Baby Face" by Jan Garber, "The Girl Friend" (Olsen), "Hello, Bluebird," Art Landry, okay?

Saturday, 24 September 1960

God! I'm very sorry I've put off writing so long, really I yam. I've been utterly swamped with homework. It's awful! I've never done so much homework! Me and Charles just sold out the remaining copies of *Foo* number one today (about a hundred)... Made a good ten bucks... Went door to door... It's miserable work but worth the money, and besides, we won't have to look at a stack of *Foo* number ones anymore, thank ghod!!!

I'm going to try to get to Smyrna to get that race record catalogue at that place if I can (swipe it).

You said that you was gonna lettuce barrow *The Window* comic illoed by Toth... Please do so... Huh? Willya? Please? Huh? Huh?

I'm sending a pile of drawings along with this. I was gonna throw 'em away, but I thought maybe you'd like ta go through 'em first, 'n' throw 'em away if you like. I recall mentioning the fact that I'd throw some drawings away and you said I should have saved 'em for you, so, here's some… (Aren't you excited?) Hope the depravity doesn't shock you too much. (heh heh). Drawings by Charles and Sandra are interspersed withal. I thought mebbe these might help make up for this shamefully short letter.

You know you forgot your three jazz books… the ones you lent me… I'll send them to you soon as possible.

Are ya gonna go back to Kent State University or go to New York? Let me know the outcome of that scholarship mix-up.

Did you find out anything on that *Blackbirds of 1928* LP? Didja find it in New York? (wishful thinking)…

Well, I'm sorry but this about winds up this miserable excuse for a letter. I wouldn't feel so bad, only I get big eight-pagers from you… typed! Forgive me… I'll try to get a longer one to you next time.

……… Well, anyway, that's a nice sunset.

Yea'm.

Your Vigor for Life Appalls Me

October 30, 1960
Dover, Delaware

Dear Marty:

It's hard to believe it's the end of October already. Time certainly flies when you're busy. Yeh, that's right, I've been terrifically busy these two weeks since I got your letter. Artwork, homework, and deep meditation (heh heh) have been keeping active nights. This is about the first completely free day I've had these two weeks.

Sorry.

It'll probably happen again.

Tis a nice brisk October Sunday. The trees 'round about are all golden and the ground is covered with leaves. Ideal atmosphere for jack o' lanterns and all that Hallowe'en jazz.

Your last letter was a real morale booster to my work... It's comments like yours that give one the courage to go on. Your quote from Larry Ivie is really flattering! I ought to write to that fellow. I probably never will though.

I'm sending a dollar along with this so you can send me my records (mine all mine). I'm awfully anxious ta git them. Be sure to put in a big stack of extra ones (good too, none of that Benson Orchestra type) for that Clara Smith and for the fact that I think, by your ingenious way of talking, that you managed to get the better end of the deal on those records, so send lots of extras: any that you can spare. Haven't gotten a single old record since I last wrote... Things are bad around here in the way of old records. I got that LP *Duke Ellington at the Cotton Club* and an old 45 Victor of *Three Little Words* a 1930 Ellington reissue. I like about half of the LP... I'll get to like the rest after hearing it more.

Yes, that Patsy Young Velvet tone is good, very good trumpet solos, both "Sentimental Baby" and "Sweet Jennie Lee" on Clarion are good and have good solos. "Say It Again" by the Harmonians has alot of solo work on it too. Also good. Be sure to send all the stuff I mentioned in muh last letter.

Dover has reached a plateau of cultural advancement, a real bookstore has finally been opened downtown. Kind of a potty place, but maybe they'll improve. What they'll probably do is go out of business.

Delain sent us a copy of *Gamut*. Ghod, they messed up my "Winnie the Phoo" artwork! Toobad they had to print it in mimeograph. Your "A Sad Fable" is by far the cleverest bit in the whole hopeless effort. "Dick Swinnercault" by Bridwell is just plain dum... I mean, strictly CORNBALL, in my opinion.

I'm enclosing an article clipped from the Sunday, 23 October edition of the *Philadelphia Bulletin* that might interest you. I'm going to try to get my hands on some of the National States' Rights literature. It would be interesting to read. If I do, I'll send it to you. No need to send back this clipping.

Charles just told me to remind you to send the *Chuck Crumb's Funnies* and the three issues of *Arcade*, hokey?

No, I haven't gotten the Victor race catalogue yet, but I'm still determined! I hope I can get up there before those two old people die.

Have you seen the latest *Help!* (number four)? Kurtzman putting his moniker on the cover, yet! Toobad they have to plaster the covers with useless pictures of celebrities to sell the thing. How much better 'twould be to have covers like those little masterpieces on *Humbug* and the old *MAD*! A pity! This is a pretty good issue of *Help!* actually. Very clever! The satire by Shir-Cliff is pretty much of an achievement in the photos-with-captions technique. Generally I think it's the best issue yet!

Comments on the drawings you sent: they range from very good to somewhat hideous. One thing I'll say, you have a sense of volume, form in action. This you're good in. Also faces. Proportion is something we all have trouble with. Your ball point pen work is very good. Good shading. A couple of the faces are very stylish, and attractive.

Concerning your poem, shows ability, is amusing, if you're a jazz record collector. You might be able to write outstanding poetry someday, that one you sent shows promise.

Glad you can send me a tape soon. I'll send you one back or pay for the one you send. I've got lots of records to tape. You overlooked quite a few good ones that didn't have obvious names (Joe Candullo, Miami Society Orchestra, etc.) when you were here that I could put on tape, along with a few new ones I've gotten.

Glad you got to go back to the university! Got the scholarship business straightened out, eh?

What's the story you've been illustrating, something original? Tell me about it, fellah!

Yes, I know what you mean about inking in with a brush. You can go so fast, and you are inclined to with a brush, that you get sloppy. That's why I don't do it much. I always got carried away when I tried it. Heh heh.

What are you taking in college this year? What in the way of art?

I got two old pulp magazines at Carroll's Market: *Detective Action Stories* January, 1937, and *The Shadow* July first, 1936. Do you know if Thailing or anybody would want them? I got no use for them.

I'll try to get out to Ohio this Christmas, I really would like to, I just don't know 'bout the money. I hope I can.

Ever listen to Jean Shepherd on WOR radio on Sunday? Yechh, wot an idiot! Quite entertaining though, and he plays good music, though he gets wearisome after a while.

Have you seen that new series called *The Roaring Twenties* on television? Ghod, what commercial krap! Violence, sex, the usual disillusioning baloney. They have un-authentic 1920s style music. Very bad exaggeration, stereotyping to the extreme. A real let-down... Disgusting.

I got a children's book at Carroll's Market recently called *More Really-So Stories* (1929) with beautiful, really great illustrations and lettering by a fellah named John Rae. Ever hear of him? There are some beautifully done silhouettes in this book by him, and paintings in color that have a really great style. If you know anything about him, fill me in, will ya? ...John Rae.

I'd like to sit here and fill up ten more pages trying to express some strong things I feel about life and the world and people and all of it (ar, techin'), but I realize it would be a fruitless effort so I might as well end this letter here and now... Yea'm.

So good-by, send everything, *Arcade*s, old magazines, RECORDS, and a letter. I wish I could make this letter longer, but I'm afraid to start in on any long-winded subjects. Sorry. I'll try not to put off writing this late again.

Oh, a word or two about the cover. Everybody around this town is running around like a chicken with its head cut off predicting the all-out war that seems to be in the near future, and how millions will die and we'd better wake up and the terrible Communists and the "yellow horse-men" are going to kill all the women, old people and children, and make slaves of the rest, or that civilization will be wiped out. Actually, I'm not in the least bit moved by all this, whether it may happen or not, I don't care. Best not to get involved, I say. Stand by and watch, but stay out of it. So they get you, kill you, what of it?! It doesn't worry me at all. If savages want to fight each other, let them! Well, so much for ridiculous philosophy.

Flub flub flub flub...
The dollar is in here someplace.

March 18, 1961
Dover, Delaware

DEAR MARTY:
    WELL, MARTY, I'M AFRAID I'VE GOT AN EARLY CASE OF SPRING FEVER. IT'S BEEN... LETSEE... THREE WEEKS SINCE I GOT YOUR LETTER..... AND.... ACTUALLY MY HEART HASN'T BEEN IN ANYTHING FOR ABOUT THE PAST MONTH.... I'VE BEEN DEPRESSED, CONFUSED, AND FRUSTRATED. THIS LEADS TO DISCOURAGEMENT IN ANY ATTEMPT, LETTERS INCLUDED. NOTHING SEEMS INTERESTING OR WORTHWHILE. I HATE TO KEEP YOU WAITING SO LONG WHEN YOU USUALLY ONLY TAKE ABOUT A WEEK TO ANSWER MY LETTERS.... FOR ABOUT A MONTH I HAVE DONE NOTHING... (EXCEPT A DAMN TERM PAPER). NOTHING SEEMED WORTH DOING. I THINK I'M PASSING OUT OF THIS DISMAL PERIOD I DUNNO.... MAYBE I'LL SINK BACK INTO IT IN A DAY OR TWO.... MAYBE NOT.... I'VE PROMISED IN THE PAST TO WRITE MORE OFTEN 'N' ALL THAT JAZZ... GUESS I'M JUST "SPORADIC"...
    THINK I'LL WRITE THE REST OF THIS LETTER AS A COMIC BOOK... JUST FOR A CHANGE...

YES... I AM TROUBLED OF LATE... TRYING TO FIND MYSELF AND ALL THAT, YOU KNOW.... IT SEEMS THE MORE I EXPLORE MY POTENTIALS THE MORE DISCOURAGED I GET.... WELL, MAYBE SOMEDAY THE LIGHT WILL HIT ME... WE HAVE MANY THINGS TO REALIZE AND MUCH TO DISCOVER IN OURSELVES... IT'S NOT EASY AT FIRST, AND I'M JUST STARTING, I FEEL,

THERE ARE TIMES WHEN THE WORLD AND LIFE SEEM SO GOOD AND GREAT AND JUST BEING ALIVE IS A WONDERFUL THING, AND OTHER TIMES IT ALL SEEMS TO BE JUST A FRUSTRATING MASS OF CONTRADICTIONS.... IN SHORT, I'VE GOT TO GET MYSELF STRAIGHTENED OUT. GOT TO COME TO DEFINITE CONVICTIONS ABOUT THINGS. GOT TO FIND SOMETHING TO LIVE BY....

I GOT RID OF TH' COAT SO I DON'T HAVE TO FILL IN ALL THAT BLACK IN EVERY PICTURE... WELL... SO MUCH FOR MY PETTY TROUBLES ...

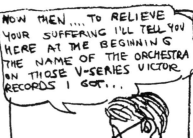

NOW THEN.... TO RELIEVE YOUR SUFFERING I'LL TELL YOU HERE AT THE BEGINNING THE NAME OF THE ORCHESTRA ON THOSE V-SERIES VICTOR RECORDS I GOT...

I'VE NEVER HEARD OF THE NAME BEFORE... AND I DOUBT IF YOU EVER HAVE... IT'S "TAL HENRY AND HIS ORCHESTRA"... A GOOD BAND ... "MY LITTLE OLD HOME DOWN IN NEW ORLEANS" IS REALLY A GREAT NUMBER... ARRANGEMENT-WISE AND SOLO-WISE... REALLY A JOY TO LISTEN TO! I FOUND THEM IN SMYRNIA AMONG THE RED-SEAL VICTORS... I HAD NEVER LOOKED THROUGH 'EM BEFORE...

TRIED TO SWIPE THAT RACE CATOLOGUE BUT THE OL' LADY CAUGHT ME...BUT I HAVEN'T GIVEN UP...I FOUND SOME ORCHESTRAS ON SONORA RECORDS AMONG THE RED SEALS TOO, BUT DIDN'T BUY THEM...WAS THERE EVER ANYTHING GOOD ON SONORA LABEL...

GOT A FEW WORTHWHILE RECORDS SINCE MY LAST LETTER... "BLACKBIRDS OF 1928" FOR ONE...FOUND ANOTHER COPY OF IT IN THE SAME PLACE YOU GOT YOURS...WAS IN WITH THE CLASSICAL STUFF...ONLY COST ME 2.19...HEH HEH!

ALSO, I GOT SOME RECORDS AT THE WILMINGTON SALVATION ARMY...THE 1927 VERSION OF "RHAPSODY IN BLUE" BY PAUL WHITEMAN; MINT CONDITION BUT NOTHING TO RAVE ABOUT...

THEN, THERE'S AN OLD FAVORITE OF MINE, "LET'S DO IT" BY IRVING AARONSON (1928), WHICH IS QUITE GOOD, ONLY ITS CRACKED, DAMN!

ALSO, "I'M COMIN' VIRGINIA" BY THE CAROLINERS (LINCOLN-2608)...NOT AS GOOD AS ONE MIGHT THINK FROM LOOKING AT THE LABEL...ON THE FLIP SIDE, "A SHADY TREE" BY SAM LANIN'S TROUBADOURS...FAIR NUMBER...ALSO "YOU WERE MEANT FOR ME" BY TED WHITE'S COLLEGIANS ON ORIOLE....VERY GOOD BUT SCRATCHY AS HELL...AND ANOTHER OLD FAVORITE OF MINE, WHICH I WILL CONTINUE TO TELL YOU ABOUT ON THE NEXT PAGE...

Your Vigor for Life Appalls Me

YES... WHEN AND/OR IF I VISIT YOU COME SUMMER I'LL WANT TO MEET DOUG STOCK...SOUNDS LIKE HE'S GOT QUITE A BIT ON THE BALL... ALSO, I'LL WANT TO MEET YOUR OTHER FRIENDS... I WANT TO SEE EVERYBODY, AND DAMMIT, IF I HAVE THE GUMPTION, I MIGHT SPEAK TO THEM NOW AND THEN...HEH HEH... YOU'RE RIGHT ABOUT THAT DAM VALENTINE COVER I MADE...IT WAS A MISTAKE.

ALSO... I THINK YOU'RE RIGHT IN THAT CHARLES AND I TAKE A "SYMPATHETIC AND WARM" APPROACH TO "LUDI-CROUS SITUATIONS." THAT PROBABLY ABOUT SIZES IT UP...
ARE YOU KEEPING UP WITH FANDOM THESE DAYS? SEEN THIS NEW FANZINE CALLED "PLAGUE"? THOSE BOYS ARE GOOD CARTOONISTS (WEST COAST ZINES GROUP), SOME REAL TALENT THERE...

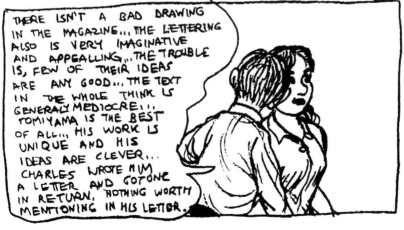

THERE ISN'T A BAD DRAWING IN THE MAGAZINE... THE LETTERING ALSO IS VERY IMAGINATIVE AND APPEALLING... THE TROUBLE IS, FEW OF THEIR IDEAS ARE ANY GOOD... THE TEXT IN THE WHOLE THINK IS GENERALY MEDIOCRE... TOMIYAMA IS THE BEST OF ALL... HIS WORK IS UNIQUE AND HIS IDEAS ARE CLEVER... CHARLES WROTE HIM A LETTER AND GOT ONE IN RETURN, NOTHING WORTH MENTIONING IN HIS LETTER.

CHARLES RECIEVED A COPY OF "IMAGE" NUMBER ONE FROM JOHN BENSON RECENTLY. QUITE A LOT OF INFORMATION CONTAINED IN IT.... ALOT OF TRIVIA, TOO, BUT STILL, IT'S A WORTHWHILE VENTURE ON THE PART OF BENSON.... I'M INCLINED TO THINK THAT JOHN WORSHIPS RUTH SOME. WHAT.

WHAT'S THIS IN "IMAGE" ABOUT SOME MAGAZINE CALLED "BOUNTY"?

A COMMENT FROM YOU STATES THAT IN 1955 THERE WAS A DELIGHTFUL SATIRE MAG CALLED "BOUNTY".. DO YOU HAVE ANY COPIES OF IT? TELL ME ABOUT IT.

THAT ARTICLE BY VON BERNEWITZ IS EXTREMELY INTERESTING, SPEAKING OF VON BERNEWITZ, CHARLES RECIEVED A LETTER FROM HIM RECENTLY STATING THAT HE WANTS TO GET BACK INTO FAN ACTIVITIES.

THAT POOR CLOD HAS SURE TASTE LIFE! GOD ONLY KNOWS WHAT I'M IN FOR!

THANKS FOR STRAIGHTENING ME OUT ON THAT THING IN "IMAGE" THAT GAVE ME THE IMPRESSION THAT DOUG BROWN WAS DOING SCIENCE-FICTION MAGAZINE WORK. YOU SEE, I LOOK THROUGH A COUPLE OF THEM AND FOUND SOME ARTWORK SIGNED "DOOG" THAT RESEMBLED DOUG BROWN'S, AND I THOUGHT... WELL....

'SO YOU THINK I HAVE MORE POTENTIAL THAN LARRIE IVIE.... HMM..... ENCOURAGING, DEAR FRIEND... ENCOURAGING!
    "HELP" SEEMS TO BE GETTING BETTER AND BETTER... MORE CARTOONS... AND THE ARTISTS ARE AT THEIR BEST AT THAT... I'D LIKE TO SEE AN ILLUSTRATED COVER, THOUGH IT PROBABLY WOULDN'T BE WISE AT THIS POINT TO CHANGE THEIR COVER FORMAT...

THE PRESENT COVER FORMAT THEY HAVE IS APPEALLING IN ITS WAY, THOUGH PERSONALLY WOULD PRE- FER AN ILLUSTRATED COVER...
    DID YOU READ ABOUT THE DEATH OF NICK LA ROC- CA OF THE ORIGINAL DIXIE- LAND JAZZ BAND?
    THE RUSSIANS ARE NOW CLAIMING THEY INVEN- TED JAZZ. IT BECAME SUCH A POPULAR FORCE THAT THEY COULD NO LON- GER SUPPRESS IT,

SO NOW THEY SAY THEY INVENTED IT, FOR GHOD'S SAKE!
    THANKS AGAIN FOR THE BARNABY BOOK... SURE GLAD YOU COULD GET IT FOR ME... I'LL
    I DUNNO ABOUT CHARLES AND MY "ON THE ROAD" VENTURE...WE'RE BOTH STILL GAME FOR IT, BUT NO MONEY, OR HARDLY ANY... AND MY MOTHER... SHE IS DEAD SET AGAINST US!... THEN AGAIN, MY FATHER, BEING WHAT HE IS IS ALL FOR IT...

POF

GARBUTT TELLS US THAT THE MILFORD FOLK STILL TALK ABOUT THE CRUMBS NOW AND THEN. "((((... CHARLEY AND BOB CRUMB COULD DRAW GOOD BUT THEY WERE ODD BOYS' OR", THAT WHOLE CRUMB FAMILY WAS CRAZY" THEY SAY... REMINDS ONE OF KURTZMAN'S ROTTENVILLE...

WELL, GETTING BACK TO WHAT I WAS GOING TO SAY, WE JOURNEYED TO SMYRNA AND I GOT FOUR RECORDS. I LOOKED FOR THE RACE CATALOG BUT THE DAMN OL' LADY SAID THEY TOOK IT OUT,,,, I WONDER WHAT THE HELL THEY DID WITH IT...

I FOUND TWO RECORDS BY THIS "TAL HENRY AND HIS NORTH CAROLINIANS" ON THE 20000 SERIES. NEITHER OF THEM LIVE UP TO THAT ONE ("MY LITTLE OLD HOME", ETC...)

THESE TWO I GOT ARE '28, THE OTHER TWO ARE '29 AND MUCH BETTER,, THE '28 ONES SURE WEREN'T WORTH THE FIFTY CENTS APIECE. THEY HAVE A WIERDLY SICKENING QUALITY ABOUT THEM,,,

THIS QUALITY IS RELIEVED BY ONLY ONE SHORT FAIRLY GOOD TRUMPET PIECE ON ONE OF THE FOUR SIDES,,,, WHICH IS ALSO THE BEST OF THE SIDES ARRANGEMENT-WISE,

THE OTHER TWO INCLUDE A GOOD IRVING AARONSON OF 1928... A GOOD SOLO ON ONE SIDE THAT IS, I THINK, AN ALTO SAXOPHONE,,,, I LIKE THE AARONSON BAND...

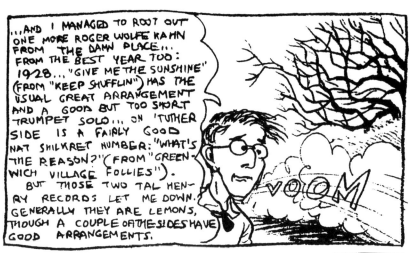

...AND I MANAGED TO ROOT OUT ONE MORE ROGER WOLFE KAHN FROM THE DAMN PLACE... FROM THE BEST YEAR TOO: 1928... "GIVE ME THE SUNSHINE" (FROM "KEEP SHUFFLIN") HAS THE USUAL GREAT ARRANGEMENT AND A GOOD BUT TOO SHORT TRUMPET SOLO... ON 'TUTHER SIDE IS A FAIRLY GOOD NAT SHILKRET NUMBER: "WHAT'S THE REASON?" (FROM "GREENWICH VILLAGE FOLLIES").

BUT THOSE TWO TAL HENRY RECORDS LET ME DOWN. GENERALLY THEY ARE LEMONS, THOUGH A COUPLE OF THE SIDES HAVE GOOD ARRANGEMENTS.

VOOM

BY THE WAY, DON'T FORGET YOU STILL OWNE ME A BEN POLLACK RECORD... HEH HEH...

I'M GAME TO WORK SOMEWHERE FOR AWHILE, IF I CAN MANAGE TO SAVE A DECENT AMOUNT OF TH' EARNINGS. BUT, LIKE, WHERE COULD WE GET JOBS? EH?

I THINK IF ONE DEVOTED HIMSELF TO THE CAUSE, HE COULD ACHIEVE TRUE EXPRESSION THROUGH COMBINED WORDS AND PICTURES... SUCH AS IN THE COMIC STRIP...

TOOOT TOOOT

IF GEORGE HERRIMAN CAN DO IT, THEN IT'S NOT IMPOSSIBLE... THIS IS ONE OF THE THINGS I MAY EVENTUALLY TRY TO ACHIEVE... I THINK KURTZMAN HAS DONE IT...

TOOOT

THE IDEAS YOU EXPLAINED FOR A COMIC-STRIP SOUND GREAT TO ME... IT SOUNDS LIKE SOMETHING I'D LIKE TO DO MYSELF.. YES, IT WOULD REALLY BE GOOD IF DONE RIGHT... AND...

SPLAT

...AH ME... IT HAS BEEN ANOTHER TWO WEEKS... YES... SO VERY SORRY FOR THIS GREAT DELAY, BUT A GREAT NUMBER OF THINGS HAVE KEPT ME FROM THIS LETTER... TODAY IS MONDAY, APRIL FOURTH.

YOU'RE PROBABLY GETTING THE IDEA I'VE LOST INTEREST IN THIS CORRESPONDENCE... THIS IS NOT TRUE...GUESS I'M JUST "SPORADIC", AS I'VE SAID BEFORE...

LESSEE... MY TIME HAS BEEN SPENT LABORING ON HOMEWORK. YOU SEE, WE HAVE THIS IDEALISTIC PRINCIPAL WHO BELIEVES IN LOTS OF HOMEWORK FOR THE STUDENTS IN THE HIGH SCHOOL), AND HOURS AND HOURS PHILOSOPHYING AND REFLECTING IN SOLITUDE OR WITH CHARLES...

AND ALL LAST WEEKEND WAS TAKEN UP DOING A QUICK OIL-PAINTING FOR A SIX-HUNDRED DOLLAR STATE-WIDE ART SCHOLARSHIP CONTEST. THREE WINNERS WILL BE CHOSEN,

THIS THING IS SPONSORED BY (GET THIS;) HALL MARK CARDS AND THE FEDERATION OF WOMEN'S CLUBS AND THE DOVER CENTURY CLUB.. GOD... AND GEE WHIZ, GOSH-ALL GET OUT I GOT MY GODDAM PICTURE IN THE DOVER TOWN PAPER!

144   *Your Vigor for Life Appalls Me*

ANOTHER CHIEF FACTOR IN THE DELAY OF THIS EPISTLE IS THE FACT THAT WE HAVE JUST THIS WEEKEND PACKED UP AND MOVED OUT OF OAK DRIVE...

YES, WE NOW RESIDE IN GOVERNOR'S AVENUE... IN A RAMBLING OLD TWO-STORY "AMERICAN GOTHIC" STRUCTURE IN ONE OF THE OLDER NEIGHBORHOODS, I LIKE IT BECAUSE WE ARE ONLY A BLOCK FROM DOWNTOWN AND THIS THOROUGHFARE IS NEVER DULL.. WE LIVE ACCROSS FROM THE FIRE STATION FOR ONE THING... ALSO, THE COLLEGE IS RIGHT CLOSE BY...

THE ADDRESS, FOR YOUR INFORMATION, IS 56 GOVERNOR'S AVENUE. WELL, TO GET BACK TO ANSWERING YOUR LETTER:

YES, I AGREE WITH YOU THAT KELLY SPOILED "OUR GANG" WITH THE CRIME STUFF... DON'T KNOW WHY HE DID IT, MAYBE THEY TOLD HIM TO... THE BEST OUR GANG STORIES BY FAR WERE THE ONES WITHOUT THE CROOKS, BUT THE ARTWORK WAS ALWAYS GREAT!

HAVE YOU RECIEVED YOUR COPY OF ALTER-EGO YET? WHAT'S YOUR OPINION OF IT? GHOD... WHAT A WASTE OF GOOD PAPER! DON'T SEE HOW ANYBODY COULD DEVOTE HIMSELF TO "DC" COMICS. AH, I GUESS I'M BEING NARROW-MINDED!

AS FOR GIRLS, AS I SAID BEFORE, AND I SAY IT NOW... BETTER, SIMPLER, PURER. TO LOVE AT A DISTANCE... I FIND THIS INCREASINGLY EASY TO DO AS LIFE GOES ON, AND ALSO, I GET INCREASINGLY MORE OUT OF IT...

IMAGINARY GIRL ←

I AM APPALLED BY THE FEMININE ESSENCE, YOU SEE, AND THIS CAN BE APPRECIATED MORE BY OBSERVING THAN BY KNOWING INTIMATELY THE GIRL AND ALL HER CORRUPTIONS.

YA SEE, I'VE GOT TWO SISTERS AGES FOURTEEN AND NINETEEN AND I KNOW THEM INTIMATELY AND I KNOW WHAT GIRLS ARE REALLY LIKE... THE SOUL OF THEIR NATURE IS OVERWHELMING, BUT THE PERSONALITIES OF MOST OF THEM ARE... WELL... FEH...

AGAIN I'M NOT MAKING SENSE... WELL, WHAT'S NEXT HERE? OH YES... YOUR FRIEND CAROL... YOU CERTAINLY MUST HAVE NOT BEEN VERY CLOSE TO HER... HOW COULD YOU SPEND A WEEK WITH HER AND NOT BE UNHAPPY... I KNOW I WOULD HAVE BEEN DEPRESSED HAVING A LIVE A WEEK WITH A GIRL WITH FALSE VALUES SUCH AS SHE HAS, UNLESS MAYBE SHE WAS FREE WITH THE SEX... HMM... I GUESS EVEN THIS WOULD DEPRESS ME (AFTERWARDS). COULDN'T YOU TALK TO HER? TRY TO REVEAL YOUR ATTITUDE TOWARD LIFE TO HER, IT'S POSSIBLE YOU COULD OPEN HER EYES TO TRUE VALUES.

AS FOR INTELLECTUAL GIRLS, AS WITH MANY VERY SMART MALES, THEY SEEM TO LACK INSIGHT AND AWARENESS, THOUGH THEY MIGHT BE TOP-GRADE INTELLECTUALS, THERE'S A GIRL HERE IN DOVER SCHOOL LIKE THIS. SHE'S PROBABLY THE TOP SCHOLAR IN THE SENIOR CLASS, BUT IT IS APPARENT THAT SHE HAS LITTLE INSIGHT. I THINK INSIGHT IN A PERSON IS MORE IMPORTANT THAN A CALCULATING MIND.

Your Vigor for Life Appalls Me

SEND ME A STORY OR TWO OF YOURS WITH YOUR NEXT LETTER. I IMAGINE YOUR RECENT WORK IS AN IMMENSE IMPROVEMENT OVER THOSE THAT YOU SENT ME ABOUT A YEAR AGO.

LARGE DRAWING ON PREVIOUS PAGE BY C. CRUMB

THEY WERE THE ONLY LITERATURE I'VE SEEN BY YOU, SO I'M ANXIOUS TO GET A LOOK AT WHAT YOU'VE DONE SINCE THEN.

YES, YES, SEND ME THE PARTS OF THE NOVEL AS YOU GET THEM DONE, I'M FLATTERED THAT YOU WOULD TAKE STOCK IN MY CRITICISM... THIS SHOULD BE AN INTERESTING AND ENJOYABLE EXPERIENCE FOR ME, AND I HOPE I CAN BE OF SOME HELP TO YOU. I'LL MAKE AN EARNEST EFFORT TO MAKE PROMPTER REPLIES, TOO.

HM. DIDN'T KNOW IT WAS SO COMPLICATED PREPARING TO WRITE A BOOK... CHARTS AND DIAGRAMS, BUT I SUPPOSE THESE THINGS WOULD BE USEFUL. I WOULDN'T WANT TO BECOME OVERLY BOGGED DOWN WITH THEM THOUGH, MIGHT INHIBIT YOU.

MM... CATTISH...

GEESE... YOU SURE PLAN TO WORK HARD ON IT! YOU MUST HAVE A LOT OF CONFIDENCE IN YOURSELF... OF COURSE YOU'RE KIDDING WHEN YOU SAY FIFTEEN HOURS A DAY OF WRITING FOR FOUR MONTHS... THIS IS PHYSICALLY AND MENTALLY ALMOST IMPOSSIBLE! ONE WOULD CERTAINLY HAVE TO BE PASSIONATELY INSPIRED, TO DO EVEN HALF THAT MUCH. ARE YOU REALLY EXCITED AND ENTHUIASTIC ABOUT THIS NOVEL? I SHOULD THINK SO.

Your Vigor for Life Appalls Me

THIS THING OF SHOWING HOW CHARACTERS ATTITUDES DEVELOPE OVER A LONG PERIOD OF TIME IS GOING TO BE A DIFFICULT TASK, AND WILL TAKE SOME HARD, DEEP THOUGHT.

UNLESS WRITTEN WITH ABILITY, THIS THEME COULD PROVE INEFFECTIVE. THE POINT COULD GET LOST, I MEAN. THEN AGAIN, IF WRITTEN WELL, IT WOULD BE A GREAT NOVEL. I LIKE THE IDEA OF WRITING IT AS THE CHARACTERS' THOUGHTS

I WISH I COULD BE AS FREE WITH MY OPINIONS AS YOU ARE. BETTER TO LET PEOPLE KNOW WHERE YOU STAND THAN TO LET THEM THINK YOU'RE SOMETHING YOU'RE NOT, OR BE SUBMISSIVE, AS IN MY CASE, AND LET PEOPLE DOMINATE YOU. YOU MAY LOSE FRIENDS, BUT ANY YOU HAVE WILL BE SINCERE, BECAUSE THEY ACCEPT YOU FOR WHAT YOU REALLY ARE.
GENERALLY I GUESS I LOOK AT PEOPLE ABOUT THE SAME AS YOU, AS INDIVIDUALS AND UNIVERSALLY, BUT THE SENTIMENTALITY I FEEL FOR PEOPLE AND THE WORLD IS SOMETHING UNEXPLAINABLE, I WOULDN'T KNOW WHERE TO BEGIN.

IF YOU CAN GET A COPY OF THE "OBESE TOAD" FOR ME WITHOUT TOO MUCH BOTHER I'D 'PRECIATE IT.
HAVE YOU SEEN "YAK YAK"? A MAD-IMITATION COMIC BOOK PUT OUT BY DELL...NEVER THOUGHT I'D SEE THE DAY! TERRIBLE TEXT, BUT THE ART IS COMPLETELY BY DAVIS, AND MOST OF THIS IS HACK STUFF.
I FOUND TWO BOUND VOLUMES OF "COSMOPOLITAN" FROM 1893 TO 1896 IN A JUNK STORE, GREAT OLD CARTOONS BY KEMBLE IN THEM...

THANKS FOR EXPLAINING YOU POEM ABOUT KRAZY KAT TO ME... YOUR SYMBALISM IS GOOD AND THE IDEALS BEHIND IT GREAT, BUT I THINK PERHAPS YOU OUGHT TO TRY BEING A BIT LESS COMPLICATED, FOR THE SAKE OF THE UNWASHED MASSES (LIKE ME), I DUNNO, MAYBE YOU'VE GOT A GOOD THING GOING HERE AND IT JUST NEEDS POLISHING.
WELL, LOOKS LIKE I'VE FINALLY REACHED THE END. FORGIVE ME FOR THE RIDICULOUSLY LONG DELAY OF THIS LETTER, AND AS I HAVE SAID MANY TIMES IN THE PAST, I'LL TRY TO WRITE SOONER FROM NOW ON.
P.S. I JUST GOTTA READ MORE KRAZY KAT STRIPS. YOU GOT ANY BOOKS?

56 GOVERNOR'S AVENUE

May 28, 1961
Dover, Delaware

Dear Marty:

This is getting ridiculous! A month and a half this time. As soon as I get out of school, I'll write to you within a week after I get your letters, I can assure you. That is, if I'm home. As it stands at the present, though, I'm afraid I'm going to have to make this a short letter, since I'm now in the midst of doing a term paper and I still have what looks like a vast sea of books to wade through before the year's over. But then... ah... leisure... nothing but time on my hands... to write, draw, create, and think... and feel.

So little has happened here... next to nothing, actually. No records, no comics, no books to report on.

Anyway, it looks like it will be a nice summer, regardless of sexual frustrations and/or "if the Russians don't get us" as Taggart would say. The spring here certainly is beautiful. The air reeks of fresh plant life. I'm sitting here on the roof of the front porch and it is very pleasant... The tall trees roundabout, the people going by... My right hand is bleeding... the damn cat's claw-work... He's out here with me on the roof... For some reason he's licking the damn tar paper... Every time he sees a bird his mouth starts quivering... Looks funny.

Charles wants me to write this down before I forget: You know that issue of *Chuck Crumb's Funnies* that he gave you a long time ago? He wants to borrow it for a while. He's doing this pictorial history of his comics and he wants to use all of them for it. So he wants you to lend it to him in your next dispatch, and I'll send it back when he's through with it.

Well, so much for that. Now to the answering of your letter. Glad you appreciated that comic book type letter. It took an extra bit of patience to turn that out.

Now, now... don't give up on your artwork. I think one of the main troubles with your art is that you don't spend enough time on it. Only by constant practice can you learn to express yourself through art. The thing is, I think, that you just tend more toward writing as a means of expression and the art is secondary. It's a wonder you're as good an artist as you are, what with most of your time devoted to writing and studying. You certainly possess the ability to express yourself to some extent in art. That has been proven.

I appreciate your advice. It helps. It really does.

I don't think you understand what I meant by convictions. You say, "the best thing to do is develop a positive attitude." This itself is what I meant by convictions. I should have put it more clearly. Saying "yes" to life is a conviction that I'm trying to reach. I want to develop a strong inner life, so that I won't be easily swayed by the outside world and other people's opinions. I want to be something inside. A real person, not just a shell of a human being.

That's vague isn't it... I don't want to be a half-baked human being. I want to be a whole person. I want to have faith in myself, in life. At present, I don't. I can sense the lacking, the emptiness of my present state of existence.

One of the Tal Henry records is a gem, arrangement-wise. Three of the sides have some good solo work on them, though brief. All are the same orchestra, I know. The arrangements are alike, kind of weird on all but that one.

Yes... it is toobad about the race catalogue. I felt sick when th' ol' lady stood there telling me I wouldn't find it on the shelf anymore and cackling as if the whole thing quite delighted her.

I envy you for some of your recent finds: especially that Goldkette's "Idolizing" / "Hush-a-Bye" and "Crazy Rhythm" / "Imagination" by Roger Wolfe Kahn. Is that Austin Wylie's Golden Pheasant Orchestra any good? I recall you recommending me to pick up any records I see by them last summer. Also, some of my favorite songs are on the list: "Together," and "Crazy Rhythm."

Hm... A Ku Klux Klan record... What do the Rhinehart Brothers sing about? Anything of significance, stating Klan views or something?

Don't forget to get my Ben Pollack EP. Heh heh.

Never heard of Leyendecker, ey? I'm sure that you'd like his covers if you saw them... At least I think you would... He didn't work in the usual style... He had a style quite all his own. I think he's dead now. We have seventeen covers by him. What charm! What warmth! He creates a beautifully sentimental world of fantasy with folkways of America as one ingredient, fairytale symbolism as another ingredient. It's a world of innocence, a world without cynicism. I hope you can get the old *Life*s and *Judge*s... or have gotten them by this time. Mayhaps you can sell me a few, at a (slight) profit, of course.

I have a small tape, about half the size of a regular one, that I could tape records of mine on for you, and you could send me one in exchange with your good music on it. Does this sound okay with you? This, I think, would be simpler than cutting a regular reel in half.

I'm sending along a book of drawings done by me in recent months. I'm sorry that I can't send you any of Charles' recent work. I think you'd be fascinated by his unique style, but he wants to save all the drawings he does now. We don't throw them away anymore like we used to. He's afraid they might get lost in the mail or something, and he doesn't want to risk it. Anyway, here's mine.

Thanks for the tip on drawing girls' noses. I'm following your advice and it has improved my drawings of women. Know any more helpful devices I could use?

The last issue of *Help!* (ten) has some very fine cartoon work in it. The German, I forget his name, really held me... Great artistic satire... his stuff. Have you seen it? Funny they don't sell it in Kent...

What can't you stand being at home? If you can't get any money, won't you have to stay at home to write? Well, I hope you can get somebody to put up the money for you.

Chees! You work out a deep, complex plot, then you give it up for another one! Well, I s'pose it's good to be changeable, not rigid in your thinking and creativity. Like you say, this new plot of yours seems to hold together better than the other one, but it all depends on what you do with it. I know what you mean about not being able to describe the effect you want — and the effect is what will be all yours alone, and make it what it is. Anyway, you've got a good plot to work with. You say the kid gives up religion. Do most kids who go to a university give up their religious beliefs? What do you mean by thrusting himself out of the womb? I have a vague idea, but explain it to me. What sort of person is the kid? Do you plan to have any love affairs in the story?

As you might expect from us two clods (Charles and me) the "on the road" plans of ours seems to be fizzling out. It's just that we don't have a penny, and our mother doesn't want us to go without money. Oh well... I'll spend the summer drawing and, if I can get paints, experimenting with painting.

You say you crave other experience than strictly scholastic. I do too. But where would you go? What would you do in Canada or Mexico? I wish I had the stamina and eagerness to face life that you have. I want to see it all, even the bad parts, but, I dunno, I wouldn't get along. I'd be lonely. Do you have a "lust for life"? Is every experience exciting, interesting? Do you enjoy life and what you see and do? You're fortunate to be out-going enough to get in there and be a part of it all — see it for yourself.

I'm glad to see that you're giving up politics. I watch people fume and fuss and debate political issues and they seem so futile! No matter what they do, man doesn't seem to change. This is the way I've felt about politics since I was about fifteen or so. But still, I enjoy observing and commenting on political issues, from an artistic viewpoint.

So you think the country is dying on its feet, eh? Is this a common view in the universities now? Tell me about it. I'd like to know. What's happening here anyway? What has gone wrong in this country? Is it the business interests, as Taggart says, or what? What's wrong with the intellectual attitude? I wish the country would wait until I'm dead and gone before it falls apart. Heh heh. I don't want to be caught in the middle of the chaos! I don't want to be around when the bombs start falling. All my life I've had a sort of terror in me.

I feel that the root of much of the suffering and pain in the world (that is caused by men) goes deeper than people acting as a unit. Of course you are right in saying so, and that people should act more as individuals than in groups, but the meat of the matter is that people don't take the time to become aware of what they are and what the basic truths are. Some people never even try, though I think most people could become aware if they wanted to... Lack of awareness and its results (understanding, tolerance, love) leads to group action, both as mobs and as organizations. Awareness would lead, I feel, to people getting together to help each other, and men would see the tragedy and utter uselessness of fighting, killing, hating, and even competing. But, I dunno. I wonder, sometimes, if people as a whole are ever going to start looking within and searching for the true values of life. I have my doubts.

Frustrated geniuses — that's rich! I had to laugh when I read that... It boosted my ego for about a week...

I guess you're right about concentration and feeling... But anyway, too much concentration on method, on the mechanical end of it, tends to push out the original and pure passion, doesn't it?

I'm convinced that you have the potential of turning out a good comic strip, if you could only spend more time on your art. Otherwise you'll have to stick with writing I guess. Have you ever tried writing a play script? I think you'd be good at something like that.

I was confused on that damn art contest thing, or rather, my art teacher was. He told me about it. Actually, what it was is this: three winners would be chosen in the state, first, second, and third, you know. No prizes or nothin'. First place painting went to Kansas City to be judged nationally with the first-place winners of all the other states. Then three winners would be chosen and each would get a 600 dollar scholarship. Hell, if I'd ha' known it was national, I wouldn't have entered it. I can't compete with kids from big culture centers and I know it! Anyway, I won in this damn puny state anyway. (Four kids entered in the whole state. That's Delaware for you.)

I don't have anything against girls. In fact I'm what you would call an "ardent feminist"... I worship the feminine nature (who doesn't?). It's just that most of them are like your friend Carol... They're devoted to artificial happiness. The thing they think they want isn't what they really want at all. There are a few exceptions, I suppose. But I just can't get along with girls because I don't fit in with their illusions. What I want to give, they don't seem to want. I dunno. Maybe when they get older...

Your friend Carol is pitiful. I s'pose she isn't very happy, is she? I s'pose you're right in saying that it's useless to try to drum your ideas and attitudes into other people. For one thing, how do you know you're right, and another thing... it doesn't work.

Your vigor for life appalls me. You say "comfort" is the thing you don't want... that it would even hurt you! Explain this to me. I want to understand this enthusiasm you have to face all of life.

Can you think of anything this Herbert Gold has written? What kind of stuff does he write? How'd you meet him?

Now to your story "Wayne." I find it difficult to sum up my opinion of it. It's a great portrayal of a way of life and a way of thinking. The main character, the girl (is she supposed to be something like your friend Carol?) is a clearly expressed human being with definite attitudes, desires, frustrations. I like the way you bring out the environment and its effect on the girl — and you're achieving the unity you told me you were trying to get... The story holds together pretty well. The conversation itself is quite an achievement. The way the characters talk, their wording, clichés and so forth, is very natural — only slightly affected. The story shows you know what you're talking about... life and people. All you need is a little more warmth... I liked the ending... That has lots of warmth... It really touched me.

Who's "Wayne"?

Send me some more stories. Send me "The Ford" if you can.

We went up to Philadelphia recently. Charles and I spent a couple of hours walking around the old neighborhood we lived in back in 1947 and '48 — 53rd Street between Market and Chestnut. It hasn't changed much, except more negroes inhabit the area than in the '40s. I can't describe the feeling that overwhelmed me during the whole visit. God! I wish I could paint! There was so much to express — everywhere we gazed... the houses... the people... all kinds of characters... kids... old men... young men in their gaudy Sunday clothes... as Charles called it — "An artist's paradise!"

Well, what else can I say!

P.S. Believe me, Marty! This summer I'll write more often, and longer letters. I promise!

P.P.S. The last letter we got from von Bernewitz was in February. His address then was 12006 Remington Drive, Silver Spring, Maryland.

~ 2 9 ~

September 29, 1961
Dover, Delaware

Dear Marty,

Guess what? We got a typewriter! So I'll probably be typing my letters from now on... I'm a pretty miserable typist, but it's easier than hand-printing... Also, I'm not very fast but I guess I'll get better... Anyway, this'll make letter writing quite a bit easier for me.

I've been on a real creative spurge lately. I've filled a whole notebook since my last letter... forty-four pages... one thirteen-page story about Jim and Mabel (which kinda flopped) and a twenty-one page story with the animals… concerning the Synthetic Man which was a bit more successful. I'm getting sort of bogged down with obligations… A kid wants me to draw him a picture of his girlfriend (I've got a regular portrait business going here), some church group in Smyrna wants me to do a mural for their church… I'm flattered, really, but, I dunno, I don't feel adequate for such an undertaking… Also a guy at Latex wants me to do some posters… I'll try to get this letter sent off before I have to get started on all this stuff.

Got some bristle-board for the *Obese Toad* material, but so far haven't done anything… It's like you say, big projects scare me… wish I could get over that. It seems I feel most at home in the little note-books, where I have complete freedom to do as I please… I thought of several political-type cartoons for the *Obese Toad*, but they don't satisfy me anymore… I want my work to have feeling, humanity… which I can't put into my political cartoons…

As you can see, I'm a hell of a typist… I'm about on the verge of giving it up and going back to the hand-printing…

Glad to hear you might make it here this Christmas… I'm looking forward to it… I might make enough money on this mural to do some traveling… I hope so…

Something odd here… Do you notice anything different about the way my writing sounds now that I'm typing? I do. It seems more mechanical, less expressive, than when I write with a pencil. Maybe I'll get over it… It's lousing up the letter…

You must be spending quite a bit of time on your art lately… Did you send editorial cartoons in to the newspaper? Did anything come of it? I'd like to see some of the stuff you've been doing lately… Haven't seen any of your recent art-work. Well, I guess some. It will be in the first issue of the *Obese Toad* which should be coming out soon, shouldn't it?

Got the rest of the race records from that store — some are pretty good… I'll list 'em later… only six or seven…

Yes, that last letter of mine was pretty long, but then look how long it took me to write it! Really, I feel that my work is but a feeble expression of something that in itself is vague and doubtful… Sometimes when I probe myself I find that my intentions in art aren't as sincere as they should be… I realize that I'm fairly good at drawing, but you see that's only because I've done so much of it, and it seems sometimes that the only reason I have stuck at it so diligently is because I have to sort of get even with society for not accepting me… Subconsciously I want to make myself immortal among men, leave my mark on the earth to compensate for social inadequacy… So I draw… If I got rid of my greatness complex, I probably would lose my desire to draw. It seems to me that a true artist is a man who is passionately in love with line, form, color or some aspect of life… While these things appeal to me, I don't find any real burning passion for them within myself… The only burning passion I'm sure I have is the passion for sex…

A greatness complex can certainly be a hindrance when one is trying to look reality in the face... It always gets in the way. How can I be sincere in my work if subconsciously I'm only concerned with living up to the standards of greatness? I hope I can get rid of this drive for fame... It's false and stands in the way of knowing myself...

I don't think it hurts a person to take out a few months, if they are fortunate to get the opportunity to dream and think about things. So many people go through life never really knowing what they are or what they want because they think it's wrong if they are not constantly accomplishing something... constantly achieving things... My father is that way... Life to him is how much you can do and how good you are at it... The only way you can reach self-understanding is by getting away from it all... work, even books... You have to withdraw into yourself as much as possible, and concentrate only on getting at truth. I don't mean that you should do this all the time, but if you have the opportunity, take it, because in this country such opportunities are few, what with the emphasis everybody puts on getting out and working, and getting up in the world and all that... It's too bad people measure your worth by what you are achieving outwardly instead of what you are achieving inwardly. Anyway, I think taking long periods to dream and think have helped me considerably in my work... Most of the improvements that I find in my work are due to something I discovered in a period of dreaming.

I want you to send me something you've done artwise lately... You say you're beginning to perceive a style in your work... See if you can find something you've done recently to send me. I'd like to see it.

This method you've worked for ink illustration sounds rather complicated... all that tracing and re-tracing, but the results should be good. The spontaneity (spelled right?) of a sketch combined with the refined quality of an ink drawing... I think I'll try it, only leaving out some of the steps... My ink work always did have alot of stiffness about it...

I think I'll send my recent issue of *Arcade* along with this letter... Haven't had my morale boosted sky-high lately... heh heh... The cover of this one is supposed to be Mabel, but it came out kinda hideous... I've got a long way to go yet before I perfect the female face, and figure too... Anyway, skip the cover, it's just an experiment anyway... not a very successful one. The usual dum drawings of Mabel and Jim throughout the book, and a couple of comic strips about them... I'm not too good with Jim and Mabel yet, but I'm working on it. After a few more years with them, I should be able to project them pretty well... heh heh. The little character with the hair parted in the middle is supposed to be the inner me sorta... With him I portray actual experiences of my own, with emphasis on the lovelorn side of my nature. "The Life and Times of Fritz" is another flop. It wasn't coming out the way I wanted it to, so I gave it up. Anyway, that big panoramic slum scene came out good. Toward the end of this book I was entering a period of self-doubt, so the stuff at the end didn't come out too good. I have another completed *Arcade* that I did between this one and the one I just finished that I'll send next time. Let's have comments on this.

That fourteen-page story I told you about is in the *Arcade* I did after the one enclosed. It's about Jim and Mabel, modern-day... The format now is this: Miss Purity owns and operates a luncheonette in an average American city. Jim, whose parents are dead, lives with Miss Purity... she adopted him. Mabel works at the luncheonette and has to take care of Jim while Miss Purity is busy in the kitchen... Jim sees the image of his dead mother, who died when Jim was only four or five, in Mabel. Jim goes to a Catholic school called St. Christopher's. His main childhood friends are Elizabeth Strong, the daughter of a wealthy businessman, and Jeffrey Malcolm, who comes from a lower middle-class family. Elizabeth is in love with Jim, much to Jim's bewilderment. Charles has written one or two short stories about Jim and Elizabeth and the Catholic school... Mabel is still the ex-prostitute, and still remains somewhat of a tramp. So far my comic stories about these characters have been rather ineffective, but, like I say, if I stick at it, I think it will improve. My understanding of myself and people in general must improve first, though.

In the latest issue of *Show Business Illustrated* there's an article on Jack Paar by Roger Wolfe Kahn.

The U.S. gummint recently put out a booklet concerning parents guiding children's TV watching done completely by Walt Kelly... Of course, I immediately sent for it (only twenty cents). It's quite good... Kelly wrote it as well as illustrated it, the usual Kelly nonsense, but good. Something like 25 pages.

Yes, the fact that Okefenokee is a unique little society in itself contributes a great deal to the charm of *Pogo*, and also the fact that this little society represents the so-called American way of life — such characters as P. T. Bridgeport, the circus man, and Deacon Mushrat are representations of American characters, of an era and its attitudes... This aspect of *Pogo* holds great appeal to me, and probably to you too. That's why I always look forward to seeing new characters brought into *Pogo's* society. They add to the color of the strip. *Krazy Kat* is something else again... just the opposite in some ways. Herriman was after something timeless, universal, from what I gather, even though I don't quite understand the strip yet... whereas Kelly was interested in this particular age, and its many aspects. Kelly touches on the universal only indirectly, rarely directly.

The only thing I don't like about Hal Foster's[1] work is that stiffness you mentioned, he's very stiff... I think he was better years ago, his stuff was looser (such a word?), more expressive, I think... Like most comic-strip artists, he's gotten in a rut... He still does very good on backgrounds, and panoram-

---

[1] Hal Foster abandoned his job drawing the *Tarzan* comic strip for the Sunday pages in order to create *Prince Valiant* in 1937. He continued drawing the series until 1971. See bibliography.

ic scenes, though. As for his text, to me it seems to be rather stereotyped, and kinda old stuff, but it's okay now and then... Once in a while Foster will touch on some truth or beauty. You know Daumier, the great French satirist... He had it just about right... His work had great zest and humor, and showed great skill too. His work really appeals to me. I wish I could find more of it... His faces have such charm, warmth, and satire... and his characters are the essence of France of that period. It seems to me that all the guys who illustrated for *Puck*, *Life*, and *Judge*, and those other late-nineteenth century magazines were all trying to imitate Daumier. Either that, or Daumier was the best in the movement or something. I guess Kemble, A. B. Frost and Nast were original. A couple others.

Oh, there were lots of good Carl Barks stories in '54, '55, and '56... They were fewer and farther between, but every bit as good as the earlier ones... I remember one *Uncle Scrooge* story in which the ducks all went hunting for the philosophers' stone, and another really great *Uncle Scrooge* story in which Uncle Scrooge wanted to get away from his money so all the ducks went to a land called Tra Lalla where there was no money or greed... This is really one of my favorite of Barks' stories. It came out in 1954, June... There are many others I could tell you about... But it is true, and sad, that Barks hasn't done any really good stuff lately, in the past two or three years. He's even done some stories over again, with only slight changes. That one about Flippism came out in the February 1953 issue... Yes, that one was a gem... Every story that came out in 1952 and up to about the middle of '53 was a gem... I've read them all at least a dozen times.

Yeh, trace the *Phantom Blot* cover, and write in the colors on backgrounds... That's the way we used to do it with Britt when we sent him traced covers to make him jellies. The only explanation I can think of for Barks' decline is the fact that he always had to do the same characters and they probably wouldn't let him make any changes or bring in new characters. And of course, there are many more taboos put on a cartoonist now than even ten years ago... Barks would never be able to do something like "Voodoo Hoodoo" nowadays (this came out in '49, was actually about the negro Voodoo cult).

I wish I could find more *Animal Comics*, they must be awfully rare. I only have five, and one doesn't have a Kelly story in it. I have an annual that came out in 1953 with reprints of *Pogo* stories in it, and an *Albert and Pogo* comic that came out in 1946. This is one of my best comics... 's in mint condition. I got all the sixteen issues of *Pogo Possum*... Hah... Jellies... The early issues were the best. You know anybody who's got old *Animal Comics*? If you ever see any, get 'em for me... Hmmm... I guess you're already aware that I want them.

The *Weird Fantasy* number 16... I think I told you that it has a great story in it by Kurtzman about TV. Do you have it? My copy is in mint condition.

Hmmm... So you like working with a brush, eh? I always got discouraged whenever I tried the brush... Always made a big mess of it. What kind of a brush do you use? A real thin one? I like to do delicate line shading, which can't be done with a brush, can it? I think I'll do some experimenting... doing all the main outlining with brush, filling in details with the pen... That should give a nice effect... Yeh, I always found it hard to keep from shaking when drawing with a brush... They say you get over that.

Ivie seems to be a good example of some aspiring young artist who devotes himself too much to the work of others and not enough to his own. What he needs, I think, is to get away from Williamson and all those guys for awhile, and concentrate on himself, and finding out his own individual approach to life and art. He may come into his own, anyway, I suppose. I admire alot of artists and cartoonists but I try not to imitate them... It's hard, but if I can be original, it's much more rewarding, spiritually, at least.

Once in a while I used to start reading *Little Orphan Annie* every day, but for some reason I always lost interest after four or five days... The same with most comic strips. I never was an avid comic-strip reader, actually, I only read a very few of the daily strips... *Pogo, Peanuts*... Gave up on *Rick O'Shay* and *Dick Tracy*... Got tired of them... Same with *Dondi — the Child of Infinite Wisdom and Love*, and *Juliet Jones*... They don't seem to get close enough to reality in human life... too idealistic, and stereotyped. Sometimes I think it's impossible to portray reality in a comic-strip. I don't think it's ever been done... All the great strips have either been satire or poetry... I can think of no really outstanding strip which has dealt with real life... Can you? Feiffer's is, I guess, in a symbolic sort of way.

You're right about *Skippy*. Crosby was rather pretentious... tried too hard to be "cute" and sentimental. Never heard of *The Bungle Family*.

No, I'm not in any hurry to see your English comics. We'll wait and see if I can make it out to your place this Christmas. Hope I can.

I don't know why the syndicates don't drop some of their old strips that have gone bad, like *Dixie Dugan*, and put in some new talent... I guess they have some kind of contract deal or something. Maybe there isn't any new talent worth putting out... Hmmm... There must be!

Market analysis be damned!!! It's choking art to death in this country. Not only comic strips, but everything... movies, TV, magazines... 'Tis a pity. That's the chief reason I'm reluctant to try to sell anything. Alot of market-analysis people have to get their noses into it and smother expression.

Hmmm... I'd like to see the book with the "Vie Parisienne" cartoons in it. What's the date of the *Playboy* issue with them in it?

You recall some of the comics that Charles and I did had sex talk in them... Would you call this stuff of ours pornographic or "frankly but healthily erotic"?... Such things as Jim and Elizabeth talking about sex, Miss Purity telling Jim about the facts of life, Jim asking Mabel to have sexual intercourse with him... it's part of life, ain't it? I mean, people talking about sex... little kids being curious about it and all.

So you think this nation is becoming more liberal about sex, huh? Of course, you're right, and thank heaven... The taboos on sex of the nineteenth century (and before) were harmful in a way... All the unnecessary fear and shame that they caused. It is foolish for man to try to cover up sex. Make it look like something it's not... another example of man trying to escape reality. Yes, you hear alot nowadays about how we're all going corrupt because sex is becoming more open... My own opinion on it is enjoy all the sex you want to (you only live once), as long as nobody gets hurt, including yourself. It seems this rule can apply to just about everything... Do anything you want as long as you're not hurting anybody. To tell you the truth, I'm rather modest myself... I know it's foolish, but I think it is the result of my parents' attitudes toward sex... They always tried to cover up the facts of life from us kids. Whenever anybody said anything about sex, they acted shocked. I learned the facts of life from a kid in school. My mother is no longer that way, but to this day, I have never heard my father say one word about sex.

I read an article about Mark Twain's daughter who is still living. She's about in her eighties now, and she doesn't want any of her father's more erotic works printed... I guess that would include 96... Also, his opinions on religion that he put into some later works. Luckily, I found a very early edition of *What Is Man?*, one of the books that they aren't allowed to print anymore, I think. It was this little book that first gave me some things to think about that eventually led to my heresy.

Well, you're back in college by now. What are you taking this year? Gad... only three years older than me and a college senior... less than three... Speaking of college, Charles is finding that, much to his disappointment, the one he's going to isn't much different from high school... All the kids are interested only in getting to that fat desk job at the end of the road, and all the teachers are academic robots who don't really give a damn about the subjects they teach... Charles says it's all very discouraging, and that he regrets that he ever got himself into it. He says he still wishes that he had two years in front of him to meditate and draw and read as he pleases, but of course he knows that our father would not allow that so he has to do something. It's either college or a job. As for his determination to get an education, he says he'd rather educate himself... read and write and think... Charles has been reading a heck of alot lately... brings new books home from the library all the time, and actually reads them... He says he's better off this way than going to a college where a bunch of crummy teachers just discourage you...

Also, some of the folk down in dear old Milford have found out that Charles is going to a negro college and they're saying he ought to be shot and that they always knew he was an odd sort but they never suspected that he was a communist agitator but now they remember that alot of the things that he said were straight out of certain communist books... God... Charles had to convince ol' Bill Garbutt that he wasn't going to the college to stir up trouble, because Garbutt said it was dangerous for him to be associating with Charles and that he wasn't going to have anything to do with him (Charles) until he got rid of some of his radical ideas. Well, Charles managed to persuade Garbutt that he was being small-minded, so Garbutt still remains our last connection with the open-hearted little town of Milford.

Well, there goes the fire siren... It's right across the street, ya know... Makes a hell of alot of noise... I can't hear myself think!

It's stopped now... When that thing goes off in the middle of the night, I wake up in a fit of panic and fear...

Did you get any good records in your last trip to Cleveland? How far is it from Kent to Cleveland? Here's the race records I got:

"Black Diamond Express to Hell" — parts I and II — Rev. A. W. Nix & His Congregation (sermon) — Vocalion 1098

"Stop Pretending" / "Hey! Stop Kissin' My Sister" — Fats Waller & His Rhythm — vocal and piano by Fats Waller — Bluebird 10829

"Who Was Job?" — parts I and II — Rev. C. D. Montgomery — Columbia 15023

"I'm a Pilgrim" / "I'm in His Care" — Taskiana Four — quartet — Victor V 38029

"Sleep On, Mother" / "Our Father" — Silver Leaf Quartet of Norfolk — Okeh 8644

"There's Room Enough in Heaven for Us All" / "Steal Away and Pray" — Pace Jubilee Singers — solo by Hattie Parker — Gennett 6072

"What a Friend" / "Nothing Between" — Pace Jubilee Singers with Hattie Parker — Victor 21655

"Jesus Gonna Make Up My Dying Bed" / "Motherless Children" — Joshua White — vocal with guitar — Oriole 8268

"Jonah and the Whale" / "Rich Man and the Needle Eye" — Rev. J. M. Gates with Deacon Leonard Davis and Sisters Jordan and Norman — sermon with singing — Okeh 8478

There were several others that were cracked or broken... Toobad... Some of these are quite good. I especially like the Joshua White, which sounds almost like blues... The singing groups I like, too... They each have their own style. The Fats Waller record is good too. You can have all these in trade. Some are in good condition... most in fair condition. Only the Rev. J. M. Gates is in poor condition. I can hardly make out the label.

I guess I forgot to tell you that the Arizona Dranes record is cracked... but playable... This will reduce its value considerably. Also, that Five Red Caps Gennett has a chip in it about a half an inch deep. All the others you want are okay... The Lonnie Johnson is in nearly mint condition.

Yes, those trips we make to Philly are always a big mess... We never get anything done. The last time we went up there we spent about an hour going around in circles on the goddamn Schoolkill Expressway... It was really a mess... I remember the one we made when you were here last time... We got there just when all the stores were closing and spent most of the time just going round and round the streets in the car.

Recently I went to Spence's Bazaar, the old auction place here in Dover where all the farmers gather to buy second-hand furniture and tools and stuff... Many times I've found good records there... This one time I'm speaking of I found a whole stack of old blues records... mostly on Bluebird and Victor's V series... I was looking through them and some guy came up and said they were already sold... I went looking for the owner, but couldn't find him. So I went back to the records, but to my surprise, they were gone... Sigh... It was a great disappointment.

About the trade... generally it's okay with me, except for a few things... I have some of the records you proposed...

"Down the Old Ox Road" by Bing Crosby

"Sunday" / "Havin' Lots of Fun" by Abe Lyman (I recall playing it for you last summer. You said you didn't like it.)

"Tiptoe through the Tulips" / "Painting the Clouds with Sunshine" by Ed Lloyd & His Rhythm Boys I have on two different Banner records.

Also, even though you offered me some good ones for the Patsy Young, I kinda hate to part with it... Both of the songs on it are favorites of mine, are good versions, and the only versions I have of them. If you have other versions of both of these songs, I'd be willing to trade the Patsy Young for them. I think Patsy Young was a pseudonym for Annette Hanshaw... They sound exactly alike. If you don't have other versions of those two numbers, I'll want something really good in trade for it... Oh yes, I also have "A Faded Summer Love" and "Where the Blue of the Night" by Bing Crosby. I do want the Roger Wolfe Kahns, Ben Bernies, and Ipana Troubadours you offered me... How about if I pick some of the records from the lists in your letters that I'd like to have in place of those four I already have... okay?

"Lily Lou" — Missouri Jazz Band / "Mon Homme" — Rose Room Orchestra — Banner 6267

"Cheerful Little Earful" — Grant Warwick Orchestra (favorite tune of mine) — Superior 2570

"Time on My Hands" / "Lucille" — Hotel Commodore Dance Orchestra — Harmony 1385

"Hoodoo Voodoo Man" / "Big City Blues" — Dubin's Dandies / Hollywood Dance Orch. — Banner

"Rainbow round My Shoulder" / "When Summer Is Gone" — Selvin / Columbians

"Dusky Stevedore" / "Sweet Susie" — Shilkret — Victor

"Sunny Side of the Street" — Bernie Cummins — Victor

"I'm in the Market for You" — George Olsen — Victor
"Alice Blue Gown" / "Beautiful Lady" — Troubadours
"Me and My Shadow" — Astorites — Diva
"Betty Coed" / "You'll Never Know" — Lloyd Keating / Louisiana Collegians — Clarion
"Little White Lies" — Hotel Pennsylvania Music — Clarion

Well, any of these you'd care to part with? How 'bout a good Kahn or something for that Patsy Young? C'mon... Be generous... Don't stick me with a bunch of lemons, bwah!

How about "Crazy Rhythm" for "Nagasaki"? Yes, send the Bix album if you can't find the Pollack EP... though I'd still prefer the latter.

I've passed a hell of alot of old country music records in the past... old Columbias, scroll label Victors, Perfects, and so forth. I'll get them from now on, if they're collector's items as you say they are. There are lots of them around here.

I know a girl, a friend of Sandra's, who says her mother has a bunch of old English jazz records that she got as a girl in England. You think it's worth looking into?

That Red Heads record I have is called "Dynamite" / "Hi-Diddle-Diddle" and is on Perfect 14639... I never got the postcard you said you were going to send with a trade on it.

I sent my thirty cents for *Record Research*. Haven't got it yet... Do you get it regularly? Sounds like it will be good... I only wish I could find more old records.

My typing is getting worse instead of better...

I have been very UNlucky when it comes to old LPs... dammit...

You say X came out with a Ben Pollack LP? What all was on it? There's a record I wish I had! I guess it was comprised of the same numbers that were on the EPs.

You mean that the copy of "In a Mist" that you have is not a double?

Of all the LPs you listed, the volume one of *Thesaurus of Classical Jazz* interests me most. Is Miff Mole's Molers strictly Dixieland style? I don't care much for pure Dixieland jazz... I like bands that use alot of arrangements, as well as solos, such as that Clarence Williams Orchestra, King Oliver's Band, Ben Pollack, Frankie Trumbauer, that type... Red Nichols, The Charleston Chasers and those type are good, but I don't like them as much.

Nothin' But the Blues interests me too... Where could I send for it? I know for sure none of the measly record stores around here are going to get it in...

Weren't Perfect and Pathé Columbia labels? I'm glad they're planning to go into another big re-recording binge... I just hope I'm able to find the LPs they put out... I'll probably have to go to Philly to get them, and they're grabbed up real quick up there... I'd like to get that Fletcher Henderson LP when it comes out, since I don't have any late twenties records by his band at all, and I've never heard any either. I'll probably miss it, living out here in the sticks. Perhaps I'll send for it.

Carol's still working at good ol' Latex… She's sort of engaged to some clod and they're making big plans to get married and all… Carol is using all her paycheck to send away for alot of junk for her future household… frying pans, dishes, all that stuff… She must have about a ton of it stored away by now… Carol used to be very artistic. She used to write stories and poetry all the time, back when she was thirteen, fourteen and fifteen, but then she started to get herself involved in a big social life and she seems to have lost her identity because of it. It's really a shame… If she had kept at her writing, she'd really be great at it now… I can remember it happening to her… She gave up all the high dreams, the solitude, the exuberance she seemed to possess for nature and all… Milford did it to her, but I suppose it would have happened anyway. Being accepted came to mean more to her than being an individual… Now she seems to be lost forever to those dreams she had five and six years ago… Her life is now devoted to that boyfriend of hers… No need to write anymore. She still draws clothes sometimes though. I can see the same thing happening to Sandra… She's fading away into the social world. As an individual, she seems to be dissolving. I think it's because they (girls) find that they don't need art and all that truth stuff as soon as they find that boys accept them and want them. I dunno, maybe I'd find that I wouldn't need it either if girls accepted me. Maybe I'd give it all up too, and devote myself to the opposite sex. That's probably the only reason I do draw… as I said earlier… compensation.

I don't know if Carol is still a Catholic or not… It's hard to tell what she believes anymore. She probably is, in a luke-warm sort of way. Yeh, Sandra has officially apostated. She refuses to go to church anymore, and is getting in trouble for debating points of theology with the priests and nuns. That isn't all she's getting in trouble for. She's getting kind of wild these days… I find that Sandra has leader tendencies. She now has taken the position of the leader of a group of rather weak-minded teenage girls. They consent to her leadership and she gives the orders. And when she says not to do something, they don't do it. Most teenage girls are pitifully gullible. I feel sorry for them. They're so docile, like a herd of sheep… I wish I could help them sometimes… but they don't really want to be any different… They like to be led, to be treated like sheep. Poor souls.

You'd be surprised how many big squabbles evolve out of petty, insignificant trifles around here. But we all put on our best side when ever anybody visits… Alot of people are like that. You'd be surprised how different most people are when they're just around the members of their family… I know what you mean about your family bringing out the worst in you. Around Max, I can be pretty intolerable, downright mean at times… but I'm the gentlest of creatures outside the family. Nobody would think I'd ever strike another human being... but me and Max are always getting into small quarrels in which blows are exchanged, though not as much as we used to... I'm trying hard to overcome it. As for the rest of the family, Max and Sandra are always quarreling, and my parents... God... life is just one long fight between them... They've been on an arguing binge for the past eight years or so... with short intervals of peace now and then... They used to get very violent, but they don't anymore. Gettin' too old I guess... That's the only thing I don't like about living... their arguing... Otherwise, it's okay.

Yes, I'm developing a "seize the day" attitude, but the only trouble is, I don't seize it! I let it pass, unappreciated... Well, I'll get better at it, I guess. If only I didn't have to be sexually frustrated... heh heh... sob...

Your family sounds to me like a bunch of proud Germans... Pride seems to be the root of the trouble... That's what causes grudges and big stinks to be made over trifles... and, like you say, they have to learn that life is too short to waste time worrying about insignificant trivia... They should rise above it. Same with my family... My parents concern themselves too much with such trivia... Also, this kind of thing is the result of not looking reality in the face. People can't get along because they don't try to see their problems as they really are. They try to evade them. Their pride won't let them see the truth. Another thing I'm trying to overcome... Pride stands in the way of truth. By truth here I mean personal truth... the absolute truth about myself.

The fact that people, in the United States at least, don't take religion as seriously as they used to is another thing that has caused so many people to think we're going to the Devil, whereas actually, as you say, it's because they don't need it anymore. Look at Sweden... Hardly anybody goes to church there anymore... I think it's three percent... but yet Sweden has about the lowest crime rate, the lowest sex-attack rate (they also have a much healthier attitude toward sex than most countries) in the world. Their prisons don't even have locks on the doors! Sweden has one of the highest suicide rates in the world because the people there don't worry about going to hell anymore. Toobad such an ideal society won't last... They'll go corrupt sooner or later and be just as mixed up as the rest of the world... if "The Bomb" doesn't get them all first. Also, they have very beautiful girls in Sweden who don't concern themselves with rock'n'roll idols. Maybe I'll go to Sweden... hih hih... They are having a juvenile delinquency problem lately, though... Toobad... It's probably due to American influences.

The Company had replaced the Church, in my opinion. Charles and I attended a Seventh-Day Adventist revival meeting one night here recently. The hall was full of mostly old folks... old ladies especially... While the "Doctor" who was nothing more than a ham actor, ranted and raved, the old folks shouted out their "Amen"s and "Praise the Lord"s "Ohh Yes"s "So right!"s, and finally, near the end, one woman came running up to the alter sobbing hysterically, and knelt at the foot of the preacher, who was shouting something about having yourself purged by God... He really gloried in his message of salvation... really hammed it up. These hell-fire type Protestant religions still seem to be holding a tight grip on the farmer class in this country, but it's mostly the old people who don't have much time left and are afraid of death and what it might hold.

Yes, the *Delaware State News* does print alot of controversial stuff. The editor, Jack Smyth (originally spelled Smith) likes to get big controversies going... His letter column is always full of crackpot stuff... and sometimes his editorials are also. This Smyth is quite a character... Besides being the town drunk, he does everything but lead a lynch-mob against the city police force, the council, the mayor, and just about every other official.

You've helped to clear up my vague understanding of what art is — art is not done purely for a useful purpose... It is not a utility, but it is partly. It is also done for the pleasure and beauty it affords... This is art?

I still believe that you shouldn't do anything that will effect other people unless you are sure you are right... But, since you can never be sure you're right, I believe that you should never take sides in a conflict between factions... This is what causes wars... Each man, I feel, must seek the truth for himself, and learn to love his fellow men, whether or not he thinks them in the right... Hmmm... Then on the other hand, it seems that we have to prevent our fellow men from doing something that is a threat to our own survival... It seems we have the right to step in and put a stop to the doings of other men in this case... But how do we know we're right and they're wrong? They might think we're a threat to their survival... Yeacchh... What a world! I haven't been giving this thing enough deep thought. I'd better drop it for the time being.

I'm trying to get over that malady of being reluctant to start on a big project, or doing anything big, like writing letters to you. This to me is always a big project. This fear is mainly what has kept me from starting the *Obese Toad* stuff... It has kept me also from doing long stories that I've thought about... and paintings and stuff.

Anything and everything can be beautiful if you want to see it that way. It's just that our environment and temperament make us so that certain things appeal to us greatly, enthrall us, so to speak, more than others... Yes, I suppose that "beauty is truth, truth beauty" is sort of the way I feel about it... It's the way I approach my work, too, I think... You see, I'm not really sure about my motives, like I said earlier, sometimes it appears to be one thing, and sometimes another. I guess it's both.

So you think the United States will turn to socialism, eh? Do you have any idea when? You think we're as sensible as the British, in that they adjusted themselves to reality, sort of? If we're not wiped out by the Russians first, do you think the switch-over to socialism will be without violence? Look how prejudiced most Americans are against socialism. Most of us in this country hate it with a purple passion... They'd rather die than live under it. Communism and socialism are all one and the same to most Americans.

Yes, my memories of the Church are pervaded with the gloom and solemnity of it, too. I had a kind of fear for all the priests and nuns when I was a kid... They were so pious, so solemn... sometimes almost not human. I went to a Catholic school in first grade that was extremely gloomy. It was in Philadelphia... one of those typical, old, dark, big-city schools. All the nuns were mean. We had to wear starchy white shirts and ties every day... The playground was a little asphalt lot with a high iron-bar fence all around it, and only the girls got to use the swings... We had to go to church every day, and the first grade had its mass down in the basement, with only wooden boards for pews — my knees always killed me after mass. It was all quite dreary and frightening. I was always afraid some nun was going to pounce on me and beat me to death. Later on, when I started to become aware of all their traditions and ceremonies, I was depressed, but yet fascinated, by the medieval atmosphere about it all... the songs, the great organ music, the old statues, the designs on the robes of the priests, the processions, the incense, the chants at High Mass. When I was little I actually used to think that the priest was really talking with God up there on the altar jibbering away in Latin, and that God was whispering back to him from up in Heaven. You're right about one thing... there certainly was no love... only strict rules and tiresome, painful ceremonies, like mass and confession, that you were ordered to go through. How can a bunch of forbidding, cold people teach you to love a God who will send you to Hell if you don't willingly and humbly partake in something you don't have the faintest understanding of?

That's a good point you brought out, about the freedom a child has who is unaware of any supernatural element... Gives one something to think about. Such things as the Church hold men back from developing and exploring their full potential, it's a mental block, which holds unnecessary fears and limits on man... confines his thinking... tries to kill all imaginative and natural thinking, all universal questioning. I know this from experience... Whenever I would ask questions of an explorative nature, it was treated as something wrong, I was disdained for it. Imagine the freedom I would feel now if my mind hadn't been trained not to step outside certain limits... I hope I can achieve this freedom.

Did your parents give you books and encourage you to read as a child, or did you do it on your own? I was quite rational when I was very young, until I learned that I was supposed to accept certain things and not rationalize. Now I'm making an effort to regain that lost questioning, probing nature. I think this is the same with most people. As children we all explore life, question it, try to get to the bottom of things, but as we grow older we learn to accept without question... Our inquisitive side is smothered... by traditions, by society, and so forth. I never read books at all till I was around thirteen and fourteen, not seriously at least. Except comic books, of course... At first I just studied the pictures, and drew my own, then I began reading them around eight or nine... I was too lazy mentally to read before that.

I used to collect all kinds of stuff, but, like you, mostly for artistic reasons... like marbles... I used to try to get the ones with the beautiful designs on them and get rid of the plain ones. I used to collect cards, concentrating on finding as many different kinds of designs on the back as I could find. Spools, too, I used to hunt for... I would draw faces on them and give each spool-man a name and personality of his own. I had a regular little spool society going on for about four or five years... Charles did the same thing with blocks. We were always acting out adventures with our spools and blocks, making it up as we went along. This pastime dominated a large part of my childhood. Then, of course, the comics came along, and now, old records.

I'm afraid I really don't know what kind of relationship I want with a girl. How could I? I'll know after I have a few relationships with them, I guess... It seems to me that I want a mother-type, that's all. I dunno, maybe if I got to know a girl, I'd be like you... want the girl to look up to me, depend on me...

So you've never been in love, eh? Ever been infatuated with a girl? That's a little different thing... as you probably know. Infatuation is sort of being in love with some sort of idealized image of feminine beauty (or masculine, if you're a girl) that you see in the person who is the subject of your adoration. This has happened to me about twice... I was in love with an image, not a real person. In both cases I hardly even knew the girls, but to me they were sacred and pure. I desired to make love to them, to kiss and all that, but, since I never was able to get that far with them, my passion never reached the point of desiring to get them in bed... It seemed to me they were precious jewels or something... One of them is the "Joanne" that is mentioned in one of the comic-strips in the *Arcade* I'm sending you.

Why psychologize, you say? For the very reason you mentioned, because you aren't out participating. That's the best time to sit back and examine yourself, subjectively and objectively. Then go out and participate with a better understanding of yourself, and the whole human race, too. Constant participation is just as harmful as constant reclusion... It takes a substantial amount of both to get the right perspective. I need more participation myself... I know so little about real life that I'm inclined to idealize too much... Ah well...

... Well, so much for one letter. Sorry this isn't as bountiful as your generous helping of eighteen pages, but I always comfort myself with the knowledge that you love to write... Hih God! All I've done is talk about myself... You can do the same if you like... I'm willing to listen.

R. Crumb

November 5, 1961
                                         Dover, Delaware

Dear Marty:

I shouldn't talk about late letters. Most of mine are just as late or later than this recent one of yours. That postcard I sent you was just one day too soon... Got your letter the very next day... Certainly was a relief to hear from you. I was really worried.

I guess you noticed the new address on the postcard. Yes, that's right, we've moved again... Third time since I've known you, I think. This time it's a modern, split-level type suburban home, located in the midst of a couple hundred other modern, split-level type suburban homes. Very dreary surroundings... I look out the front door, nothing but the same monotonous neat little clipped lawns and evenly spaced houses as far as the eye can see... I look out the back door, the same scene confronts my eyes. The address, again is 937 Sunset Terrace. That address is so typical of modern suburbia... Anyway, you do see some beautiful sunsets from here, so I guess the name is appropriate.

Right now outside my window I was observing a seven-or-eight year old boy furiously beating a fire hydrant with a croquet mallet... I can't figure out for the life of me what he hopes to accomplish. Now he's gone and attacked the lamp-post... making a hell of a racket... It's all sort of amusing... The lamp-light blinked on just now and the little brat scampered away. Sort of charming or something... I dunno.

I've been reading various and sundry things lately. The autobiography of Mark Twain, Philip Wylie, *Franny and Zooey*, and a little of alot of other stuff... I enjoy Mark Twain thoroughly, as always. His stuff is easy to understand, contains much insight, and is beautiful... Philip Wylie is something else again. I read this book by him called *An Essay on Morals*... It is quite difficult to understand, but presents a challenge and contains alot of interesting stuff. Have you ever read anything by this man? If so, what's your opinion?

I also enjoyed *Franny and Zooey*... Very interesting, very human... I only wish I could understand it better. I never could get the gist of all this mystic stuff. Especially the very end of the book... last few paragraphs... about everybody being the fat lady and the fat lady is Jesus and all that... I just don't savvy... I guess you haven't had time to read it yet, it's not too long... 200 pages. I read it in a day... If you have read it by now, please give me your opinion and analyzation of it. It seems the more I read, the more I feel that the only way to get at reality, if such a thing is possible, is to ignore everything you've ever read in books... start looking at everything completely objectively, including all the advice handed down by the great men.

You are pretty loaded up, aren't you? All those obligations! Sheee! Doesn't it sort of get you down and make you want to cut yourself off from it all? That's what alot of obligations always does to me. Guess I'm just afraid of responsibility... It was unfortunate that you lost those three pages that you wrote to me. I know how you feel... I did that once myself... It's very disheartening to start over when you have already written half a letter.

Whenever I think about what a nice guy I consider myself to be, I get sick... You see, now I consider myself a nice guy for admitting this fault. Jesus! You can't fight your ego... Right now I pride myself upon my honesty with you. I pride myself on that previous statement... ON THIS ONE!! But why am I fighting it... I'm so confused. What shall I do with myself?

Somehow or another, I must find the true nature of myself and accept it for what it is.

I was exceedingly relieved to know that those drawings I did for the *Obese Frog* were gotten to you on time, and am very glad that you and the rest of the staff found them acceptable... I had my doubts... For awhile there before I sent them I was considering tearing them up, but your note sounded so urgent that I supposed you needed material pretty bad... Actually, I thought the small one-panel thing was the best. Somewhat pessimistic, though, I guess... I'm anxiously awaiting the *Obese Toad*. I'd wait and comment on it in this but I don't want this correspondence to drag as much as it used to... now that I have this typewriter... I'm anxious to see the work you did for the *Obese Toad*, and the rest of the gang, too. I dunno, maybe by the time I'm finished with this letter the *Fat Toad* will have arrived... So maybe there will be comments on it at the end of the letter. Putting the gray shading on the comic strip I sent was a good idea... It looked rather blank and empty. I was going to put those vertical lines in all the panels, but that would have looked monotonous... Besides, I had my doubts as to the quality of my line shading... That's why I didn't put much in. As to putting the library in the last panel... that's okay wid me.

Be sure to send me a copy of the *Kent Quarterly* when it comes out. Should I send money? Just what are you going to do in this study you're working on of Proust and the rest? You going to analyze their work or what? Book-length... Gad... How long is "book-length"? Such scholarly undertakings give me the willies. Especially where somebody so complicated and deep as Proust is concerned... Who knows? Maybe it'll get published. When do you hand it in? What do they do, just put a grade on it and give it back to you? Greek philosophy sounds interesting. I've done a tiny bit of reading on the Greeks. Took one look at the *Encyclopedia Britannica*'s translation of Plato and gave it up. I wish I had the intellect to grasp this kind of stuff, at times. At times, I say, because at other times I feel I'm better off left in my simple, uncomplicated state. Just how far do you intend to go with this education business, anyway? All the way up to a Doctor of Philosophy?

My mural has not seen the light of day yet, due to my procrastination... The lady in Smyrna has been waiting a month for me to call her and tell her how much the materials are going to cost... Damn, I want the money too! Like you say, I'm afraid to tackle anything big. What I have to do is I have to paint some kind of religious scenes on these two walls in this little room in back of the church that is used for Sunday school purposes... The church is Episcopalian or something... supposed to be one of the oldest standing churches in the state. It has alot of really beautiful stained glass windows in it. Anyway, this Sunday school room is rather small and dreary looking, so they thought some paintings would brighten it up. I don't know why they just don't go to some junk store and buy a bunch of cheap old religious paintings... Anyway, the lady wants my murals to project some sweet, pleasant, scenes, since the room is for children and all... Also, I'm supposed to put these gold-engraved prayers all the hell over the walls... I've got to get started on the damn project pretty soon if I want to get paid for it by Christmas.

If I do go back to Ohio with you, you'll have to overlook my inability to conduct myself properly around your friends... Also I'm very helpless... Can't do much for myself...

Nope, never seen Pittsburgh... not in the daytime, anyway... We stopped there to eat on the way to Delaware in '56. It was even interesting at night, now that I think about it.

I am anxious to meet all the people you know, though. Girls included... heh heh... Also, I'm anxious to pore over your record collection. And comic collection... And there are plenty of things I want to talk to you about...

Your comments on the *Arcade* I sent were greatly appreciated. Very rewarding and satisfying and ego-boosting to hear... So I'm sending another one. Heh heh... I thought anyone but me would consider that big Mabel-face on the cover freakish. Glad you appreciated it. I guess it was worth the effort after all. Those excellent colored pencils had alot to do with it.

Yes, yes, I'll do that TV strip for the *Obese Reptile*! Glad you liked it... I hope you can talk the staff into letting me do it... I was sort of proud of it myself. Some of it... I don't even live in Ohio, let alone go to the University, so I consider it quite a lucky break to get my work in the magazine... my best stuff, too. And a slick magazine, at that... (all is vanity)... I'll probably make a few minor improvements on it. Thanks very much for getting my stuff accepted... Did the rest of the staff see that TV strip? What were their opinions of the strips I sent? Thanks again.

Yes, I did lose interest in that "Life and Times of Fritz" thing pretty fast... Actually it was because I got sort of stuck. It was getting too complicated... in my mind, I mean. It was too difficult to handle. I decided to wait a couple years before trying to put so much into a story. All the plans I had thought of and tried to work out for that story were just more than I can handle right now... Too hard, much too hard, to express.

Yes, this particular *Arcade* does have quite a variety of stuff in it... mainly because I was very confused there for a while and didn't know just what to do with my artwork. That was just before I laid off for a long period. I was very confused. I still am to some extent...

That slum scene in the Fritz story took me a couple of hours to do, and was quite tedious work, but worth it, I suppose. Yas, I still intend to keep working with the animal characters… I can express something with them that is different from what I put into my work about humans… I can put more nonsense, more satire and fantasy into the animals. Also they're easier to do than people. With people I try more for realism, which is probably why I'm generally better with animals. Have you ever done anything at all with animal characters? I don't suppose you have.

That "Happiness Is Within" bit, as I said in my last letter… is a personal experience of mine… as a matter of fact, an experience which has taken place a number of times. That lady-killer character you noticed is supposed to be Mister Typical He-Man Teenager… I see and know many of them… Yes, it is the same type as that guy in the Feiffer strips. I've got some good ones about that guy. One from *Playboy* in which he expounds on how girls like to be pushed around and take abuse… I've heard guys say that in real life. Seen it too… Down in Milford there was a guy like this… used to lead his girlfriend around by this little chain which she wore around her neck… Very sad.

The simple-minded cat blowing bubbles is Fritz's side-kick, Yimmy… another cat we used to have… You remember Yimmy… He's the one that got killed while you were visiting us in '59… the one we had the funeral for… Actually Yimmy's smarter than Fritz, but he just doesn't know it…

The negro in the top-hat and dapper clothes with "Maple Leaf Rag" written next to him was from that Hoagy Charmichael show *The Ragtime Years*.

Sandra keeps on improving on her drawing, but she really doesn't give much of a damn about it… All she draws is boys, boys, boys… nothing else. We try to get her to take more of an interest in her art, but… what can you do when someone has such a satisfactory social life that they have no need to compensate with something like drawing… Sandra also writes a bit of poetry… not as good as Carol was at her age… Carol's poetry showed more feeling and genuine expression… Of course, Carol didn't have all her energies wrapped up in a big social life at fourteen like Sandra does.

For chrissake… we got this goddamn huge lawn here at this new place, and my father, a fanatic about lawns and things, is going to make us keep it in perfect condition… Jesus… One thing I liked about that other house… the lawn was so small that it wasn't worth cutting…

I'm sending you another *Arcade*, since you are so anxious to see more of my work… heh heh. This one was done through the rest of the summer. The first fifteen pages or so are full of alot of miscellaneous stuff… the only stuff I did for about a month… The rest of the book is Jim and Mabel… the first time I attempted to do any long strips about them by myself. I'm more proud of the cover of this book than the inside… I think I got my point across pretty well in this cover… trying to bring out typical teenageism as I see it… I can't put it into words but it's there on the cover… At least I see it there… This Jim stuff is of doubtful consequence… I keep working on it, though. I may be able to perfect it. Well, maybe not perfect it, but make it worthwhile, at any rate.

Right now I'm holding our cat "Creep" on my lap while I'm typing... Creep love...

I did my first all-text fiction story recently... only about ten pages long (hand-printed in one of the *Arcade* books)... about Jim. Rather a crude effort, but, as Shaw said, a man must stagger about like a fool before he learns how to skate... Oh well, I consider the story a worthy effort, anyway, and a step in the right direction. I dunno, maybe it isn't the right direction at all, maybe the whole aim of my life is completely wrong.

We used to have a 1944 *Tip Top Comics* a long time ago with some very old *Tarzan* strips in it which I thought were quite good art-wise. I don't know whether they were by Foster or not. *Prince Valiant* has that common fault of most fiction... Some of the characters are gods and others incarnations of evil... goodies and badies... This gets on my nerves... Some people, it seems, are influenced by this kind of thing, and divide up the people in their life into good guys and bad guys... I guess this is a natural human trait... The only comic-artist I can think of that doesn't do it is Feiffer. His characters, as you pointed out, are the most human of all comic-strip characters. Feiffer now has a strip in the *Sunday Bulletin Magazine*. It's a regular feature and I'm saving them. So far two have appeared. Both good. They weren't about neurotics and beatniks, either. One concerned a suburban civil defense man, the other was about wife, so maybe Feiffer's broadening his scope... Or maybe they told him to, because it is one of those family magazines... Feiffer, I think, is mainly concerned with contemporary society, its effect on man's nature. His strips are never the type that could take place in any time in history... Well, I don't know why I'm telling you all this, it's perfectly obvious.

Ivie's theory about Barks is probably about right... Most of the stuff he does now just lacks heart. He could probably do so much better if they'd let him.

Yes, *Animal Comics* are rare. In *Comic Art in America*, it said that children were asked why they didn't like *Animal Comics* (this was after they quit it due to lack of sales). They were told by kids that *Animal Comics* was too dull... no violence or excitement... just alot of little bunnies with blue bowties... something like that... I like them... There are some other good stories besides those by Kelly. A regular feature in *Animal Comics* was a story called "Jigg and Mooch" by Biff... It concerned two dogs and was sort of charming... Nother good feature was "Hector the Henpecked Rooster"... Kelly also did several other stories besides "Albert and Pogo"...

I have one *Albert the Alligator and Pogo Possum* comic, 1946, and mint condition. It's quite good. I don't think it's the same one you're talking about though. No story with the word "Daze" in it, but the last panel does show all the animals sitting around a big fish fry (on the back cover), but then, so do alot of other Kelly stories... Pogo gets caught in a pot in this one, but not Albert. I also have *Pogo Possum* number one, (coverless) which ends up with a big fish fry... which goes to show you how repetitious Kelly is... Nobody

gets caught in a pot, though. *Pogo* #1 is 1949... We used to have the cover...
It sure was neat... a parade scene... lost it about 1955 or '56.

Right you are about *Rick O'Shay* being too repetitious... That's one of the
reasons why I quit collecting the strips... The strip lost the zest and liveliness
that it had when it started... It became stiff... Those soap-opera type strips
seem empty and lacking in genuine human reality — the adventures, or stories, come and go and leave nothing of significance, nothing for you to think
about. In short, there's nothing to them...

Yes, I'm trying to put into my work the every day human realities that I've
never found in a comic strip yet, though Feiffer has come the closest. It's an
extremely difficult thing to do in the comic strip medium... There are so
many delicate little things that, when I try to express them in comic strip
form, come out awkward... Alot of things, it seems can only be gotten across
right when you write them down, explain them out with words... I consider
it a challenge, though, to be as human, and real, but yet interesting and with
my personal ideal toward life, as possible in a comic strip. Charles and I have
had a few debates as to whether you can express reality to its fullest in the
comic strip... He says it can't be done. I say I'm going to try it... So far, I
haven't really gotten at stark reality, the bottom of life (as I see it) in my
work... I might end up giving it up and going over to writing alone, if it does-
n't seem to be doing any good to try to do it in comic strips. But then, who
knows, I might succeed?!

We did sort of over-do the cussing and stuff in our work when we dropped
all inhibitions. You see, this was right after we both dropped out of the
Church and we were taking full advantage of our new freedom. But then, in
real life, people talk about sex and everything... Sex, we figured, was just like
anything else... so we put it in our work as we saw it... as we saw people's
attitude toward it... I guess we did over-do it though... Ah well, a man must
stagger about like a fool before... etc... etc...

In what way is Mark Twain's attitude in his later years pessimistic? I don't
follow you. In what respect do you disagree with his attitude? How was Swift
a pessimist?... I've only read a small part of *Gulliver's Travels*...

I've forgotten what all we put on that tape last time you were here... I
recall alot of the stuff was rather mediocre. Which of those All Star Orchestra
records do you want? "Steppin' Along" I presume... I like that one...
What've you got for it? ... Somethin' good I hope.

Yes, I have those jazz books of yours... So sorry I haven't returned them...
I've had them out for the last eight or nine months, planning to mail them to
you, but I never got around to packaging them up... I'll have them for you
when you come here... I was wondering when you were going to ask me
about them. I've read them all, by the way. Hee hee.

Is the colored cover going to be on the issue of the *Obese Toadstool* following this one? That's a good deal that you can have a colored cover for it... Is
it going to be the same or different every issue? Is the variety of color limit-

ed? What is it done in, paint or what??? I'd shore like the opportunity to do a cover in color that will be printed... Do you think they will let you do any covers? I suppose they will since you are the major artist of the staff...

Didja get any records in Akron? Huh? Didja? Gee, "Where the Sweet Forget-Me-Nots Remember"... I sure liked that record. I can't figure out why I ever traded it to you. Well, now that you and Ski both have a copy, the next one you find you can save for me... heh heh... sigh. I recently got Victor 22223... the Gene Austin with Thomas Waller accompaniment... He also has a long solo on the side "My Fate Is in Your Hands." He's not on the other side at all. Got this record in a great big strike I made recently... biggest strike I've made yet, as a matter of fact... More of this later.

I'll let you have all the gospel and spiritual records except "When the Saints Go Marching In." Do you still want that Arizona Dranes record, with the knowledge that it's cracked? I found a record on the rare Champion label recently... A quartet rendition of "Old Black Joe" and some other song... nothing great, but the label is rare, isn't it?

Yas, I notice Annette Hanshaw's similarity to Ruth Etting. I sort of had suspicions for a while that the former was a pseudonym for the latter, but I guess not. Hmmm, toobad Ruth Etting records happen to be scarce... I only have one side with her on it... "Keep Sweeping the Cobwebs off the Moon" by Ted Lewis with her doing the vocal. I like her... They'll probably put out an LP of her if they haven't already.

This new strike I made recently is going to put a new light on this trade deal we've been working out, so I better not make any more propositions right now.

In an auction at Carroll's Market recently (they've put up a new building in place of the one that burnt down), I saw a whole album full of middle thirties Victors... all in the 25000 series... all Benny Goodman... One odd looking scroll label with "Swing Classic" across the top of it... Unfortunately, I had no money, so I let them go... I would have made off with them, but I don't want those kind that bad... Ah, I'm an unscrupulous sort, I am...

I saw a Hoosier Hot Shots record once... On red label Oriole. The lady at the shop wanted fifty cents a record, so...

Hmm, interesting record, that Melotone that you got. Was the style of the label any different on one side than it was on the other? When did Melotone start, anyway? Never seen any of them...

You can have any country music records I have if you want them... I'll give them to you when you visit here. Hm. Four volumes of Fletcher Henderson... He certainly must have recorded alot of good stuff! Do you have any listing or anything of what's on them? If so, write it down for me, will you?... Like you did those others... I'll ask that girl about those English records next time I see her. She hasn't been around here since her steady boyfriend slapped Sandra in the face... God! Did that ever lead to one hell of a big stink!

I still haven't gotten the *Record Research* I sent for… Are you sure thirty cents was enough? How many back issues did you send for, anyway?

Charles has become acquainted with one of the students at Delaware State College, or rather, this kid became acquainted with him… A friendly sort of negro, one Thomas Freeman… Also quite intelligent… We have engaged in long discussions with him, about religion, and people and so on, in which he did most of the talking… Very talkative person! He's really a very interesting person to talk to, or listen to, I should say. He has this very extremely optimistic outlook, he says he loves everybody, and the world, and everything, and he puts all his faith and trust in the Lord. We've had many, many arguments on this point of God. He believes in it like iron. Of course, his father is a minister, so what can you expect? Sometimes he sounds like he's just repeating his father's sermons, ver batum (whatever that means). Anyway, he is quite intelligent, and not intolerant of anything, be it atheism, homosexuality, or what have you… He says he couldn't possibly hate anything… He's also very energetic… Takes part in all sorts of church activities and other organizations… He is a member of the NAACP and makes speeches at meetings concerning the race question. He lives with his father and mother and large brood of brothers and sisters in a miserable little shack down in the negro section of town. There are fifteen kids in his family in all. He's full of interesting stories… injustices he's seen against his race in his time. His trip to Greenwich Village was very interesting. Maybe you'll meet him when you come out here. The only trouble with the boy is that it's hard to make him absorb your ideas and opinions… He has alot of certain fixed ideas and shuts the rest out. As Charles says, he has his ego shut up in this little room, and he won't let anything else in the door. Anyway, he's a nice guy, Tom, and easy to get along with, and one of the few people who tolerate me and Charles, so…

Charles is doing worse and worse in college. He doesn't give a damn anymore… and only two months… He's done alot of smart alecky themes and gets Fs on them, naturally… Anyway, he writes with honesty, and as he pleases, and not the way some robot of an English professor wants him to write… He's planning to quit after the semester. College just ain't for him. What Charles wants to get out of life they don't offer at any college… Charles wants, so he says, wisdom, not a brain bogged down in technicalities… The purpose of college, it seems is to prepare you for life economically… prepare you for that fat desk job, as you so beautifully put it in the *Kent Quarterly* that time. Academic learning just doesn't lead to true wisdom and understanding… It almost seems, and Salinger agrees with us on this, that you have to push all that you have learned in school aside to get at the true meaning and proportion of things… The Buddhists say that a high point is reached when you take all your books out and burn them.

I used to go down to the Wesley College soda shop with Charles and we would sit and watch the goings on… like you say, just a bunch of teenagers, only the layers of phoniness are thicker... By the time a poor soul reaches college they've been trying to be something they're not for so long that it becomes a part of them and they start adding new layers of falsehood on top of their smothered self... To think, I'd be the same way if I had been accepted by society. Since I am not accepted, I go against the modes of the society which rejected me. These college kids are nothing but impressions on other people, on each other. Their real selves got lost somewhere around the age of eleven, twelve, thirteen. It's all sad.

What happened to that novel you were going to write? Have you written much of it? I guess you haven't had much chance to... but you said you were going to work on it this summer. It looks like you won't be working on it at all now, with this big English project of yours... Oh well, you can still find time to do short stories.

There's a theater group at Delaware State but Charles isn't joining it... Charles has developed a negative attitude toward theater groups, after two years in the Kent County Theater Guild... I used to go and watch the rehearsals and I can see why he has developed a negative attitude toward them. We went to one of their last-night-performance parties... Everybody was drunk and doing the "twist" and it was quite amusing but got boring so we left. Charles actually got up and danced with this one youthful looking middle-aged woman. I don't think she would have danced with him if she hadn't been drinking. He asked the only sober girl in the whole place to dance and she refused.

Charles told Garbutt one time when he was up here that he'd bring Tom Freeman down to see Garbutt sometime. Garbutt said something like "If you bring that damn nigger down to my house I won't let you in the door!" He says it's not that he's race-prejudiced or anything, it's just that the results would be that he'd get stones thrown at his house and people would stop associating with him... He really got sore about it. Charles said he might bring Freeman down anyway just to see if Garbutt would really do it... Garbutt is still friends with us, but he thinks we're a couple of nuts... Poor Garbutt, he's such a gullible clod...There's some ol' guy named Ellis that he practically worships. According to Garbutt, this man Ellis can do or think no wrong. The guy is pretty bright, Charles has talked to him, but mainly he's a convincing speaker.

I can imagine how you felt when that air-raid siren went off, being unaware that it was just a test run. They tested a new air-raid siren here a couple of weeks ago. I was walking along downtown while the damn thing was blaring away... very loud. I looked in all the people's faces, wondering what they were thinking about... if they were thinking about Dover being blown off the map as I was. Nobody looked too happy about it. I could tell that. I felt pity as I looked at all their faces, all their pitiful lives that could be snuffed out by the Bomb... It was one of the few times I have felt genuinely sorry for humanity as a whole.

Hmmm... Interesting account of intuition you told me about concerning Hammerskjold. I wonder if there's anything extra-sensory in something like that or if it's just coincidence. I experienced something similar with Clark Gable. I started thinking one day that it was about time for him to kick off and I kept thinking about him dying for a while and then a couple of days, maybe a week later, it happened.

That clod Carol is planning to marry and her and Pat aren't getting along as well as they used to... They argue quite a bit, so maybe there's a chance that she won't marry him after all... She can save all that junk she's accumulating for the next guy who comes along. I was listening in on one of their private arguments recently (eavesdropping is a hobby of mine) and I get the impression that they hardly understand each other at all. I can't see how two people can be in each other's company for a period of two years and be so distant as those two seem to be from one another. Their relationship seems to be based on a mutual sexual understanding. All this is affording me with a great many lessons, and also material for my comics.

I'm afraid the same thing is happening to Sandra that happened to Carol... loss of individuality, dissolving into society. I can still have intimate talks with her, though. Carol has completely cut herself off from the rest of us. She, too, considers us all a bunch of nuts. I say "too" because everybody in Dover that knows Charles and me considers us a couple of nuts. Most of them, anyway.

You're right about my mother... She refuses to be passive. My parents both want their own way, consequently there is continual friction. They understand each other about as well as Carol and Pat understand each other. My father is probably like your uncles... He's so consistent it's sickening... He's got these certain fixed ideas about everything which nothing can penetrate... completely rigid. Not in the least bit flexible. At least my mother is somewhat flexible. The fact that you are aware of this assertive trait in you is good enough... Of course, you can't eliminate it if it's hereditary (or can you?), but you can keep it from getting out of hand, so to speak.

I'll look for *The True Believer*... Sounds interesting... Maybe it's in one of the libraries around here. If it was on the newsstands I would have noticed it by now.

So Doug Stock is a believer in the faith, huh? Does he have his own version, or does he adhere to one of the traditional religions? I imagine you and he have had some heated debates. Does Stock insist on spreading his beliefs? I think most people feel that what they believe should be heard by their fellow man... Everybody wants to be heard... Everybody's got something they must say... some opinion, some belief. It makes the world interesting. I wonder what it would be like if nobody expressed what they believe... There'd sure be alot more individuality around. It's all part of the evolutionary process. First man accepts one belief, then he goes on to another one, a better one. He spreads his beliefs, and other men, of future ages, improve on this belief, or go beyond and above it entirely...

It seems that there is no such thing as good and bad, right and wrong. Everything, including violence, death, suffering and all, is necessary to the evolutionary process. As you say, violence is necessary to achieve certain ends. It always has been, it probably always will be.

All I hope is that the United States fares as well as England in these changes. I hope there aren't any mass executions or anything. And I hope there isn't any great economic collapse which results in mass starvation or something... mainly because I might be affected personally by all this. I hope we can go on leading relatively peaceful lives, like they have in England all these centuries. As you can plainly see, I crave security and comfort. I relish my present state and don't want anything to prevent it from continuing. We'll be lucky if we got over the hump without being blown to bits by the Russians and Chinamen (Yellow Horsemen?). Have you read about the latest terror weapon? Both Russia and America are in this frantic race to see which country can perfect it first... The Neutron Bomb, it's called... You explode it in the air over a city and this fall-out kills all the people... No buildings destroyed... plants unharmed, just all the people drop dead... and the stuff penetrates the thickest steel walls so that no fall-out shelter is safe... You can't hide from it... You're dead if you're under the explosion. The deadly fall-out goes away after awhile and loses its effectiveness. What won't they think of next?

What would you rather be: Red or DEAD? Heh heh...

Your advice on shyness was appreciated. I realize that all you say is very true, but I've tried to no avail to overcome it. I make an ass of myself in the process. I, too, seek out introverts rather than the other kind (more than the other kind, I should say), the trouble is, I never meet any introverts. There just aren't very many of them around. Yes, most people make, like you say, acquaintances easy, but it is something else again to have a real, genuine friend... somebody who accepts you for what you really are, and not just because you are living up to certain conditions. You say you could count your true friends ALMOST on one hand? I can count mine on two fingers!

No need to tell you how good the orchestras of Fletcher Henderson and Tiny Parham and Jean Goldkette sound... "Nothing short of great!" as you once said... But alot of names I never heard of turned out to be good too. Francis Craig, for instance, a name I can't find in any jazz books, is a really good band, with good solos... also Warner's Seven Aces... See if you can dig up anything on these obscure names for me. That Louis Armstrong record has a beautiful trumpet solo. "Up and At 'Em" by Ben Bernie is the best record I ever heard by his orchestra. Good hot arrangement and solos. Alot of unlikely names turned out to have good solos on them, Hal Kemp, Charlie Straight, Ted Weems, McEnelly, Art Landry, and so on. That odd Puzzle[1] record with three popular songs on both sides has a couple of hot arrangements and solos... Each number plays one minute or so. I don't care much for the Original Memphis Five, but some of the numbers by them are good.

That McKinney's Cotton Pickers is as good as any of the numbers on the LP in my opinion.

"Mood Indigo" by Calloway's Orchestra is good. And no vocal.

I'm glad I got another version of "My Kinda Love"... It's a good one too... vocal by Crosby.

Do you know anything about The Little Ramblers? Sounds to me like the same group as The Cotton Pickers... Both groups are good.

The Halfway House Orchestra is rather unusual, but very good... good solos.

Louis Dumaine's Jazzola Eight is weird... A really odd group.

Don't care much for Whiteman's "My Blue Heaven."

Both sides of the Moten record are good. Clifford Hayes is another name I can't find anywhere.

I guess this is all for this time... Write soon and all that jazz... Looking forward to the *Obese Toad* and the *Kent Quarterly* and seeing you this Christmas... If you have time, how 'bout doing a cover on your next letter? I'm really curious to see what your artwork looks like these days.

P.S. I got some doubles that you can have if you want them:
"That's Just My Way of Forgetting You" — Goldkette
"Birmingham Bertha"— Goldkette
Both in good condition.

Well, again, I hope you can write soon. I'll try to keep answering promptly. You're my only contact with the outside world... This correspondence is necessary to my well-being.

rcrumb

Are you still writing to Alan Dodd? You said one time that he got a letter from Britt after Britt quit writing to us... Did he give you Britt's address? Write and ask him if he knows where Britt is now. The last address I have is Miller Trunk Highway. I want to see if I can contact Britt again, see what he's doing now... I can't figure out why he quit writing to me.

---

[1] Victor released the Puzzle series during the Depression to boost sagging sales. Each side of the record had three different selections, mastered on adjacent grooves. When the stylus was placed on the disk, one of the three selections would play at random.

Dear Marty,

Received your airmail letter last Thursday.

I've taken your advice about half way to heart. I'm now making a feeble attempt to get a job. I'm not what you'd call "anxious" to go out and work, even for a week, but I guess the trip will be worth it. There's alot to gain from such experiences. The main thing that holds me back is fear. I always have such a rough time when I'm out on my own. I guess I'm my own worst enemy, as they say.

But I really don't know what made me a recluse. Is society to blame, or am I? When I go out among people, I get the feeling that I just don't belong... The effort to adjust is too painful. Yet I want experience, I want to see life and people and all. It's that battle going on inside of me that I told you about. I don't know what to do. Anyway I'm making a half-hearted effort to get a job. I guess you have to try things out, experiment, at least.

So you've been making plans for my visit, eh? That makes me feel kinda guilty, because I haven't planned one single goddamn thing for us to do when you come here... which proves how self-centered I am. Not that there's much to see around Dover... You saw it all in the summer of 1960. Well, we can draw and stuff, make a trip to Philadelphia if one of my parents would be so kind. We'll probably spend most of the time sitting around talking. There's so much to talk about.

According to my folks, you can come any time after Christmas, and stay until they decide to kick you out...

No, I wouldn't want to come if it had to be on your money. Not because of any noble guilty conscience or anything, but mainly because then I'd constantly be worrying about the obligation of paying it back... Well, I guess there's a bit of noble guilty conscience involved too. But it isn't really noble, at all, as we both well know, it is merely a trained mental process, this conscience. And the feelings of nobility is merely pride. One gives oneself credit because he has listened to his conscience, because one has felt guilt when he is supposed to feel guilt, and not only that, but... yea'm...

Anyway, you sort of put me to shame there... The fact that you so desire my company that you would put up your own hard-earned money to have it. I doubt if I'd do the same if I were in your place... I'm not that unselfish.

To tell you the truth, I don't know why you're so anxious to come and visit here, and have me visit you. It seems to me that I'm a rather dull person to be around, self-centered, self-pitying, taking and not giving. You have so many companions already that are probably infinitely more interesting and willing to give of themselves than me.

I'm not trying to discourage you or anything. Certainly not! By all means, come!

I hope I can make it out to Ohio... I really do! I hope I don't have to let you down by not coming. There's so much I want to do and see!

Gee! They'd actually let ME do the colored cover for the *Obese Toad*? Gosh... Even if it's only in part, it's quite a lucky break... I really feel fortunate! I really do! Think of it! A real pro-magazine cover, in full color, by me! (at least in part) Boy! This really increases my desire to pay you a visit! Heh heh... How many copies do they have printed?

Anyway, I'm touched, I really am, that you want me to visit so much that you'd offer to lend me the money and all... No kidding... Your letter sounded almost pleading...

I suppose that Fritz story was about the best I'd done up to that time. I labored long hours over that story... I liked the way it turned out... I don't know about the stuff I've done since then... whether it's better or not. I haven't done any Fritz stories since that one. You'll see all of my recent work when you come here. Thanks for the compliment on that story. When you come here, you can advise me on how I can improve my "Jim" work. It really needs it.

I got some old records recently... I'm sure you'll want at least one of them... A few are quite good... Looking forward to hearing from you... and seeing you...

Your Vigor for Life Appalls Me

Dear Marty,

At last! At last! It has finally come, as I knew it must, someday. Every night, for at least two months, as I climbed under the bed covers, I said to myself, "Well, who knows what might come in the mail tomorrow..." but the next morning it was always the same thing, bills, advertisements... but then, at last, it came...

I was certainly glad to get the nice long letter, and the *Arcade*s, and the *Phantom Blot* comic, and hope to receive the other stuff very soon.

Choke... The air-raid siren just went off... How terrible it sounds... Why do they have to keep testing it all the time... It depresses me to no end...

The letter was very good... very interesting... a feast of words it was... gave me plenty to think about... I admit that I became impatient and frustrated waiting to hear from you and get all the stuff all these weeks... but if I was in your place I would probably lax off altogether... I mean, what with all the work you have to do and, mainly your new found LOVE. Gee, how can you do anything, now that you have that?

Of course, I want to know all about this love of yours. I want to know just how it makes you feel inside and just how it affects your thinking process and all. How strong is the love between you and her? You're intelligent, perhaps you can explain to some extent this thing that is such a great mystery to me... to everyone, I suppose. Sometimes I try to figure out what love is in my mind but I always end up realizing that I'm not going to get anywhere until I experience it... experience it fully and greatly, I mean. God, I wish I had your ability for talking my way into a relationship. It is a skill I am utterly without. Well there's much more needed than the ability to talk in getting a girl. But it certainly helps.

You certainly have layed off letter-writing lately. You used to be such a prolific (I think that's the word) letter writer. Who all are you writing to now, besides me? Do you still correspond with any of the old EC-Kurtzman fans? That reminds me, did you see that latest issue of *Help!?* It has a cartoon in it by Kenny Winter. That boy has become quite an accomplished cartoonist... His work is quite professional looking... In fact, I didn't even notice his signature on it until a week or so after I got the issue. I like Kenny's humor in *EChhhh* alot... Great stuff, some of it... The joke he did for *Help!* is fairly good... a satire of Mort Sahl

Hope you can send me the *Obese Toad* soon... God, it's been so long since they were first going to put it out... I have an old note here from you, written in long hand, which starts out, "Can you do some stuff for the *Obese Toad* in a hurry?..." dated 29 Sept. Heh heh... It took me about two weeks to get the stuff to you and I was worried as hell that I was too late... It's a shame that some of the stuff you did is now out-dated. I hate that kind of enterprise where they keep putting it off and putting it off.

Don't the professors ever bawl you out for doodling during classes? I was constantly being reprimanded for this in high school. I also had the bad habit of drawing all over the desks.

That sounds wonderful, even though it would take alot out of me, walking twelve miles with a girl... Must have been a very pleasant experience. This Barb sounds like a rather unusual girl... I certainly never heard of any high school girl like her... I've always longed to meet one that didn't give a damn about all the stupid social conventions... Oh, how I've searched for such a girl... but never had the privilege of finding such a gem. You're a lucky bastard. Does Barb go in for rock'n'roll and all that other teenage crap? Does she read *16* magazine? Heh heh.

Oh, curses upon my typing! Goddammit... I never caught the knack for this thing.

xxxxxxxxxxxxxxxxxxxxxxxxxxxxxxxxxxxxxxxxxxxxxxxxxxxxxxxxxxxxxxxxxnuts

You say this picture of Barb that you sent me is only a couple of years old? Are you sure? She looks like a child of about nine or ten in this picture... If she looks like this in real life she must be very beautiful.

When I saw the newsreels on the big youth peace march in Washington I searched for your face in the crowds... I knew you'd be in there somewhere. Weren't there something like four-thousand kids in that thing? Anything interesting take place while you were there? I've never been in Washington myself... never been south of Georgetown, Delaware... I intend to make a tour of the whole south one of these years... Everybody says it's really beautiful down there. Bill Garbutt and his brother traveled all over the south about a month ago. I asked Garbutt to tell me all about everything he saw, but I guess the clod's not very observant. All he talked about was some girl he screwed in Texas.

The way I figger it, if you leave home and move around alot and don't intend to settle down for a long time, and your folks won't let you leave your stuff at home, the best thing to do is to just sell it all. Sell all the good stuff to other collectors and the rest to auction or antique dealers. That's what I intend to do when my collection becomes too much of a burden. I'll only keep a few very personal things, like my own artwork... My parents will probably hold on to that stuff for me: my home-made comics and all. Anyway, when you start moving around you won't have any use for all your records and comics and books. You'll never bother with them so why keep them?

Actually, I hope to go beyond collecting material wealth someday... I look forward to the time when my sense of well-being will no longer depend on having a closet stuffed with records and a big trunk full of comic books. Sometimes I feel very burdened down by it all. Don't you? I wonder sometimes if the moments of happiness and satisfaction that all my stuff give me are worth all the trouble it takes to accumulate it.

I suppose my old records wouldn't be such a "fixation" with me, as you call it, if I had a more adequate social and sexual life. I guess that's why they don't mean as much to you as they do to me, because you are able to satisfy these basic needs and the need for compensation is not as great. I have come to realize that one of the main reasons why I've always been collecting things like mad is because I feel lost and I need something to cling to, something to live for and devote myself to, to take the place of a social life to some extent. I think I would give up all my material possessions without hesitation for the love of a woman.

You say this latest published story of yours "The Grin Unclosing" (???) was done very spontaneously. This can be a good thing, because it gives the subconscious a better chance to come through, will be more truthful, less pretentious, and not as laborious as a creative effort which is meticulously planned and carefully thought out. Doing this is liable to make you inhibit yourself, make your work seem unnatural. It's very difficult to know just how much to plan and think out in detail and how much to be spontaneous and let your work come from the heart. I think that's one of the main problems of creating a work of art. It's that old problem again of getting rid of your self-consciousness and letting sincerity come through. I'm anxious to see this latest story of yours. Have you written much creatively lately? Was that the first time you did a story without planning it all out ahead?

This reminds me... have you done anything on your big creative project lately? The novel, I mean. I hope you can get started on it soon... From what you told me of it this Christmas, it has great potential. Are you going to put off starting it till this summer or what? I hope you don't let it go too long, or your ideas might turn stale on you. I've thought a great deal about all you said that one night about your plans for this novel and about the state of civilization and all... It depressed me to a great extent at the time, but I'm coming to accept it I think. I mean all that stuff you said about the inevitable doom of the United States and how there isn't much hope of avoiding a nuclear holocaust and all. How does Barb feel about all this? Is she optimistic about it, or pessimistic? Is Barb generally a happy, optimistic person, or is she melancholy? I suppose, from all that you've said, she's more the former.

I've read that *Raise High the Roof Beams, Carpenters*. I liked it every bit as much as *Franny and Zooey*. In some ways, I liked it even more. Have you read Salinger's latest published piece? It was in an issue of *The New Yorker* sometime in 1959. It's called "Seymore, an Introduction." It's quite long and quite difficult to grasp. It is quite different from his other stuff, much more wordy and all. He wrote it in the character of Buddy Glass, first person. It tells all about their childhood and alot of complicated stuff about Buddhism and whatnot. I read about a fourth of it and gave it up. Charles read all of it and so did Maxon. They said it got simpler toward the end, but it was just too much for me. That's interesting about Salinger writing incessantly, but keeping most of his work to himself. I guess we'll have to wait till he dies to see alot of what he has written. I heard somewhere that *Catcher in the Rye* was originally more than a thousand pages in length before they cut it down. According to that article in *Time* magazine Salinger enjoys watching television. Strange man. I also read somewhere that *The New Yorker* pays Salinger a steady salary just to keep writing, even if he doesn't turn out anything publishable.

I'm looking forward to getting this philosophy guide you're sending. I hope you don't forget. Do you want it back or can I keep it? I agree with you that it is best for a man who is trying to find some of the answers in life to read and think about what men of the past have thought and said about life, but I think that for him to fully appreciate and understand what these men believed he should work from nothing, start from scratch, as if he were the first man on earth, or a visitor from another planet, who has come here to observe the earth... I can't explain this right... The heck with it. It just frustrates me to try to get it straight in my mind.

You see, a man can open his own insights, sometimes, or he may discover for himself something that someone else, or many people, have already discovered, by using this method of starting from nothing, using only the senses and the reasoning power to figure life out... In other words, start with no knowledge. When he finds an answer in this way, it will mean much more to him, and be far deeper in him, than if he just read it out of a book and worked it over in his mind from there. I think it is good to engage in this method, while also, now and then, learning what other men have said... Both are good ways of learning. I don't know why the hell I'm telling you all this. You've probably already thought about it so much, and gone so much deeper into it than I, that my writing it down like this probably appears dreadfully trite to you.

That is one of the chief problems I have to cope with in writing a letter to you. It is so difficult to find something worthwhile to say because I realize that just about everything that comes into my mind has already been well thought out by you a long time ago and that you've gone so much further than me. My beliefs and what I saw are just vague attempts at finding things that you have already studied and thought out and eliminated, or accepted, a long time ago. In short, what can I possibly tell you that you don't already know? And know more about, to boot.

Ho Hum. Sometimes I wonder if we can ever really understand anything... As time goes on I just seem to sink deeper and deeper into a mire of confusion. But, like you say, just because all is confusion doesn't mean we can't enjoy life. Or does it? I dunno. The main reason I don't enjoy living very much is because I'm socially and sexually inadequate, I think. Again, I don't know. Maybe I was born with a pessimistic temperament.

Yes, you are right. Charles and I do have a negative attitude toward formal education. I don't know whether this is wrong or not. I don't know whether a college education would help us or not. But when I think of college, I think of alot of loathsome responsibilities weighing me down, I think of having to cram my mind with alot of useless drivel; I think of the terrible ordeal of having to try to get along with all the people I would have to come in contact with in college, and the torture of having to act like I'm interested in what they are saying when I'm not... of having to say things when I really haven't got anything to say. I think of how sexually frustrated it would make me, seeing all the beautiful and charming young girls, and knowing that I could never communicate with them, or enjoy their company. I'm pretty sure all this goes double for Charles.

I realize that I should be willing to accept responsibilities for my own good, but what's the use, I ask you? Is it worth all the effort it takes? I love freedom. Right now I have it. Even though I am depressed and in despair much of the time, it is bearable because at least I'm not trapped under any obligations. While I was going to school, I was twice as miserable as I am now, because I loathed all the burdens of school work which seemed so useless to me. Maybe it was because there weren't any compensations for it, I dunno. But tell me, please, what you have gained from four years of college? What immense good has it done you? I'm speaking of the learning itself, not the social side of it. In what great way have you benefited?

I don't quite understand what you mean by "discipline and guidance along certain areas of learning" and "other fields that will be simply inaccessible to you without the rudiments you'll get in college." What other fields? Define. You've often spoke of this discipline. But I don't think I quite understand what you mean by it. Self awareness? Will power? You say "we need something which will allow us to take ourselves by the shoulders and guide ourselves." Guide ourselves toward what? A certain goal, or what? I think there is something here which you know and understand from personal experience that is beyond my comprehension. Cannot a person become an integrated whole without a "regulated pattern of formal education"? It seems to me that any self-understanding I have was reached without the help of my high school education... I could be wrong.

Tell me, if you can, how has your viewpoint changed from when you first went into college? Has going to college in itself changed your outlook on life to any great extent?

I doubt if going to college would help me any in the aspect of personal contact. It would probably be similar to my high school years, in which I was fairly isolated from the rest of the people, teachers and students both. My personal contacts were few and very awkward most of the time. It seems that some people have a knack for creating antagonism without being aware that they are. Most people seem to resent you if you are not sociable, if you don't act interested in what they are saying or doing. I agree with you that you have to learn to go halfway with people, and I've been trying to learn how to do this all my life. Most people are good actors, I guess. Just to get along, just to be part of the group, they can put on a mask, they can act a certain way so as to be accepted. I want to be accepted and a part of the group as much as anyone else, but when I try to go halfway, try to put on a mask and act in the manner that people expect me to act, it seems to come out all wrong, and awkward, and people don't like this, it makes them uneasy, so they make every possible effort to avoid me. So around most people I try to be as inconspicuous as possible. I wish with all my heart that I could get along, because I need companionship and attention as much as the next guy. Another reason I have trouble getting along is because I'm very self-centered and egotistical. I find it very difficult to be interested in other people. I mean, in the way they <u>want</u> me to be interested in them. I find it extremely difficult to give of myself to others. I <u>want</u> love and attention, but I can't give it myself. Of course I don't want to live in an ivory tower, but do I have any choice? What can I do? God knows I've tried to get along with people, tried to get girlfriends, tried to be a nice, likable guy. But most of the time, my attempts have ended in bitter feelings. I've read all the books on getting along with others. I've heard all that "be yourself" stuff. When I'm myself people think I'm nuts. I'm not repelled by people. It's just that when I get around them I lose my composure, my mind slips out of order, I become confused, nervous, I don't know what I'm doing. I don't think I've deliberately cut off the social side of my nature... I need this as badly as anyone. I'm not a natural born hermit. I've just failed at it, that's all. No matter how I try, I can't do it. So I have to rationalize. I have to make the best of the situation. I have to try and be content without this social life. You said once that people who try to live only on the mental level frighten you. I'm trying to live on the mental level alone because I have to, not because I want to, not because I don't need people and don't need physical experience.

Phoo... All I do is feel sorry for myself. I've always been full of self-pity. I guess you'll have to tolerate my self-centeredness or cut off the correspondence, because I'm certainly not going to change. Thank heaven you're not like this. Thank heaven you show an interest in other people. Self-centered individuals get on my nerves.

I realize that there's nothing odd about this greatness complex of mine, but it is a foolish "chase after the wind" and I dislike it intensely, and am trying to rid myself of it. It stands in the way of peace and contentment and makes a man a slave. It leads to great frustration and is liable to make all that one does a pretentious lie. It would be wonderful to be free of it. But can one ever be free of it? It's such a deep rooted part of me. What is your attitude toward this thing, this great vanity? Do you find it to be part of your motive for writing? I know that it is probably the chief reason why I strive to be a good artist. Can one love his work without feeling swell-headed about it? Pride is such a basic part of human nature, but yet it bothers me, I feel guilty after feeling great pride. There seems to be something false in it. Something wrong. Why should I give myself credit for doing anything? What right have I to consider myself great? All that I do and feel is the result of a force greater than myself... call it circumstantial evolution or God. But whatever it is, it deserves all the credit, not I. If I could reach the point where I could love what I do because it is good in itself, without feeling proud for having done it, I think I might have great peace.

Hi ya, Marty!

Sandra has to add her two cents.

Everybody needs something to live for. If not a creed, then a political cause, or just about anything. If you have something else to live for, then you don't need to look for a point to life. But if your life is empty and you feel lost and alone, then naturally you look for something to cling to. If I were socially and sexually adequate, I think that my approach to life would be very similar to yours. It's very hard when your life is so confined and in a rut to be fascinated, to find life always exciting. I have come to realize that life is pointless. I know this and I've given up looking for any great meaning behind the scheme. But because of this I am left with nothing to live for. My existence seems futile, not worth all the struggling and frustration and anxiety that it brings, because the joys I have are few and small. Maybe this is my own fault. I dunno. I think that gradually I will find peace and acceptance of my existence, and be satisfied to live just for the sake of existence, because it's better to exist than to not exist, even though it is a struggle. I'm constantly wondering whether or not a man can do this. I suppose it is what the Taoists do.

I think the main reason you find life worth living is because you are able to satisfy basic human needs. If you weren't able to satisfy them, all the things you see "lurking down every street, behind every door" etcetera would depress you and seem empty and dreary. I dunno. Maybe it wouldn't. Most of the time I don't know what I'm talking about. Why say anything? "A fool's utterance comes with many words."

The family situation has gotten pretty bad around here. I have often been tempted to end my life, but I can't find any means which are quick and painless enough. I'd get out of this miserable, sterile place, but the rest of the world is just as bad. "There is no happy land." The whole world is a jungle. You can't run away from it. My parents have been at each other's throats constantly for the past month or so. They have had several serious fights, which even led to blows a couple of times. About a week ago my mother left the house and didn't come back for three days. She took the car with her. When she came back, I found something in the car I wish I hadn't found. It was a birthday card that she was going to send to Maxon, but on the back of it was scribbled a suicide note... Can you blame me for feeling depressed about life? I don't want a bed of roses, but even so...

I hope you're not on the brink of despair. You did seem rather down in the dumps about things when you visited this Christmas, but now that you have found you-know-what, I think it'll be a long time before you are unhappy again. Anything is bearable when you have love. I'm sure that this great discovery of yours has made college more bearable for you. Remember when you were here how you talked of being sick and tired of college, how you would like to just leave it all? Remember how you talked about running away to Mexico and all? All this probably seems ridiculous and far away to you now. Now that you have found the one thing that can make everything look good.

Who needs a "Point to Life" when you have a girlfriend?

Dean Moriarty had a goal of a sort. I think his goal was to get as much out of life, to use up his complete human capacity while he had the chance, to do all that offers sensation and not worry. I guess you can call that a goal. Sometimes I think I'd like to live like Dean Moriarty, but I haven't got it in me. Not by a long shot. I think this character Moriarty is more of a dream than a reality. If there are any people like him at all, they certainly must be rare. Either that, or, I dunno, maybe they're quite common and I'm just ignorant of their existence.

I recall you telling me about Freud's belief that civilization has been a failure. I wonder if the town library has the book. It would probably depress the hell out of me. Do you think you could explain to me just what Freud believed to be the root of this failure? Didn't it have something to do with man trying to suppress the aggressive side of his nature or something? Do you have a copy of the book? Does Mr. Freud have any remedy for the situation, or does he believe that it is hopeless, that we are destined to fall back into the caveman stage?

I think I have a vague idea what you mean by man warping his own nature by "rigid institutional forms" which leave him struggling all his life, lost, confused, and all. Could you go into this further? I'm not quite sure I know what it's all about. I guess the churches would be one aspect of these "rigid institutional forms," wouldn't they?

Very interesting, those paragraphs on "disaffiliation." To feel free of society, but yet be a part of it to the extent that your survival depends on it, right? This is a very difficult thing to achieve, I think. Especially in the extremely complex system of society that exists in this country today. There is constant pressure being put on the individual, pressure that is trying to make you a part of society, pressure that is trying to make us think and act in accordance with standards and traditions: the churches, the industries, the military. If you don't fall in line, you are looked down upon, disdained. You are no good. Take this great old American tradition of ours that most of society considers sacred, "Making Good," ambition, getting up in the world, and getting in there pitching and competing. If you have no desire to compete, to get up in the world, you are sneered at, resented. By the middle and upper classes, that is.

I don't think there is as much emphasis put on this in the poorer class. And of course it's the same thing with... well... just about everything, the way you act, the way you dress, and so on. If you don't dissolve yourself into the accepted way, life can be made pretty miserable for you.

My aunt came over a little while ago. She brought her brood of spratlings with her, ages two, five and seven. I look at them, watch them run around making noise and acting like the little demons they are, and I can't help feeling sad. They have such little chance of leading worthwhile, full lives. The cards are stacked against. Their heads are being filled with alot of tripe. Their minds and imaginations are being suffocated, molded into narrow, petty, pitiful confines. Their lives will become sterile, empty, futile, dull, full of prejudice and superstition. Pathetic creatures. I wish I could do something for them, but it would be like trying to stop a waterfall. Even if I knew what to do, how to handle the situation, there are simply too many other forces in their environment that are working against them. It makes me sad. I suppose gradually one comes to accept these unpleasant aspects of life.

I don't know about writing. I've become discouraged. It's so hard to be really honest, for me, at least. Most of what I write comes out very pretentious. To ever really be able to turn out anything worthwhile, I'd have to write and write and write like a madman, like I was obsessed. And what's the use? Why add to the mountains of writings already done in the past, why heap more junk on vast piles? I think it is better just to enjoy being alive. When you were here you made an interesting remark. You said that a man must live for his life or for his work. And I think you also said that you'd rather live for life, if you could. So would I. We were discussing your friend David Tabor at the time, I believe. I just don't know. I've lost heart where writing is concerned. Besides, I don't feel that I have anything worthwhile enough to say right now.

Sigh... April... It just rains and rains and rains... Life is sad and beautiful.

I like what you said about not determining to pursue one particular objective, but to just _evolve_. I must remember that.

Has R. D. Stock ever explained to you what god (God) is to him? Does he profess to _love_ this supernatural being? When I was on my big religious kick, I tried to find God, tried to love Him, and sometimes I really thought I did love Him, but deep down I knew I was kidding myself. I never really got a grip on faith. I realize very well that there are people, many of them, that really do have a genuine faith and love for God. Tom Freeman is one of them. But I can't get him to explain it to me. Charles and I ask him about God. What is God? He says if he knew that, he'd be God himself. Then how can he love something he doesn't know and can't know anything about? From what source does this love and faith flow? That's what I'd like to know. Can R. D. Stock answer these questions?

Even if you crave to find some point to life, you just can't pick faith and love for God out of the sky. Not even a rigid Catholic training can give it to you. It certainly didn't give it to me. And needing a point to life didn't give it to me either.

I don't think these black Muslims have much of a chance. If they think the white southerners would ever consider giving up any of their great beloved homelands, they're plum loco. Not in a million years. Does their plan include the idea of all the negroes being forced to live in this separate homeland, that they will all have to stay out of the rest of the country? Many white folks will gladly agree to this, but the big argument will come when they have to decide which states the negroes will get. An argument which will go on forever. That is, if the idea ever reached that stage, which it never will. The black Muslims will never get anywhere, except maybe to cause a little more trouble and confusion. Well, I guess they could make great strides if they organized battalions of storm troopers.

There was this terrible sense of competition between me and Britt. I think that was the root of the trouble. But we were growing out of it, as our relationship mellowed. I sure wish he hadn't stopped writing. I wonder what he's doing now. Yes, I had a very good time when I visited him in Northampton. I really liked that town. It wasn't any bigger than Dover, but yet it had so much more... big library, book stores, junk stores, beautiful quiet places of nature, a girls' college. I often think about my relationship with Britt. It had a great deal of influence on my life. It was very turbulent, full of good times and bad times. The more I think about it, the stranger it seems to me. Britt was a strange sort of person. I wish I could explain it. He was deep, no question about that. I wonder if he still draws or anything, still collects comics. Keep trying with those relatives of his. We might find him yet.

There's a new book out called *The Village Voice Speaks*. Charles just got back from downtown and told me about it. Sounds interesting. Have you seen it? We're going to gather up the little bits of money we have and purchase the book.

I like that "Blue Turning Grey over You" alot. I'd want something good for it in trade. The records you owe me include that Henderson / Ellington LP, "Baltimore" by Fletcher Henderson on Velvet tone, that album of Bix reissues (78s), "She's No Trouble" by Benny Moten, Orch., and you said you would try to get "She's a Great, Grand Girl" by Roger Wolfe Kahn Orch., from R. D. Stock. Also, you said you were going to send us a couple of Mickey Mouse Big Little Books. Do you think it would be safe to send that LP through the mail? I'm very anxious to get it. The others I'll wait to pick up personally. If you don't think it's wise, I'll wait to pick up the LP too.

I like most of the sides you picked out in Smyrna. Good songs, and some good arrangements.

This Manolo Castro's Havana Yacht Club Orch. sounds interesting Is it a twenties band? Is it good? When you talk about the records you got got from me, it makes me regret trading them. There were some very unique sounds (like "Voodoo") that I'll probably never hear on another record. But that Folkways LP that I got for most of the best ones is worth it. Excellent LP.

Francis Craig, I found out, became a popular band leader and piano player around the late forties. His record, "Near You," was very popular. (I found a copy of it recently.)

I have that Leo Reisman record you mentioned. Yes, they do a good job of those tunes, both of which I like very much.

You say you have some good doubles for me? Hold on to them. You said when you were here that when I visited you I could take some of your doubles for the stuff you got this Christmas. Also, we may have a trade going by this summer. What are some of the doubles you have?

The Ted Lewis record sounds good. When did that band start having good jazzmen in it? What are the Mound City Blue Blowers like? Is it a regular orchestra or what? Is the Red Allen Orch. an arranged group? I'd like to hear that number. I really liked his trumpet solo on "Saratoga Shout" by the Luis Russel Band. Is "Why Was I Born?" by Teddy Wilson Orch. in the pre-swing style, or is it later?

I got a few good records since you were here. Got a whole batch of old Oriole label stuff out of a Victrola cabinet at the used-furniture place on New Street. The best of these were "Pa's Old Hat" and "Steppin' It Off" by the Dixie Jazz Band, both on black label Oriole. And also "Doin' the Raccoon" / "Cryin' Blues" by Ted White's Collegians, which you already have. Both of the Dixie Jazz Band numbers were very good, excellent arrangements and solos. Are these Dixie Jazz Band records listed in the discography? I'd like to know who made those records. I like "Cryin' Blues," too. It's similar to that "Cat's Kittens" which was also written by this Willie Kreager character. "Cryin' Blues" is better though, I think. "Doin' the Raccoon" is a very good piece of Americana besides having a good arrangement and some fair jazz. It's better than the other version I have of that song by the Levee Loungers.

The Oscar award show is on television right now. What a farce. All those greedy, prestige-mad, fame-maniacs sitting there in the audience waiting and hoping to get their sweating palms around one of those precious little statues. This is what they've worked so hard for, licked so many asses for, stepped on so many faces for, given up everything for, including their humanity.

Also in that Victrola cabinet I found a few scroll label Victors. *Birth of the Blues* by Paul Whiteman, which I found to be somewhat of a disappointment. Generally, Whiteman's band had corny arrangements, except for those by Bill Challis. "Hard-to-Get Gertie" by Irving Aaronson's Orch. has a good arrangement. And then there's the Five Harmaniacs, a real weird group. Corn mixed with jazz, it sounds like to me. Fiddle, harmonica, ukulele, banjo, kazoo, and whatnot. The tunes they play are "Coney Island Washboard," which they wrote themselves, and "Sadie Green."

Among the rest of the records I've gotten are "Angry" by Ted Lewis. I like the tune. Glad I got a version of it. "Harlem's Araby" by the Metropolitan Dance Players on the Nadsco label. It's the only record I've ever seen on that label. It's a small jazz group, better than I expected, from about 1925. The other side is "Collegiate" by some mediocre group.

Got a Cliff Edwards & His Hot Combination on Pathé label, with some good solos on one side. "Isn't This a Lovely Day?" and "Top Hat, White Tie, and Tails," two Cole Porter tunes from the movie *Top Hat* with Fred Astaire and Ginger Rogers. Good tunes, by Archie Bleyer & His Orch., vocals by Chick Bullock on Melotone. "Saint Louis Blues" / "Beale Street Blues" by Eddie Peabody on the violin. God, how obnoxious! An original version of "Alexander's Ragtime Band" by Prince's Band, which I like. Several other good dance band records.

Once in a while I see an old early thirties movie with some really great sounding band in it, hot trumpets and clarinets and all. And it makes me wish I had a tape recorder on hand. Maybe someday they'll put some of the best jazz from old movies on records. I hope so.

Yes, I much prefer the early Walt Disney strips to the later ones, much more expressive, more mood, more unique and fascinating. I like the *Phantom Blot* comic you sent. The cover appeals to me alot, too. Like you said, simple, but well-planned and colored. It's a shame *Mickey Mouse* has fallen into such a dreary, static rut. Thanks muchly for the comic. Well, you certainly got enough for it. Didn't I give you a *Little Lulu* comic along with the Disney stuff?

I guess I'll send you the double of *The Spirit* comic that I have. I can tell that two of the stories in it are definitely by Will Eisner[1] and two of them are not. Are these *Spirit* comics rare or anything?

Must be great, having your ideal girl just walk into your life like that. It must have really sent you flying into outer space. It makes me very happy to hear that Barb liked my work. It's very seldom that I get any female appreciation. I hope you were telling the truth when you said she was "really moved" by that story. It does my heart good to know that I am capable of stirring feminine emotions. So she's anxious to meet me, eh? Hmmmm... I have the feeling that she'll be anxious to get <u>away</u> from me after she does meet me. For some reason girls become antagonistic toward me after being in my company

---

[1] Generally considered one of the four defining classic American comic-book cartoonists (along with Carl Barks, Harvey Kurtzman, and Jack Kirby), Will Eisner created *The Spirit* series as a widely distributed Sunday newspaper insert in 1940. Distinguished by Eisner's masterful control of narrative, timing and page layout, it featured a beguiling mixture of drama, action, satire, and sex appeal. *The Spirit*, many episodes of which were written by a young Jules Feiffer, ran until 1952; it has since been reprinted in a variety of formats, mostly by Kitchen Sink Press. After retiring from comics for 25 years, Eisner reinvented himself as a creator of serious fiction in comics format with the 1978 release of *A Contract With God*, and has released over a dozen graphic novels in the past two decades; at the age of 80, he shows no sign of slowing down.

for a while. Maybe it's because I'm not very masculine, or because they think I'm a snob or something, I dunno. I certainly hope with all my heart that I can make a successful relationship with Barb, that I can communicate with her. It certainly shouldn't be as difficult as it is to communicate with most teenage girls, if she is all that you say she is. Do you feel that you have found your "Other Half," that you are now a whole being?

Thanks very much for the wonderful four-page comment and analyzation of my work. That you put so much time and thought into it really appalled me... It certainly gave my ego a great boost. Without these encouragements of yours my work would certainly dwindle to a great extent. And I mustn't let that happen. I'm duty bound to leave my mark. I'm a slave to my work.

Some of the work in those four *Arcade*s looked sort of strange to me after not seeing it for so long. Some of the drawings of Mabel are terrible. The picture of W. C. Fields was in a book written on his life. I forget the author. Anyway, I sort of traced it. I put the photo underneath the page and could see through it just enough to get the basic outline of his features. I like the way it came out. What a great comedian! Yes, the one of Tshombe came out good too. One of the best pencil shading jobs I've ever done.

I got a great laugh out of those little caricatures you did of Charles in the margins. Excellent satire. I also got a kick out of the one of Maxon and Fate pointing out at me. I'm glad you put them in there.

I like to do surrealistic stuff... gives me a sense of freedom. It's very difficult at times to break through inhibitions... fantasy-type stuff comes out best when you're not concentrating too much on what you're doing, when you're just sort of playing around.

Well, here I am on the last page already. I should have included more sheets in this letter. Maybe I ought to not fold 'em anymore.

Hoo Boy! Three pages on that "Synthetic Man" story. I was overwhelmed by so much devotion! Don't laugh when I tell you my eyes watered as I read those pages. You see? I don't love my work, I love the attention it gets. Really though, I think you have found alot of meaning in that story that I didn't really set out to put into it. And of course, you discovered alot of things that I put into it sort of subconsciously. The whole idea "came to me in a flash" you might say, and I set about it quite enthusiastically, more enthusiastically than I ever was before about a story or have been since. I'll admit I was proud of it. I thought it was pretty hot stuff. But NOW!! At first I was sorry I put the spider in it at all. I sort of made him up on the spot when I reached the part where Sniff went through the hole in the wall. And I regretted it because he didn't seem to fit, he didn't have anything to do with the story. But then when I got near the end, I saw that it would be perfect to have him come back and save the day. I'm certainly glad it worked out for the best, and was surprised at your enthusiastic reaction to it.

Yes, I was trying to get the idea across that we're becoming robots with synthetic personalities, or something like that. It's hard to explain. I never thought of using this spider character again, but after all you've said, I guess I will. If I ever find a place for him to show up again. I suppose the spider is something I would like to be, but I now realize it is beyond my power to be such as that. I didn't realize it when I did the story.

I did a term paper on the Faust legend in my senior year. I found it quite interesting. I read a little of Marlowe's play, a little of the story by Goethe, but I found it difficult to understand these authors. But it is a fascinating thing, which I thought about a great deal back then. But I just can't explain what it all means to me, how I feel about it. If I tried, I would get tongue tied.

As soon as I can get the money I'll send you the *Spirit* comic and the May 1962 issue of *Arcade*. I'd send you a couple of other issues which have been completed since your visit, but they have work by Charles in them and he doesn't want me to send them out. May is the latest completed one, and contains the only long comic stories I've done this year. These things get harder and harder for me to do, and it's even more difficult to come up with a worthwhile story idea. One is a Fritz story, the kind that rambles on without any plot. It's not as good as some of the previous Fritz stories. I got discouraged and turned it into a two-man with Charles at the end. Then Charles quit on me, so it comes to no ending. It just stops. The other is, of course, a Jim and Mabel episode. I think it's the best one I've turned out so far with human beings. But I still got a long way to go yet before my efforts with these characters are worthwhile. Also in this issue are some writings by, inevitably, Maxon! It was bound to rub off on him, this greatness mania. I dunno. I wonder if it's just a stage he's going through, or whether his writing will ever come to anything good. These are some of the first things he's ever written outside of school, so they're pretty pretentious and all, but he is intelligent and I think has what it takes if he devotes himself to it. He improves. But, like I say, what's the use of adding more on to the vast, infinite mountains of writings that have already been done? Oh well, if it offers gratification...

On the February and April issues of *Arcade*, are covers by Charles, colored and inked by him, and very beautifully, I think. And I think you'd like them very much too. It's toobad Charles won't let me send them. He's afraid something will happen to them. What do you think of Charles's work, what you've seen of it? He thinks you don't care for it. Do you?

Sandra got booted* out of Holy Cross again. I think the priests feel she's a bad influence on the rest of the students. Sandra has managed to convert a couple of her friends to some extent, and one of them got up in class one day and started reeling off all this anti-Catholic stuff that she learned from Sandra. Sandra has given up her idolatry of Bobby Darin. Now it's Rodgers and Hammerstein... Now she's driving us all mad by constantly playing Rodgers

*permanently, this time.

and Hammerstein records and singing the songs from their shows all the time. God! When she goes out for something, she goes all the way! Poor Sandra. I think this turbulent home life is beginning to take its toll on her. She's taken to drinking now, ya know. She's come home tipsy several times in the past few months. I hope she can keep it under control.

She had this big party here a few weeks ago. Everybody was drunk. Sandra and Dot Muzic were staggering around, knocking things over and all. Jackie Newton, that Sex Siren of Sunset Terrace, crashed the party. She was tipsy herself and was being really noisy and was very affectionate with everybody. She even came up and embraced me and kissed me! On the cheek, that is. It was delightful anyway. I guess she was amused to do that to such a cloddy fellow. Dear sweet Jackie. If only... well, nevermind... Anyway, I've never been so excited as when she gave me that hug. She even let me put my arm around her waist.

Yes, Marty, sometimes in real life it comes like a vision, a wish-fulfillment... though not usually, as you say. But you should know. That's just what Barb was, just how she came into your life.

I'm saving that war bond of mine for the trip to your place this summer. Anytime is fine with me. My father is putting pressure on me and Charles to get jobs, though, so maybe I'll have alot of money to throw around this summer, and maybe I won't be able to visit you at all. I guess I could always quit the damn job... It doesn't mean that much to me... especially not in the summer. I could always go to Atlantic City and do portraits if I got hard up.

Do you think that eventually you might marry this girl? What would you do for a living in that case? Do you have any idea?

Creep has finally led Franny astray. But he has had to compete with alot of other tom cats for her favors. It won't be long now before Franny has a blessed event, or two, or three, or more. Write soon... SOON, fella.............................Opps no more room.

~ 3 3 ~ *August 6, 1962*
Dover, Delaware

Dear Marty,

It was good to get a nice long letter from you again. That's the first full-length letter I've gotten from you since March. I'm certainly glad I made that trip out there. Now I know Barb. Her letters are extremely charming and delightful. What a rare find she is! I hope we can all get together sometime and be a clique or something — in New York, possibly.

I hope you can send me the records soon — I'm really anxious to play some of them — the King Oliver for instance. I hope the two dollars will cover the charge, for most of them, at least. Thanks very much for giving all those to me, and also I really appreciate your going to all the trouble of packaging and sending them for me. Thanks, Martimus.

No more typewriter. My father took it back. Says we can't afford it. Too bad. A pity.

My liking for jazz has taken a big leap recently, partly due to the visit at your place and listening to hundreds of good records. Especially early negro jazz. Generally, I prefer the negro bands of the twenties over white, though I'm crazy over alot of white records. The negro stuff seems to me more wild and inventive. It seems to have more of the essence of classic jazz. To me, anyway.

Also, the more I hear of early blues records, the more I like them, and the negro country bands. I got a few of these kind recently, like the Famous Hokum Boys which I really like alot.

I've gone and overhauled my record collection. I got rid of most of the junk and mediocre stuff. I held on to some of the lesser George Olsen, McEnelly, Nat Shilkret records to sell to Garbutt. He's buying them from me at twenty-five cents apiece. Good deal! And I've cut up about half the albums and made separate cases for all the good records, and put them all in one box, in alphabetical order, like you have yours. At this point, there are two rows of records in cases, each a foot and a half long. These are all I'm keeping. The rest are in about ten albums, which I intend to sell or trade. My collection is only about half of what it was, but it's all the better stuff. I decided that since I've got to move them all to Philly I just couldn't keep all of them, not even the ones that were fairly good. There were just too many. What a feeling of relief to be rid of all those records that I never played! I'll wager I got rid of about five-hundred or so.

But now record-hunting has been booming and I've been bringing in records right and left. I've gotten nearly a hundred since I overhauled my collection. About fifty of these went into my collection. Some I'm keeping for trade, some I got rid of.

So there I was, walking down Governor's Avenue, and happened to glance in the window of an old, locked up door. Boy, did my eyes pop! There, sitting on an old stairway, was a mint-condition copy of "I'm Gonna Meet My Sweetie Now." Well, I ran into the radio-repair shop next door and asked a guy about the records. I ended up buying them from an old, bent over character who lived upstairs (ten cents apiece). He says he has thousands more records in Cheswald, and suggested that I give him a list of the kind of stuff I look for and he'd have a guy he knows who has knowledge of old records look through them for me and pick out ones I'd want. I'm still waiting on that prospect. He said he'd phone me when the guy brought the records down. It's been a couple of weeks now.

Here's what you've been waiting for — a list. This isn't all of them. There were alot more — lesser stuff — a few sermons — J. M. Gates and such, hill-billy bands and singers, a Bailey's Lucky Seven version of "Flag That Train" on Gennett, two clarinet solos by Wilton Crawley on Okeh which sound exactly like your old buddy Boyd Senter, but the singing and guitar are good on them — lots of other stuff which I'll trade you if you want, or sell.

Some of this will be in alphabetical order, since I've put 'em away. Some won't be. Well, here goes:

Okeh 8261 - "Gut Bucket Blues" / "Yes! I'm in the Barrel" - Louis Armstrong's Hot Five

Okeh 8680 - "Beau Koo Jack" / "Mahogany Hall Stomp" - Louis Armstrong's Savoy Ballroom Five

Columbia 2544 - "Time on My Hands" / "You Call It Madness" - Smith Ballew & His Piping Rock Orchestra

Columbia 14205 - "Barbecue Blues" / "Cloudy Day Blues" - Barbecue Bob

Perfect 020T - M & O Blues - "Big Bill & His Jug Busters" / "How You Want It" Big Bill (guitar acc.)

Perfect 15468 - "Minnie the Moocher" / "Star Dust" - The Blue Ribbon Boys (vocals - Chick Bullock)

Perfect 12594 - "St. James Infirmary" - Chick Bullock Orchestra acc./ "Calamity Jane" - Adelyne Hood

Perfect 15506 - "You Rascal You" / "I Can't Get Mississippi off My Mind" - Chick Bullock's Levee Loungers

Perfect 15490 - "The Levee Low Down" / "Blues in My Heart" - Cab Calloway & His Orchestra

Oriole 2396 - "Corrine Corrina" / "Down Hearted Blues" - Cab Calloway & His Orchestra

Perfect 15757 - "Stormy Weather" / "Let's Call It a Day" - Bob Causer & His Cornelians

Victor 19997 - "Better Get out of My Way" / "Floyd Collins Waltz" - Vernon Dalhart Trio

Pathé 32491 - "Dustpan Blues" - Walter Dalton / "Farm Relief Song" - Lone Star Ranger

Oriole 8013 - "You Can't Get Enough of That Stuff" / "Nancy Jane" - Famous Hokum Boys

Perfect 169 - "Come on Mama" - Famous Hokum Boys / "Terrible Operation Blues" - Georgia Tom & Hannah May

Victor 20676 - "Positively-Absolutely" / "You Don't Like It, Not Much" - Jan Garber & His Orchestra

Harmony 827 - "My Sugar and Me" - Golden Gate Orchestra / "Dream Mother" - Carolina Club Orchestra

Perfect 15786 - "Smoke Rings" / "Sophisticated Lady" - Earl Harlan & His Orchestra

Perfect 15481 - "Sugar Blues" / "Black and Tan Fantasy" - Harlem Hot Shots

Oriole 1885 - "What a Funny World This Would Be" - The Home Towners / "Stew Song" - Holden Caufield & His Orchestra

Columbia (illegible) - "Preachin' the Blues" / "Black Water Blues" - Bessie Smith (Jimmy Johnson, piano)

Columbia 14343 - "Mother's Children Have a Hard Time" / "If I Had My Way I'd Tear the Building Down" - Blind Willie Johnson

Brunswick 80047 - "Creole Rhapsody" Part One / Part Two - Duke Ellington & His Orchestra

Oriole 1998 "If I Could Be with You" - Ben Pollack & His Orchestra / "Because I'm Lonesome" - Imperial D. O.

Oriole 8106 - "Slow Mama Slow" / "New Salty Dog" - Salty Dog Sam

Columbia 14179 - "Young Woman's Blues" / "Hard Time Blues" - Bessie Smith & Her Blue Boys

Columbia 14137 - "Money Blues" / "Hard Driving Papa" - Bessie Smith (Fletcher Henderson - piano; Joe Smith - Cornet)

Columbia 3885 - "Baby Won't You Please Come Home Blues" / "Oh (illegible) Blues" - Bessie Smith (Clarence Williams, piano)

Columbia 3936 - "Midnight Blues" / "Bleeding Hearted Blues" - Bessie Smith (Henderson - piano)

Okeh 8536 - "Miss Annabelle Lee" / "My Blue Heaven" - Lillie Delk Christian (with guitar and clarinet acc.)

Decca 1546 - "Alice Blue Gown" / "Cuddle Up a Little Closer" - Ben Pollack's Pick-a-Rib Boys

Victor 22115 - "Doing the Boom Boom" / "Look What You've Done to Me" - Leo Reisman & His Orchestra

Oriole 8059 - "That Stuff I Got" / "You Do It" - Famous Hokum Boys

Like I said to Barb, the Jelly Roll Morton is my favorite of the lot. Both sides are simply beautiful! A great record. Has "Jungle Blues" been reissued at any time? Gad! Victor oughta put out an LP of the Richard M. Jones Jazz Wizards! Both sides have just what I like best — the blending of a great arrangement with solo work and the heavy, driving rhythm. Never heard a better record. With it I would rank "In dat Mornin'," "The Boy in the Boat," "Skagalag" / "Voodoo" and a few others as my top favorites — some of the King Olivers too (the later ones).

I like the "Hot Five" alright, but it's rather beat. A shame. "Beau Koo Jack" / "Mahogany Hall Stomp" is on blue label. Was this blue label early reissues or what? I like both sides, but "Beau Koo Jack" is my favorite.

The Smith Ballew & His Piping Rock Orch. is fair... not as good as yours. That reminds me. Sitting in the Pittsburgh bus depot waiting for the Philadelphia bus I heard "I Love Louisa" playing over the loud speaker. I couldn't help snickering to myself. I found that I have a version of "What Is It?" by the High Hatters on Victor, but it's not nearly as good as the Smith Ballew.

I like M & O Blues alot. Interesting, weird band accompanying "Big Bill." Good blues record!

The Blue Ribbon Boys' renditions of "Star Dust" and "Minnie the Moocher" are excellent. Really beautiful. I wish that Bullock bastard wasn't on them. Anyway, they're the best versions of those two songs I've ever heard. They have good hot solos too.

"St. James Infirmary" has a hot trumpet but Bullock is so corny... The other side of this is a comedy song.

"You Rascal You" is good but not as good as "Dixie." Bullock corns it up again.

Both the Cab Calloway records are quite good, except, of course, for Cab Calloway. Some good tunes, too. I like "Blues in My Heart" (you have a version of this by somebody, don't you?) and "Corrine Corrina" alot!

"Stormy Weather" is good. I like the tune and they do a nice, pleasing arrangement of it.

Funny thing, I really got a kick out of "Better Get out of My Way" by the Vernon Dalhart Trio. It's mostly instrumental, with violin, guitar, mouth harp and so on, and the vocal isn't as obnoxious as that Dalhart usually is. I like it. I put it in my collection.

"Dustpan Blues" is a good country vocal, and "Farm Relief Song" reminds me of that Ku Klux Klan record of yours, an interesting social comment. Too bad the record's cracked.

I really like the Famous Hokum Boys. I like the tunes they play, sort of country-negro style, I guess. This Georgia Tom is a major voice in all the sides by them. Hannah May is in a couple of them. "Terrible Operation Blues" is one of these comic sex tunes... quite funny, too! You remember I used to have "Nancy Jane" but it was so worn you could hardly hear it? Certainly felt good to be able to hear it good and clear. I really like that group.

The Jan Garber has good arrangements on both sides, if you go for "Roaring Twenties" style music.

"My Sugar and Me" is quite good, except for the miserable volume of Harmony recording. A hot record.

I can't figure out whether this Earl Harlan Orchestra is white or negro. Both sides have good arrangements and a hot saxophone. I like the tunes, too.

Of course, the "Harlem Hot Shots" is great on both sides. Who could this be? Not Duke Ellington... Can you fill me in? "Sugar Blues" has a Louis Armstrong style vocal.

The Home Towners is typical. I like them. Especially that Arthur Fields, boy!

The "Peg Leg" Howell is a country negro band, violin, guitar, and what not... very good! Only the guitar is so loud it's hard to hear the violin... Maybe it's my record player.

That Herwin label is interesting as hell. According to the label, it comes from Saint Louis. I wonder how scarce they are. It's an electrical recording. There's a trumpet in this, but it plays pretty straight. It's a good spiritual record. Kinda scratchy, though.

God! Blind Willie Johnson! What a voice! I like his singing... His voice is a musical instrument... The words hardly matter.

Sam Lanin's "Flag That Train" surprised me. It's quite good. Better than the Bailey's Lucky Seven version. The tune is very catchy.

As a rule I don't care for the thirties swing style but this Jimmie Lunceford is really moving. Really great! It's growing on me more and more. Didn't care for it at first. Doesn't somebody in Ohio have this? You, perhaps?

Sara Martin I like, and the accompaniment too. This record is in the poorest condition of all, just about. But you can hear it alright. None of these records are beyond making out the words. Thank heaven!

"Without You Sweetheart" / "Let a Smile etc." has good arrangements and a hot trumpet, I believe.

Seattle Harmony Kings is fairly good. "How Many Times" is a catchy tune by Irving Berlin.

All three of the Ted Wallace records are excellent. Nice smooth band, top arrangements that are every bit as good as the best Roger Wolfe Kahn, plus alot of good jazz. Do you have any records by this band? These are the first I've ever found. "When the One that I Love Loves Me" is really a great tune! I think you have a version of it. The lyrics are so absurd and asinine they're almost satiric. "Get Happy" is really the best version of this favorite of mine I've heard. That band plays it just right... Perfect!

Will Weldon is quite good... nice guitar, too... This one is pretty worn.

"Side by Side" / "Pretty Lips" is pretty good. Sounds alot like "I'm Comin' Virginia"... Pleasing arrangements, good trumpet... Nichols, ey wot?

"Pretending" is fair... It has a good, but brief, cornet solo.

"Crying My Blues Away" is a weird thing... Nice tune, with a strange arrangement. Alot of hot solos. The other side, "Shake Your Shimmy" is done by a piano, bass, and drums trio. It's quite good.

Bessie Jackson is fairly good. Joe Evans I like alot. Really a good blues singer.

Of course, all the Bessie Smiths are good. A couple of them are in pretty poor condition, though. Excluding the accompaniments, my favorite is "Preachin' the Blues"... A really moving tune, and she does it excellently. The accompaniments by Jimmy Johnson I like (James P., is it not?)... And the "Blue Boys" are very good, as is Joe Smith.

"Creole Rhapsody" is good, but there's something about the Ellington band starting in 1929 that I find distasteful.

"If I Could Be with You" is good. The arrangement copies the McKinney's Cotton Pickers' version in spots, like at the end. Teagarden's vocal dominates half the record.

Salty Dog Sam is a good blues singer.

This Lillie Delk Christian record is odd... quite off beat. She has a kind of odd voice, not of much worth, but the clarinet on both sides is quite good, with a strange tone quality — almost like a hornpipe.

"Alice Blue Gown" is very good — a good swinging hot version of the tune. Do you have any idea who's on this and what year it is?

You have "Doing the Boom Boom"... a nice arrangement, fairly good tune. The vocal is nauseating.

The copy of "I'm Gonna Meet My Sweetie Now" was the same master as the one I already have, so I sold it to Garbutt for fifty cents. It must be a fairly common record.

Thanks for getting me "Ain't Misbehavin'"... Bring it with you when you come here next time and I'll give you some sermons for it, or would you like "I'm Comin' Virginia"?

Interesting trade you made with Lambdin. I had no idea that the Louis Dumaine and New Orleans Owls were such hot items. Or is it that Lambdin favors the New Orleans style? Wasn't that Clarence Williams' Washboard Band the cracked one?

You got alot of good stuff for those four. "Cherry," at last. Lucky poisson. "Milenberg Joys" is a great one. Think you could trade that to me for something? Some of the bands I've never heard of — like Leroy Smith Orch, Mississippi Maulers, Charlie Troutt's Melody Artists — what are they like? Any of them negro bands? What's the Tiny Parham like... What year is it? What's the other side like? What's the Clarence Williams on Okeh like? Ah me... Why can't I get stuff like that in trades... What kind of jazz does Lambdin appreciate most?

Well so much for record talk... I'm sorta worried about moving my collection to Philly. I hope I can take them in the car. Yah, I plan to make record hunting trips down here about every three or four months. I don't think I'll have much luck in Philly with the junk stores. My only hope is to meet up with other collectors who are willing to sell some of their records, or trade for drawings or something.

I'm going to follow your suggestion about doing up a portfolio and taking it around in Philly. Unfortunately I haven't started it yet. I saw a want ad in the *Inquirer* recently for an art student to touch up black and white portraits. Too bad it appeared a couple of weeks too soon. I hope such openings are plentiful. That'd be an ideal job for me.

As soon as possible, I plan to get an apartment of my own. I can't stand my mother and father's neurotic relationship anymore. When they start arguing I just have to get out of the house. In fact, one morning about a week ago, things got so bad that I stuck some clothes in a bag and hitchhiked to Philadelphia. I stayed with my uncle for a few days, which was almost as depressing as being at home. I spent quite a bit of time hunting for a job, but without success. Then my mother found out where I was and came up and dragged me back. The whole situation was infinitely depressing. Alot of times I almost broke down in tears thinking about it all. As a very small child I had the vague impression that civilization had straightened everything out and all of mankind was at peace and there was no longer anything to worry about. Little did I know how close was the prehistoric savage! But it made itself known to me. Even the American middle class, I now know, is subject to the ruthless, brutal, unmerciful id. If you haven't got the inner toughness that it takes to survive, you might as well have yourself committed or do away with your life. There's no room for "gentle and loving"...

Hmmm... Your comments on my last long letter (April tenth) seem very dated. My attitudes have changed quite a bit since then. Mainly in that I've become indifferent to alot of things I was concerned about then.

I've stopped ever hoping to see the *Obese Toad*. I consider the stuff I did for them mediocre and I hope they don't print it. It's a shame for you, though — you told me you did some things that were timely and effective only while they were current. Which was — about a year ago, wasn't it? It seems to be in pretty much of a mess, what with one of the partners skipping out and everything — and the printer will lose money on it.

So your folks refuse to give you any money to get started, eh? How come? How long do you plan to work in Akron before coming east? How did that job with the trade journal come out? I sure hope you got it! If you did, tell me what you're required to do. You're not going to move ALL your stuff to Akron, are you? I mean, all your comics and books and newspapers and stuff! Are ya going to take all your records? I bet you look forward to having your own place with eager anticipation... So do I... It'll be somewhat difficult at first, adjusting to all the duties you're not used to performing (at least I'm not, dunno about you) like getting clothes washed, buying household utensils and all. You're a little more self-sufficient than me, anyway. You're used to buying your own clothes and cooking. I'm completely dependent on my mother for these things. The only thing I can cook is canned soup. And I have no idea what size any of my clothes are.

Well, you'll have plenty of time for writing — no interruptions, no noise — and no Barb... Barb will be in Columbus... I guess you'll be going to Columbus quite a bit... Hey! Maybe you could get in some record hunting there. I wonder how it will effect you, being so far away from Barb.

When I was in Ohio I read an article in *Playboy* by Jack Kerouac that day you spent alone with Barb. The article was a definition of the Beat Generation, appearing in a 1959 issue, I believe. I told Charles about the article and he wants to read it. Do you think you could dig up that *Playboy* and send it here? I'll send it back as soon as we're done with it... Would it be too much trouble to locate that particular issue? I would certainly appreciate it.

Here's the date of *The New Yorker* with "Seymour, an Introduction" in it: June 6, 1959 — okay!

There was an interesting documentary on TV not long ago on the life of Bob Hope. They showed alot of candid films of TV rehearsals, back stage activities and all the frantic activity that takes place before a TV show goes on the air. It was really fascinating. How mad and ruthless show business is. Only a few can withstand it. Like Marilyn Monroe. Ah! What a pity!

Barb told me all about seeing Doug's *Dr. Caligari* and a few other films he got recently. I'd like to see it, what with the expressionistic scenery and all. What did you think of it? I expect that someday you will have a vast collection of silent movies, including most of the great ones. I wouldn't mind having some of them myself.

We got the *Ginger Man* recently. I've only had a chance to read parts of it. Alot of what I read I didn't quite understand, but I did find it very amusing in places. Donlevy's writing reminds me quite a bit of yours. His way of expressing himself is quite similar to yours, his wording and all.

Of the three stories in the *Kent Quarterly*, the one I appreciate most is "Trampoline Journey." I can't tell you in alot of scholarly words why... I guess it's because I identify myself with it more than the others. It says what I would say if I had the ability, and I think this is why most people appreciate certain literature and ignore another kind — a matter of identification.

I don't think I'm quite intelligent enough to get the most out of your writing... Maybe it's just a matter of lack of education. I think that's why I enjoy very simple literature, like *Catcher in the Rye* and all, because, while the meaning might be very deep, it is very simply stated. I have trouble understanding and appreciating symbolism, which your stories are full of. I think the theme, the story line, and the thoughts in your three stories are excellent, but the wording is just a bit too complex for me. After reading it a few times, I can appreciate it to an immense degree. Your choice of words is very good, but sometimes the sentence structure and all can be confusing. It was very appropriate, putting that passage from Anne Franke's diary at the beginning of "Trampoline Journey." It sums up the situation of the character in the story.

The first part of the story, the part about his childhood, I find humorous, but melancholy too. Very good. Yes, it has warmth... tragic warmth. I think I already told you that I really liked how you define the American teenage girl. I hope you go into this subject more extensively in the novel. Your perspective on girls is just right, and the sexually frustrated clod's attitude toward them is just right — very close to my own attitude.

In all your stories, the human situation is expressed as an undefinable combination of the tragic and joyful. This is very good, I think. All you need now is to suffer to give your work the right depth. Heh heh. And think, the longer you write, the more experience you get and the wiser you become, the more honest your writing will be. As of now, I find it to be somewhat affected and pretentious. But still, what you are trying to say is plenty honest enough... It's just the way you word it that I think is a bit overdone.

I really like the way you did the title page and the picture at the end of "And the Villains Still Pursued Her." One of these days I'm going to do something like this, but without any of my own work in it — using newspaper and magazine clippings of all kinds of old etchings, photos and all. Boy, you could really make something great if you did it right — what a neat magazine cover you could put together!

The more I read this one about Miss Pruitt, the more I get out of it... Same idea as in *Lord of the Flies*, that the savage beast is still stronger in man than his civilized side. You put it very effectively too, with the same tragic-comic aspect. Choice of words is very effective and seems, sometimes, sarcastic. The various descriptions of Miss Pruitt bring out the insipidness of civilization to a T. The paragraph about Miss Pruitt and the ape is beautifully done. The idea of the beast facing the sad end-product of civilization, contemplating each other, is quite touching. Also, your impressions of the human beasts, the hoods, are very effective. While you put the story across very effectively, I think, somehow it could have been made stronger. It lacks impact, you know? Alot could be done with this theme. What gave you the idea for the story? Anything in particular? It certainly is a unique idea.

"The Grin Unclosing" is rather difficult for me to comment on. It's very complex, very symbolic. Its meaning is somewhat hidden. Naturally, the part I appreciate most is the letter. It is simple and human and tender — no intellectual overtones, no surrealism, no symbolism — just simply stated feelings and events, so that the most ordinary of readers (including myself) can understand it.

The phone call part I like alot, too. Very realistic. The impression of the harsh and sensual "sweet life" comes through very well in that part. All the artificiality, the clichés and whatnot are quite effective. I still get the meaning here only vaguely — I mean about "The Grin Unclosing" — the last sentence in the story. Would you explain it to me again, please? You're probably agitated with my denseness. Can't say as I blame you — I'm agitated with it myself.

My only suggestion to you is that I think you should try to simplify your style a bit. You could be much more effective. I don't know how to say it clearly. I suppose gradually, as your writing becomes more polished, the meaning will stand out more clearly and sharply. It's the very same process all writers and artists go through — the crystallization of ideas, the refining of style.

Be sure to send me a copy of your latest story when you finish it. Is this one going to be all autobiographical? What is Barb's opinion of your writing?

Like I said in Ohio, I think I've just simply become numb to the bomb business... I used to worry myself sick about it when I was eleven, twelve, thirteen... but gradually you just stop worrying about something you can't do anything about, and it isn't causing me any immediate harm, so, I'll worry about it when, and if, it happens.

I don't see anything wrong with committing suicide if life is hopeless, if your life is more unpleasant than it is pleasant. In some cases, it is the sensible thing to do. If you can't get along with anybody, if living from day to day is nothing but an unrelenting struggle with no hope of relief, why go on with it?

Personally, I think I'm over my suicide tendencies for the time being. I'll tell you why. One day shortly after I came back (actually I was dragged back) from my trip to Ohio, things were looking terribly bleak and I was more miserable than I'd ever been before in my life. I can't tell you how miserable I was. "This is unbearable," I thought to myself, "I can't go on living with this terrible feeling inside of me"... So I went out walking and came to this swimming pool. Here, I discovered, was an ideal place to commit suicide. The pool was about twelve feet deep and filled with water. Drowning is quick and comparatively painless. I stood by the pool for about half an hour, trying to get up the courage to jump in. But deep down I knew I could never do it. I found that even with its misery and frustration, life was precious to me. Complete oblivion! The thought of it makes everything in life seem good and dear, even suffering.

Yes, I was starting to loosen up about the last five days of my visit out there. I was really enjoying it... especially Barb. Dear sweet Barb. She's the only girl I could ever feel comfortable around. She's honest, intelligent and sensitive. I feel something in common with her, and that's why I felt relaxed in her presence. More than relaxed. I felt warm inside, that life is good, and an adventure. Oh where am I going to find a motherly Barb, a large, plump Barb!?

I got the impression Ruth was more interested in you than she was in me. But how could I expect her to be interested in me. I was close-mouthed and boring and nervous in her presence, while you were full of fun and jocular and talkative. By the way, Barb told me about your date with Ruth... What all did you tell Ruth that night?

But after I came back to Dover, after the trip, I really felt miserable again. It's hell to go and see other people living, and loving, and enjoying life, and not to be able to do it yourself. And all because you're stuck in a place where no one, not a soul, can accept you and make you feel a part of life. Instead, you have to be a recluse. I want to live, I want variety, I want to do things and I want to love. You don't know how horrible it is to want these things desperately and to not have them even a little bit. I hope moving to Philly will end this.

Hmmm... Your motive for creating seems to be greatly different from mine. You, it seems, are detached, as a person, from your work. My work is me... it is me on paper. Which proves that I'm more of an egomaniac than you. In your work, you can be objective — you don't write as the subjective Marty Pahls, you write as a voice for our time, you write what you see as the commonly felt emotions and attitudes and beliefs. Your writing is the voice of many, including yourself (sometimes), but not only yourself. With me, it's the opposite, my work is the expression of me, as a unique and special person — my own special feelings and attitudes. Sometimes I can do what you do, but not often.

Ah yes — Robert Morley... a great English actor and a fascinating character. So Tabor is like him — I'd really like to meet this guy... Maybe I will someday. From the way you and some of the other people in Ohio talk, he seems to have what it takes to become famous. I won't say great. How is Tabor as an actor? On the stage I mean.

I sure hope you can come visit this summer. By that time I hope to have a job and lots of money. I guess I'll save some of the money, but I've got alot of LPs to catch up on, like those two five-record sets. I might not have an apartment yet, but I should know my way around pretty good, so I could show you the interesting sights.

I hope Barb can come east with you sometime soon. Charles is anxious to meet her. Hey! try to get "How about Me" / "Cradle of Love" off Dave Ski. Remind him that I still want it.

"Coney Island Washboard" / "Sadie Green" by the Five Harmaniacs is Victor 20293. An odd record.

The Cliff Edwards & His Hot Combination is "Someone's Stolen My Sweet Sweet Baby" (the other side is sweet) on Pathé 25163.

Ted Lewis's "Angry" is Columbia 416. Nothing to rave about.

I don't know if I can send you any *Arcade* books this time... Haven't got the postage funds. Oh well, I haven't done anything particularly interesting in the *Arcade*s since you were in Delaware. But, I'll try to send you one or two.

Sandra is still crazy about Rodgers and Hammerstein, but now she's branching out into other musicals — Lerner and Loewe's "My Fair Lady," Meredith Willson's "Music Man" and God knows what next. She gets madder by the day!

We're moving August thirteenth so you may as well write your next letter to our new address (isn't this getting ridiculous?) which is:

16 Wellington Road
Upper Darby, Pennsylvania

I haven't seen the house yet, but I know where it is. It's right near Market Street where the elevated train turns off, right on the edge of Philadelphia proper. A good neighborhood. The sixty-ninth street terminal is nearby. There are always alot of trolley cars and old-fashioned red and white interurban trolleys there.

Well, so ends another miserable letter. When I compare your letters with mine I feel ashamed. I stutter and stammer and end up saying nothing. Your letters are thorough, intelligent — mine are half-baked, incompetent.

If you haven't sent the records yet, you might as well send them to our Philadelphia address. I'm sure anxious to get those records. Especially that "Wa Wa Wa" by King Oliver.

Thanks ever so much for the good times I had in Ohio. Thank your mother and father for me if you haven't already. I hope to be able to visit you again when you have your own place in Akron.

Your Vigor for Life Appalls Me

Maxon has become an avid Dostoevsky fan these days. He's reading everything by the great Russian author that he can get his hands on. His favorite so far is *The Brothers Karamazov*.

Well, I guess the next time I hear from you I'll be in Philly. Write soon, if you will.

P.S. Maxon went out on a date with a young lady recently and claims he enjoyed himself. He's going out with her again this Wednesday.

Are you going to get those "Sad Fables" photostated?

~ 3 4 ~   *March 10, 1963*
                                                Cleveland, Ohio

Dear Britt:

Hello Britt. Been two years this month, I believe. You owe me a letter, Britt!... Got your address from your relations in Akron. I'm living with Marty in Cleveland. How 'bout that, eh? I'm pretty much unchanged since March, 1961. So you had to drop out of college for want of funds... sad... You always did have a hell of a time getting your hands on money... I was very glad to learn that you're still alive and that you've kept up your artwork... doing decorations for departments or something for a living... That's almost as sad as what I'm doing for a living... working for a greeting card company... Listen, Britt, ol' kid... let's get things going again... It jest ain't right for friends to break off this way... I want you to write and tell me all (ay ell ell) all that's happened to you in the past two years... What in God's name have you been doing? What direction have you taken... What is your present outlook on life... And tell me, is Bert still living? Do you have many friends? Do you make it with girls? Have you found love? Come, my friend, speak up! Let us hear the word! Marty and I have been living together in an apartment here since fall. Marty has found love and is writing a novel... but I'll let him tell you about that... Please write, for chrissake! I really want to know how you are, no shit! Our family is living in Philadelphia now... Nobody's married yet or anything like that... YOU MUST WRITE! We must get together again... talk about "old times" and all that crap...

Dear Britt:

I am alone in the apartment. All about me is silence, except for the sound of the alarm clock ticking away the precious minutes of my life, as usual, and the steady monotonous rumble of cars, trucks and busses over on the highway just a couple of stone's throws from here. Also heard is the slow dribbling of the leaking toilet and through the walls comes the distant sound of voices... The entryway door creaks open and slams, the radiator hisses, a child runs down the hall bouncing a ball. Actually it's pretty goddamn noisy around here!

Pulling your letter out of the mailbox was a joyful moment, but reading it filled me with great sadness. Britt, you are truly hung-up... It seems your frustration has just steadily become more intense over the past years. It seems to be just a giant-size version of the "bag" you were in when I last saw you... It makes me very sad, my old friend. Very sad. And you haven't kept up your artwork? This I will have to see for myself. I'm always picking up magazines like *Help!* and *Cracked* in hopes that I might find something by you in one of them. I had hoped you would develop your fine ability (I'm reluctant to say talent — what is talent?) into something worthwhile. But I know that if one is too badly hung-up, one loses heart for such pursuits. All that becomes of significance is the torment and the search for relief. Art is not enough, I know. But it also comes as a shattering blow that for you not even the love of a girl is enough. But from your letter I'd say she must do you some good. What could be making you so unhappy... What disease has gotten into you that is "rotting" you? Listen, have you thought of getting psychoanalyzed? I know plenty of people here with problems who get treatment and they say it does them good. Of course, virtually all these people have rather superficial hang-ups and consider it an "in" thing to be neurotic and getting psychiatric therapy is a status symbol... It's quite obvious that basically these people find life bearable and even enjoyable. They have little time for people with real live basic problems, because they can't stand to have stark depression and despair in their midst, and I can't blame them. Even so, I strongly urge you to get psychiatric help. I'm not saying a psychiatrist will cure you or anything, but I'm sure this would help you understand yourself better and make you better able to cope with life (what does "cope" mean? What an odd word it is! "Cope"! Hm! It just now struck me... Oh well). You might be able to get free treatment (or very low-priced) through the social service... They have that here in Cleveland... That's where all these kids go that I was telling you about. They also go to the university psychiatrists.

How did the high school in Duluth end up? Did you make any good friends? It seems to me that you must be desperately lonely. At least that's the impression I got from the letter. Does this girl give you understanding? Did you meet her in college? Describe her in detail if you will. Britt in love... ah me... It makes my heart glad... But you seem to be having a hell of a time with her... You say you're always hurting her. How, for God's sake? Of course, you're in no proper state to get married... Wait until you've straightened yourself out a bit and are financially able to set out on your own... I take it you're still living at home.

You're such a sensitive, intense fellow, Britt. It is really painful to see you in such great turmoil... It is painful to read your letter... You seem to be going through emotional tortures of some kind. I hope you come out of it as you get into your twenties... Sometimes people with unhappy childhoods and adolescences (hm) are very happy in their middle years. Sometimes not, too. But come to Cleveland and we shall see what we can do. I'm anxiously looking forward to your visit. We don't have access to a phone, so write and tell us when you're coming. If you come by bus, of course we'll meet you at the station, but I hope you bring your car... If you drive, we'll have to set up some meeting place, because you'd have a difficult time of it trying to find our place on your own, unless you're a genius. Y'know, it seems strange that the three of us have never actually been together all at one time!

I presume you have continued following Kurtzman, Elder and all in some half-hearted way.

Tuesday, March 19, 1963

I'm writing this at seven in the morning at my sad drawing table at American Greetings Corporation. Work doesn't start until eight. I'm always the first one here. I've started getting up at five, coming here around six-thirty and working on my own art or writing letters. I'm always too tired at night to do anything so I go to bed early. How sad the rapid transit train is at six in the morning, full of old people with lunch boxes grumbling to themselves.

My job here is indescribably dismal... I've always been disgusted by greeting cards. Most of the artists and writers here feel the same way. It's a strange society. We are living in the twentieth century where a hundred artists and writers must spend eight hours a day turning out artwork that is completely the opposite of what they really want to do. It's quite a phenomenon. Oh, there are a few exceptions. I know of two or three people here who like making greeting cards.

Working here is much like going to high school. You have a teacher ("supervisor") who grades your work and gives out assignments and who gets after you if you goof off. You eat in the cafeteria with your gang, or you go to a restaurant down the street if you don't have a gang. You have your popular groups and your social rejects, your intellectual cliques and dum cliques. Rumors, scandals and jealousies abound. Sex is rampant. The only difference between this place and high school (besides ashtrays) is that every Friday morning the secretary comes around and hands you an envelope which you greedily rip open, then you pull out a slip of paper which reads "Pay to the Order of Robert Crumb Exactly $53.24." Actually I get sixty-five but with deductions and all... and at that I'm about the lowest paid clod in the whole place — probably because I'm the youngest and haven't had any art school. I'm also the worst artist. <u>Greeting card</u> artist, that is.

Ah there is so much to tell, so much I want to know! You seem to be quite willing to tell all, and I'll do the same... (of course, we never really "tell all"... there are always things which we hold back). But I haven't the patience or the energy (let alone the skill) to put it all down in a letter, so I'll wait until I see you, which I hope will be soon.

Gee... here we are, writing to each other again. Seems strange... This all came about so suddenly... in a matter of a couple of weeks...

Well Britt, all I can say is come to Cleveland! Come! Come where there are warm hearts and gentle souls and twisted minds! Come and bring Bert! Bring comics (I get all *MAD*s, *Pogo*s...). No, don't bring comics — I was just kidding... You can stay as long as you want... You might even try getting a job here! Just a thought.

~ 3 6 ~

April 2, 1963
Cleveland, Ohio

Dear Britt:

So life isn't so bad after all... you are living... really living...

I'm writing this at the sad sad hour of five o'clock in the morning, which is the only time of the day that I ever feel like really doing anything...

So you'll be here in about a week... How in the name of heaven do you intend to find this place? Good luck, fella! Perhaps we should arrange some meeting place... Let's meet on the top floor of the Cleveland Union Terminal... or perhaps the old subway entrance in the deserted bank at Detroit and 25th Streets... or maybe in Cubby's 16 cent hamburger and orange juice restaurant at Euclid and 105th... or better still, at the Flat Iron Grill under High Level Bridge...

Well, anyway, it will be something to see you again... In a way I feel inadequate... You have become so mature and full of adult knowledge of the world and I'm still a kid... still shy and immature.

Your letters, by the way, and in case you don't know, are very well written, despite the fact that you still leave words out. You have a very colorful writing style which expresses your personality and the way you see life. Very enjoyable to read. Have you done any creative writing like stories or anything? Have you done any comic book type stories... What have you done with your cartoon ability? Anything?

I remember how hung-up and frustrated you used to be with girls... When did all of that come to an end? I'm glad you've found love... Now at last I can say to myself, "Ah! Britt has found love. Britt's life is complete — no longer is there reason to worry about Britt!" And it's true... just about anything is bearable, I think, if there is love in your life...

I might as well tell you what-all the family has come to... Carol is now twenty-two and has been engaged to some clod for more than a year. She lives in an apartment in downtown Philadelphia, in the old section south of City Hall where all the arty types hang out. Charles (clod o' clods) is still at home... He has done virtually nothing since graduating from high school... All he does is sit around the house and occasionally he takes walks through the city, throwing eggs at passers-by or sitting on the floor of the subway staring at girls' legs... He made a feeble attempt at college. He attended Delaware State College (which is 95 percent negro, if you recall) but dropped out after four months, saying it's all futile... The only worthwhile thing he got out of it was the friendship of a young negro fellow name o' Tom Freeman.

Maxon has turned from baseball and model airplanes to Dostoevsky and existentialism... He has become a real, young pipe-smoking intellectual... He's living by himself in a boarding house in Dover... Smart kid...

And Sandra... Ah, poor Sandra... She spent a few years going through the teenage bit, you know, dances, speeding cars, rock'n'roll records, drinking, smoking, heavy necking in drive-ins, etc, etc... But now she is a social reject (her friends in Dover think she's gone out of her mind), despises typical teenagers, reads books, wears black clothes and takes nothing seriously...

My parents are as sad as ever... All I can say is, I'm glad I left home... If I ever move back to Philadelphia, I will live by myself in a furnished room, by gum...

So you have your own "studio" now, eh? Britt has come up in the world — gets to have his name painted on a glass door — lucky lucky! My drawing table at American Greetings is in a little cell (similar to the toilets in a bus station john) in a vast huge room full of babbling, raving idiots who have become drugged by years of "color separation," which is the name for what we do... I don't think I'll be able to stand this work for more than a year... I hope to get into a better department, as I think I've already told you...

Well, enough... We can really talk when you come here — get down to genuine communication instead of this meaningless drivel... You can come anytime, since Marty isn't working and can meet you no matter what hour you show up... We'll serve you Old Crow just to make the meeting historic...

~ 3 7 ~

June 27, 1963
Cleveland, Ohio

Dear Britt:

I'll tell you the truth, Britt, ol' kid... the reason I haven't written is because I don't have anything to say. As it is this will be a short letter. I think of writing to you every day, but then I remember that all I have to talk about is my goddamn problems and I hate to think of burdening people with them. I want to keep our friendship going because I feel we still have every bit as much in common as we did in days of old (except, of course, for your success and my failure at winning the love and affection of the tender sex), but I just can't sit down and pour out bullshit on paper all the time, and nothing of interest ever happens that I could tell you about. So that's why I haven't written and I'm truly sorry. I feel bad because I value your friendship (I really do — no shit) and I hate myself because I have nothing of worth to give.

I'm writing this at a table in the Miami Restaurant, a 105th and Euclid spot which has a huge neon palm tree out front over the sidewalk and which is a favorite spot for the whores to work out of... Before me on the table is a tall cherry ice cream soda and my sad battered portfolio with old letters and drawings and other accumulated junk in it... I will stall around with this ice cream soda for maybe a couple of hours while I'm writing this letter. I can't write in the apartment... There are people there talking and laughing and drinking beer... I don't drink beer so I thought I'd leave rather than be a drag on things... "I hate to drink around somebody who doesn't drink," Maggie said, tossing back her thick black hair with a wag of her head... Ah Maggie... beautiful, plump, peach-colored, good natured, dumb Maggie...

A whorish looking colored girl with possibly the biggest ass I've ever seen just walked out of here with a very midgety puny fellow... Ah me... Outside the night air is hot and thick... Restless people walk around aimlessly... sit on doorsteps, porches — lean out of windows... Convertibles tear down 107th street at breakneck speed — run you down if you don't watch out... Sex is rampant... Drink is rampant... And here I sit with my ice cream soda pouring out self-pity to a long lost friend, trying to find the past, trying to live something that never was, never will be... always seeing before me the image of Britt in the back seat with a nymphomaniac... trying to see his face... mad comic book collector's face in the fit of lust... Rock 'n' roll comes out of the jukebox in here... Hopeless lost teenage cravings never satisfied... Twenty in two more months and the animal teenager who never was will never be... a war against myself which I've lost... an unthinking beast inside of me gets weaker and weaker... whines as it lays in my rotting heart dying... suffering from leprosy... radiation sickness... Could I make up for ten lost years in the next two months? Could I let loose and live the way I wanted my whole teenage years to be in the next two months? Once they're gone I'll never have the chance again to be a wild, unthinking animal-child... I'll be twenty... twenty years old... I despise the thought... I want to be thirteen... not the thirteen I really was in Milford walking home from school with my absurd briefcase and broken-hearted over Mary Shepard and Dolly Hensely... I want to be thirteen and running in the grass fields with a healthy young girl... I want to be bold and arrogant and full of sex appeal and independence and blind passion... I want to take big fat eleven year old Susan Kirby behind the bleachers after the football game is over and all the people are gone and the bright lights turned out and wrestle with her in the soft wet grass and feel her warm body in the chilly 1956 autumn night and feel victorious over her as she lays there panting and laughing... I have all the cravings of a thirteen year old and they become more impossible and unreachable with each passing day... twenty in two months... I can see it's going to be a sad sad day...

Now you see... I've vomited all over you... I've spilled my skuzzy old shit all over you... Now you see why I hate to write letters... I feel ashamed... Perhaps I won't mail this... but it's better than sending nothing at all, I guess... I dunno... Fuck it...

Well, I got out of color separation... I'm now in the "Hi-Brow" department... that is, the department which makes the corny contemporary-type cards... but what a relief... My new job is so much easier! It's really a relief... Now all I do is I take the verses that the writers make up and do up half-size roughs of them that go to the big boss for approval... If he approves them then they get drawn up for production... The roughs just have to be simple drawings which express the idea of the card... nothing too elaborate or finished...

Of course, much of the time I make them more elaborate than they have to be just for the hell of it... I can make up all kinds of crazy designs and characters and stuff... I don't have to worry because they aren't for actual sale... It's a great improvement over my former position... Now if I can just get a raise...

Are you sure this girl who you're seeing isn't putting you on? It all sounds pretty far fetched to me! But the main thing is, you're getting your cookies... Congratulations...

Have you seen about the old *Life* mags yet ... If not, do so at the first possible opportunity...

Tell Karleen to watch out for the toads because they're out to get her... One of these days she'll be walking down a dark street when all of a sudden from behind a tree will leap... yes... ten thousand toads! They will cover her... envelop her entire body... explore every fecund morsel of her flesh... bury theirselves in her hair, play king-of-the-mountain on her breasts... kiss her toes... jump in her mouth... It's happened to others...
It could happen to her!

Write back if you still dare to... I hope you do...

By the way, that was a very clever little postcard you sent a few weeks back — the wittiest piece of art I've ever seen from you... I liked it alot... I really did...

Oh yes... Pahls is still unemployed...

~ 3 8 ~

August 17, 1963
Cleveland, Ohio

Dear Britt

Well, I got your letter today... I'm very sorry I haven't sent you a letter... I guess the trouble is that my own writing disgusts me... Every time I go to write a letter I end up drawing a picture instead... I haven't written to anybody for a long long time... It's been much more than a month since I last wrote to you... almost two months actually... but why dwell on it...

I have before me your two recent letters... You have many problems... You are deeply involved... with girls, with financial worries... with what to do with your life... You seem to be quite worried, to the point even of depression... But let me ask you... are you deep-down enjoying this mess? I mean life... I think you are... I dunno... Are you? You make no mention in your recent epistle of Karleen... How is it going between the two of you? It appears to be a very touchy situation. From what I gather, I don't think you're ready or even want to devote yourself to one woman... It's a sad situation for both of you but what can you do? Love does not listen to reason... Ah me... I wish my problems were more of this nature...

At this moment I am lying on the bed with my foot balanced precariously on the night table which has one leg missing and stands up only because a heavy trinket box was placed at the opposite end to hold it down... While I've been writing this I have been tilting the legless end of the table with my foot, curious to see how far I can tilt it before it will fall over, sending the clock, Marty's framed pictures of his beloved Brock and several other pieces of junk crashing to the floor...

That reminds me... Marty says he'll write to you soon but told me to tell you anyway to get moving on those ECs you owe him... By the way, you can forget about the old *Life* magazines... I decided I don't need anymore... I've got quite enough...

I would like to see you graduate from college... It would do you alot of good, enrich your life, help give you direction and awaken your mind to many things... You have the potential of being a really intelligent, creative-type person... maybe even a learned intellectual, if you went through college... but it seems you're just having too damn much trouble scraping up the money... It's pretty tough putting yourself through, paying for it all completely on your own... I wonder if it's worth it... Perhaps you should wait until you are better able to pay... Anyway, whatever you do, I think that by your middle twenties you could be quite an accomplished person if you're willing to struggle and put yourself into it now... By "accomplished" I don't mean monetary success alone, it also includes having a good intellectual background, a mature approach to situations, the ability to take on responsibilities and cope with problems, the talent of getting along with and enjoying people and a readiness to give of yourself... and being sensitive and imaginative as you are, you could be a good artist to boot... I'm not kidding, you could become a very well-rounded human being... I don't think you have any problems which are so deep or bad that they would stand in your way... I mean, you have no neurotic walls around yourself which prevent you from really getting something out of life and doing much good for yourself and others... I think someday you will be ready to devote yourself completely to one woman and you will probably raise a family... The barriers which stand in the way of all this are pretty typical ones and not impossible to overcome... The financial problem can be solved if you are willing to do alot of grueling day to day hard work... A young fellow in your place simply has to hustle if he wants to get anywhere... As for the goddamn Army, you don't have to worry about that for a couple of years yet... Pahls just got the order to report for his physical examination, and he's twenty-two... Neither Pahls nor I intend to serve... Pahls, if he is not rejected on physical grounds, will take his stand as a conscientious objector... I'll probably get rejected 'cause of my eyes and being too far underweight... If not, well... who knows... Maybe they'll get me... Maybe I'll kill myself...

GOOD DRAWINGS BY R. CRUMB

It's five o'clock in the afternoon... Pahls is out with his sweetheart taking a hike somewhere... I fell asleep in the middle of writing this letter... I just got up and made myself some cream of wheat but I cooked it too fast and it was pretty awful stuff... all grainy and tasteless... oh well, I'm learning...

Gak! I'll be twenty in a couple of weeks... It's a very depressing thought... I will have had a completely kissless adolescence... a youth totally void of sweetness... I took a week's vacation not long ago and went home... It's all very sad... My mother had a miscarriage and is now in the agonizing process of losing her mind... She's just completely out of it... she's impossible to cope with... Sandra has no friends anymore and has become a reader of books... She's got to get out of there if she's ever going to enjoy life... Maxon just graduated and doesn't know what to do with himself... Carol got married recently and seems to be contented, though I fear for her 'cause the guy she married is kind of a bastard... He could make it miserable for her in later years... I hate to think of it... I hope Carol has the sense to call it quits if things get bad, but I dunno... She's awfully submissive... I don't know how Charles keeps going... It's amazing that he hasn't killed himself... He can't cope with the world... that's why he stays at home... yet I don't think he's really miserable... he's discontented though, which is natural... He spends all his time reading and writing... He writes hundreds and hundreds of pages in print much finer than this and no margins... He fills up notebooks but doesn't let anybody read any of it and the sad thing is that he always destroys what he has written... Its really a shame because he's just a great writer... He has given up art entirely, sold all his old comics and now is in the process of getting together a complete Shakespeare collection... He has fallen in love with Shakespeare... When he gets stoned he goes around reciting speeches from the plays in a very exaggerated John Barrymore style... I think he has finally come to realize that he must get away from home... I want him to make it to Cleveland... As soon as the old bearded jelly-belly gets a job I'm going to send Charles the money to come out here... I'd send him the money now but I simply couldn't finance it...

The last time Charles was down in Milford he found out what some of our old schoolmates are doing... Dennis Hazard is now a grocery boy in Green's Market... he's married and has a kid... Mike Holman is an intellectual college student who is a follower of Ayn Rand and is completely changed from what he was. Ben Tebbens knocked up Kay Isaacs and had to marry her and they are now living in a trailer on the outskirts of Milford and are struggling to make ends meet... Jackie Todd is in prison for five years... Can you imagine what a mean bastard he's going to be when he comes out?... Maxine Lord is married and works as a receptionist in some office or something... Most of the kids in our class are probably married now... especially the girls... Do you remember Fred Speakman, who everybody called "Big Fred" and who was the butt of everybody's cruel jokes and jeers and scorn and who took all that crap with a smile? Well, he put a gun to his head not long ago and ended it all...

MIKE BRITT and his faithful dog BERT

We went over to Atlantic City while I was there... It's a pretty wild town... I was offered a job doing portraits there on the boardwalk and I almost regret not taking it... It sure would have been interesting... and there were some very sexy girls working there... Ah well, perhaps it is best that I didn't... Anyway, I got a ten-dollar raise at ol' American Greetings... That'll help some... It's a funny thing... the other day the boss told me he really appreciates how hard I've been working and all the time I was afraid I was going to get bawled out for goofing off so much. God, what an easy job! The boss isn't even there half the time...

Pahls has done next to nothing with his writing, which is really a shame, and he hasn't seen Elonne probably since you were here although I had a talk with that young lady myself yesterday and am almost tempted to ask her out only I know better... Tell me, Britt, ol' kid, what do you really think of Pahls... Lay it on the line, boy... I know he's a windbag and I know he's not as funny as he thinks he is and I know he's a leech but I'm grateful to him in many ways... chiefly because he had the patience and understanding to make me his friend, to encourage me in all my pursuits and has been most tolerant of my neurosis and has allowed me to cry on his shoulder, which I take advantage of too often... I enjoy his company and because our outlooks are quite similar, we sometimes have very enlightening conversations... His writing shows sensitivities to things that he never lets on in conversation and for this reason I wish he would write...

Pahls has just come back... Now he and Barb are over on the sofa wallowing in love and lust... Oh God... What am I to do!!!

Listen, Britt, why don't you do some comics or something? Or don't you have time? Why don't you try writing some satire? You see, you have it in you to do something worthwhile in this view. You really do! So shape up, Britt! Do something with your ability! Damn lazy clod!

It would be great if you came to Ohio... I would enjoy very much seeing you more often... I don't know what it is that holds our relationship together... Our lives are so different... Maybe it's our mutual sense of the absurdity of what we are living in the midst of... and ourselves...

~ 3 9 ~   *September 15, 1963*
                                            Cleveland, Ohio

Dear Britt:

Your last letter is quite a piece of writing... I understand you considerably better now than before you wrote this... You are one of those sensitive people with a vision of life which you somehow unfortunately never found the means of expressing. Somehow you never could get deeply involved in your own art, enough to get somewhere with it... Of course you still could, very easily... For that matter, you have it in you to be a fine writer... But I think to be a really good artist or writer (and I know you wouldn't be satisfied with being a mediocre one) you sort of have to give up alot of your normal life and devote a great portion of your life to working... Your art should be your major pastime if you really want to be good at it... I don't know if it's worth it to you or not... I think most good artists were forced into making art their life's work because they found they were unsuited to the life that most men lead... They couldn't have adjusted to the norm, so they went off by themselves and built their own worlds... I find that when there are alot of people and things around me that I am able to enjoy, I neglect my art completely... I don't give a damn about it... but sooner or later I always go back to it... It's sort of a refuge from the terrible confusion and sadness of real life...

I liked that cover you did very much... I think your art has improved quite a bit, despite the fact that you haven't worked at it... I wish you hadn't cut the cover in half... Actually your conceptions are very appealing and really project something... Honest to God! You've got to get on the ball, Britt... For chrissake, WORK! DRAW! The more you do it, the better you'll get, the more you'll believe in your own ability... I'd really like to see what you could do if you worked at it... I know you could be damned good... and YOU know it too... You've just got some kind of perfectionist complex or something, I dunno...

Yes, it's strange when you think that a new crop of teenagers has come along who know nothing of Buddy Holly, Jerry Lee Lewis, Bill Haley, Fats Domino, and The Coasters... Well, I'm no longer a teenager... Ah me... twenty... Those days in Milford, in eighth and ninth grades, seem like half a century ago...

Well, by this time you should know whether or not you're going to college... I would like very much to see you come to Cleveland... I think it would be great... I think maybe we could learn alot from each other... do ourselves some good... Really, though, I think you ought to leave home... unless you're going to college... in which case you'll HAVE to live at home...

I guess girls see you as the strong, silent type... Girls see me as the weak, silent type... Oh well, maybe someday...

Perry is one of those timeless sad people... A nymphette at twelve, a sexpot at sixteen, a hag a twenty... It's an old old story... always heart-breaking to see...

In the last couple of weeks I've gotten entangled in the lives of a bunch of sad, hung-up arty-type girls... I haven't worked on my book or done anything (I'd intended to write this letter long ago but there just hasn't been time)... I've been over to their place every day this week except today... You wouldn't believe the hopeless mess these girls' lives are in... I think I've aged five years in the last two weeks... I even got to making out with one of them... the most psychotic one of the bunch, naturally... She's a real sickie, this kid... vicious too... At one time she was in a mental institution... She smashes things... Yes, it is sad... Making out with her is sad... She gets very melodramatic about the whole thing and I have to say something absurd to snap her out of it... Oh God... It's just too sad... Why can't I enjoy the company of some nice simple jolly unsophisticated type girl... I know why... because I'm a sickie too... But these girls have so many problems that I feel well-adjusted when I'm around them... In a way I guess they've helped me... I dunno... It's too hard to explain... I'm just wondering how long it'll be before I go over there and they start heaving bricks at me... Or maybe they'll seduce me and then murder me or poke my eyes out or something... Oh well, at least they are girls...

I only have twelve pages to go in my book... I'd sure like to get it done... But those girls are much more interesting... I've got another book in mind after this one... I dunno when I'll get around to starting it but it's going to be better and will take all the capacity of my imagination and skill as an artist to bring it to being... Sometimes I get very excited about it... Other times I think it's too much for me to handle... Maybe I'll tone it down and just try to do it in a limited capacity... Wow! The ideas I have for this thing... It's going to say all... ALL! But time! Time is scarce... There is a drastic shortage of time... Oh me oh my...

Well, Britt, my good friend of the golden days in the sunshine of our happy youth, I will stop now... even though this letter is only half as long as yours of 27 August... You see, there's nothing more to be sad... I mean said... except write me another superb letter... Someday I'll have them printed in book form...

R. CRUMB

~ 4 0 ~

October 10, 1963
Cleveland, Ohio

Dear Bripp:

The main reason for the big delay in writing this time was... oh hell... sheer laziness... But the second main reason is that Pahls and I have just moved to another apartment and your letter got lost in the scramble and wasn't found until a few days ago by Pahls who immediately lost it again but which finally came within my possession last night, along with a postcard about five days old which I hadn't known we even received... Pahls... every time I give him something to look at I entertain thoughts of never seeing it again... as has happened... That guy loses everything he lays his hands on... Loses it amongst his heaps of papers and books and it always takes forever to find it again and, like I say, sometimes things are lost forever... Every time he cleans the place a few things of worth are never seen again... He always accidentally gets good stuff mixed in with the trash... Whenever I can't find something the day after he cleans the place I always look through the trash... I've found so many things in there... silverware, the coffee pot, letters, books... The guy's insane... Every time we go out there's a big ritual of searching the house for his wallet, or his belt, or his shoes... One time he found a paycheck from work that he had never cashed and had completely forgotten about... It had been buried in a stack of papers for months... Very often he'll put something down somewhere and go to get it half a minute later and spend two hours looking for it and even then sometimes he never finds it... It can really be aggravating... But I shouldn't criticize Pahls... He's really one swell guy... a real prince... Yeah, Pahls is just aces with me, just aces... the dirty bastard... no, really...

No, I haven't been seduced by any nymphomaniacs... sad to say... Although one night this girl tried to take my clothes off... The only trouble was that she wouldn't let me take her clothes off... Sick sick sick... They're all sick... I'm sick...

So how the hell are you doing with your goddamn college studies? I hope you're making it... You must keep pretty busy, with studying and doing signs and all... I hope your money holds out... I hope you get something out of college... I'm pretty sure you will... What the hell ya taking?

Nothing new on Charles coming to Cleveland... I'm waiting for a letter from him... I sort of hope he comes to Cleveland but then I don't know exactly how well he'll get along with Pahls... him and Pahls have differences...

I'm not getting anywhere with those nutty girls... In fact, I've sort of given up trying... I haven't seen too much of them lately... The nicest one has left... Her parents took her away because some asshole got her pregnant, poor sweet innocent creature... No kidding... She really is innocent... This guy forced himself on her... She didn't enjoy it at all, she said... but she's so damn weak-willed, she couldn't stop him... Alot of girls are like that... They'll let a guy screw them even if they don't enjoy it just because he's a good friend and pushy and they don't want to create bitter feelings and maybe they sort of think of it as a favor to the guy... I dunno... Then again... alot of girls get a kind of masochistic pleasure out of being forced into the sex act even though they don't derive sexual pleasure... The thrill of the cruelty of the man... the suffering passive female... that bit... you know... shit... I don't know... I know nothing of the workings of the minds of women and the more I listen to them the more I come to believe nothing that they say... Women never mean what they tell you... They have a million defense mechanisms... layers of ulterior motives... conflicting emotions that dictate what they think from minute to minute... They'll say one thing and really think they mean it and say just the opposite a minute later and really think they mean it... I can't cope with women... They unnerve me... and I can't overpower them with my masculine strength (mental, emotional, or what have you) because I simply haven't got any... Women are a pushover for a guy with a strong mind and strong belief in himself... A confident man can handle any woman... Confidence is knowing what you're doing and feeling that it is right... automatically... unconsciously... This I don't have... not even in the slightest degree... Around women I'm like the guy who just got off the boat and doesn't know a word of English...

Anyway, this girl who got pregnant will have to spend five months in an unwed mothers' home... And after she has the kid her parents will make her work until she pays them back all the money they've put out to the unwed mothers' home plus a couple of bastard psychiatrists... all in all about two thousand dollars... This will take up about the next three years of her life... Then she can start over... She's an artist... A good one too... Her parents made her sell all her stuff... She has attempted suicide twice... I don't know how earnest she was about really killing herself, but she's very unhappy... and very sensitive... She has retreated from the rest of the world since she got pregnant... spends all her time sitting in her parents' apartment brooding... I tried to persuade her to get away from her parents but she's too afraid of the world now to leave them... She looks upon the world as a harsh cold cruel rat race in which she has no place... One morning recently while I was on my way to the train station to go to work I met this guy who knocked her up... I asked him what he was doing out at that time of the morning (he doesn't work and is living off a colored woman)... He smiled and told me he just got out of a party... As he walked away I looked after him feeling the most hatred I've ever felt toward anyone... hatred that was probably nothing more than fierce envy, for deep down I know the girl still loves the son of a bitch as have dozens of girls... They'll say he's no good and irresponsible and cruel and a louse but still they would run to him in a minute if he waved his little finger in their direction... I made a gift for the girl as a going-away present, a little clock... I'll probably never see her again as she is going to California with her parents...

How did I get into this story? Christ... why am I telling you all this shit? Why do I always end up crying on your friggin' shoulder in these friggin' letters? Well, probably because that's all there is to do... Do you think my view of life is basically tragic? Basically sick, is what it is...

This new apartment of ours is easier to find than the last one... It's on 115th street right off Euclid Avenue, the main street of the east side... We can see old Euclid Avenue from our bathtub... What this place is, is a third floor of an old mansion... We got the whole third floor for ninety a month (that includes all utilities, plus a linen service)... Got a bedroom, bathroom, kitchen area and a huge living room as big as all that last place put together... bigger, in fact... It's sort of a cozy place, with slanting walls where the eaves start and dormers... They just finished repairing the place and modernizing the electricity and all... a nice place... Pahls is out looking for a job and has three or four prospects going... He'll have to work if we're going to pay ninety a month...

Yeah, old jelly-belly Pahls beat the draft... it's a long story which I'll let him tell you... He also shaved off his beard... Now he looks like a plain ordinary Ohio clod again...

Well, I've done four Hi-Brow cards which will be printed... A couple have already gone to press... I'm working on a fifth one now... I'm going to get up a nice collection of my printed cards... It'll be very handy for getting art jobs... I think my work would be an improvement for some of these smaller card companies... There's one in California that looks inviting... Perhaps in another year I'll be sick enough of Cleveland...

Well, Britt, old kid, old top, old head, old hat, old so-and-so, old bean, old friend... I'm looking forward to seeing you again one day... Write soon...

~ 4 1 ~

Dear Brip:

DAYS OF SUNSHINE? What in the hell are you talking about?! Days of sunshine shit... Days of sunstroke would be more like it... days of screaming agony in the Devil's pit of living nightmares... that's what I'd call it... I think the sweetest days I can remember spending with you were in Northampton that time... But those years in Milford were nothing but a hell of a mess... A continuous and destructive state of anxiety prevailed over our lives...

Well, enough of this yak about the past... We are concerned chiefly with the present, right? You seem to be leading quite an active life, one thing right after another, always something to do... Your letter consists mostly of all the things you've been doing and all the things you want to do... You always have plenty of things to talk about. The reason I don't answer as promptly as you do is that I simply don't have that much to say... My life is rather simple and uninteresting. All I do is go to work and come home... Of course, I am fascinated by all the minute details of my everyday life but how can I talk about this? It's impossible... I have to wait for something to happen before I have anything to talk about. I ask myself!! why don't you make things happen? But it's not in me... Say, why don't we drop the subject?

The wind is fierce and blows right through the thin old window in this place, making the rooms quite chilly... I'm sitting on a mattress in the living room right now, my sleeping quarters while Barbara Brock is here... The woman who owns this joint was just here inspecting the radiators to find out why they don't work properly... I think maybe she got them working by letting the air out of them with a little key she has... At least I hope she did... It's damned cold in here... The radiators are warming up a bit...

That was a very nice cover you did for the letter... very nice indeed... Shows you have a real sense of pattern and design... Very pleasing to the eye... The way you abstracted the faces was very tasteful... You're doing quite well these days... Let's hope you keep it up...

Ahh... Things are much better now... I'm sitting on the radiator from which comes the most warmth (toobad it isn't a girl)...

Thanks for sending the strips... Both of them are quite well-drawn... Weare certainly is a good draughtsman but possesses little imagination, consequently, like you say, the over-all effect is dull... "Flook," too, was very well drawn... I like his caricatures... Toobad I couldn't make hide nor hair of the dialogue... These I will return to you... If I can find them... Pahls probably put them in with some stuff and it'll be years before they turn up...

And now... ta ra ta ra dom da dom... Pahls has a job... Yes... Pahls has found employment... He now works and earns money... He brings home approximately the same as me... a little more... What does he do, you ask? Well, he went to the Craig Employment Agency to see if they could get him a job... Instead , they hired him... to write ads for them for the newspapers... a soft job... The money scene has eased up considerably... and I'm due for another raise soon...

How come we moved? Oh, I guess we just got sick of living in the same place for so long... almost exactly a year... We both like this new place alot... We agreed before we decided to take this place that if we were going to pay ninety a month we'd both have to be working, so no sweat about the rent... Actually, it's very reasonable when you consider that the ninety includes all utilities and linen service even (geepers)... Are you crazy? It would take at least two hundred bucks to get enough furniture to fill an apartment... The junk stores aren't as cheap as you seem to think... and neither of us could afford that... And besides, who wants to cart around a bunch of furniture? No, both of us prefer furnished places... We took one piece of furniture from our other place... stole is the word... a big soft easy chair which we both cherished and which is extremely comfortable... Apparently, and just as we had hoped, the old alcoholic superintendent of the Carnegie place never missed it... At least we never heard from him... If he did notice it was gone I'm sure he didn't give a shit enough to find out what happened to it.

Yes, I was shooting off my mouth about women in that last letter... Of course I didn't know what I was talking about... We both know that... I was worked up about that mess... I dunno... Maybe some of the things I said made sense... Who knows? If I were to go spouting off again about women in this letter I'd probably say something entirely different... I'm always making generalizations... Everybody does that... People have to classify and categorize everything... It makes life look so much simpler... It makes things so much easier to understand... That's a mental habit I got into early in life and it is quite dominant in my thinking... I hope I can cut down on it... Life is much too complex and vague to draw lines and put everything securely under certain headings... which is exactly what you were just saying to me here in your letter...

I would like to see you come to Cleveland... As I say, I believe I could benefit from consorting with you... I could learn much... I don't know what you'd get out of the relationship, but mabe you'd get something out of it... At least you'll learn a few clichés —like "tis sad," others...

You may be able to get a job at American Greetings... Most likely as a letterer or graphic designer since most of your work that I've seen of late is in that direction... possibly color separation if you have a sufficient amount of various good drawings and/or paintings of people, abstract designs, commercial type art and the like to show them — you know, typical art school type portfolio... You don't even have to have a real hot portfolio if you can impress the bastards as a real level-headed guy, which I think you could... That's what I did... That would be weird, if you ended up working at American Greetings... That would be just too goddamn weird! But — sigh — you'd probably end up in Massachusetts, working there... Keep in mind that a great portion of the people at American Greetings are young, unspoken-for gurls... and just because I haven't had any luck with them is no goddamn indication that... Oh sigh...

I'll be frigged if it isn't snowing outside! I suppose it's already started snowing up there in the arctic regions... I'm going out in a few minutes (brrr). I'm going to have supper at a guy's house and then go to a nightclub with him (he can get me in free) to hear some good piano playing (I hope)... Probably won't finish this letter tonight, but I'll get it off to you before tomorrow is over...

I wonder if I should bother wasting my time telling you about the company Halloween party... It was a masquerade... Well, let me say that for the first time in my life I got staggering drunk and was very embarrassed and got very depressed and the whole thing was a lousy shitty mess... I got even more drunk the other night... Christ! These guys keep forcing the awful stuff down my throat... It doesn't make me happy... I just get dizzy and embarrassed and anxious... Terrible! Terrible!

The only piece of furniture I bought for this place was a big old Philco radio, floor model, which I paid five bucks for and which works very well... In clear weather you can get Moscow, Berlin, London, Havana, Japan and God knows where else... A good buy for five dollars.

It's one-thirty... I just got back from the night club... The band was lousy... but I did enjoy a great supper at this guy's house... His wife is a good cook... He's one of the writers in the Hi-Brow department... A good fellow... His name is John Gibbons and he's the son of a vice-president of the New York Central Railroad... His father doesn't think too highly of John's rejection of the railroad business to take up such lowly occupations as radio announcer and card writer. John has all kinds of stories about what it was like to be a rich kid in the forties with a chauffeur and stealing cars and going to fancy clubs and ballrooms and all about his father's private railroad car and all the crazy jobs his father put him into, like section gang worker. He did that for two days, then became the section inspector... He said "I really worked my way up fast!" He comes from this weird family... One brother is a Madison Avenue ad man, another is a jet pilot... an uncle is a gangster who owns the Holland Furnace Company... Crazy bunch of Irishmen...

So you don't know what you want out of life, eh? Isn't a life with the one you love and raising children enough? And possibly satisfaction with your art work... What more is there? I feel that for me personally, if I could just reach the point where I could really love someone, devote my life to someone, and receive love and devotion in return, I would have everything I really need... All else is secondary... But alas, I am far far from that goal... So far that often it often seems impossible... I dunno... You have no idea how terrible it is to realize that you are incapable of giving and receiving love... And love, to me, is the most important thing in life... Or maybe it just seems that way because I've never known real love... I dunno... Fuck it all!

Those pictures Marty took? Oh yes... I think only one of them turned out... It's a real weird picture of me and you looking down at the camera... our faces in shadow, with the alley behind us... I don't know where it is... I think maybe Marty put it in his scrapbook.

Yes, Brib, I think art school would be good for you... It would sort of be the push you need to get you fully involved in creative art, I think... Otherwise you'll probably just go on dabbling in it now and then... Art school might also help you find some way to direct your talent... help you find out what you can do, you know?

Your Vigor for Life Appalls Me

Yeh, I'll send you copies of my goddamn cards... It'll be months yet before they come out, probably... But I'll get copies of all of them...

That's a good idea — keeping a scrapbook with examples of good cartoonists' work — that's the best way to do it — of course the best way of all is to buy books of their work, except they hardly ever print books of cartoonists' work... which is unfortunate...

Well, hell... the record player is on, Marty and Brock are up... I can't think... So, I'll close now... Write soon... Hope to hell you don't flunk out...

~ 4 2 ~   *January 5, 1964*
                                            Cleveland, Ohio

Dear Britt:

I've lost your last letter. I think I left it at my folks' place when I was there over Christmas... so I probably won't be able to answer some of the comments you made... Your attempts at getting through college are rather tragic... Working and trying to study at the same time is a bad business... It rarely works out... People should do one, then the other... I think you should give up college and go to art school... but first get a job and save your money... Art school is the place for you... Now Cleveland has two or three good art schools... but jobs are not easy to find here, although American Greetings needs artists... Well, come to Cleveland if you're willing to risk it... You could always go back if it didn't work out...

I think you said you'd be in Cleveland in February... Does this still hold? If so, we'll be looking for you... our eyes squinting across the vast planes to the north... our ears to the ground awaiting the roar of the old Greyhound bus... Are you coming by bus? Are you going to sell your car?

Anyway, you're perfectly welcome to stay with us till such time as you want to get your own place... Get up as many samples of your artwork as you can and we'll get an interview for you at American Greetings... How much of a variety of stuff do you have... You should have a few life drawings, two or three washes of watercolors, couple of pattern designs maybe, some cartoons... Bring some of your better sign work too... maybe they'll put you in the lettering department... choke... Well, it's a job...

What are you going to do about this girlfriend of yours? How will she feel about your leaving Duluth? How will old Bert feel?

If American Greetings doesn't pan out there are plenty of big department stores who use sign painters, so that's another possibility... and there's always the Giant Tiger discount stores...

Charles has come to Cleveland to get a job but doesn't like the city one bit so is going back to Philadelphia to get a job there... which I hope to God he does...

As far as accommodations go we haven't nothing to worry about... We have an extra mattress and lots of pillows and blankets, so you really don't need to bring anything of that sort.

Your last letter showed that you have a great wit... It was full of pathos (pathetically comic). It is good to be able to laugh at yourself... to be able to see yourself as absurd, even while tragic or hung-up, as it were...

I have so much for you to see... I brought all my stuff back with me from Philadelphia (my father brought us in the car) and so have completely severed myself from the nest, so to speak, in a word, you might say... I have lots of notebooks full of stuff Charles and I have done, and I've finished my book, *The Big Yum Yum Book*[1]... This book went over very well and has received a favorable reaction from everyone, much to my gratification... Some have even called it genius! Ah, ego... ego...

That's what you need, Brip, a big project, a big creative work which will take you months and months and much time and effort to work on... a direction, you might say... a goal, in a word... a calling, so to speak... I don't know, maybe you feel that you're not up to the task... Maybe love is enough for you... No... it isn't... You need something more... You need something to work on... something all your own... Why don't you build a hot rod... choke...

Well, we'll talk about it when you get here... but for Chrissake, come!

Well, I'm gonna stop writing now... Got things to do... big things... important things... not really... but we can talk extensively about all this when you're here, like I say... I can't word things right in these damn letters... It comes out sounding very stoopid... So I'll see you...

---

[1] Executed in expensive-to-reproduce full color, *The Big Yum Yum Book* took a decade to find a publisher; Scrimshaw Press took the plunge in 1975. *Yum Yum* dropped out of print in the 1980s and was eventually re-released (in 1995) by Snow Lion Graphics.

~ 4 3 ~

January 19, 1964
Cleveland, Ohio

Dear Britt:

Don't be absurd, pal... I didn't say you could stay here just to be nice... I want you to come and stay with us... Frankly, I think your presence might liven things up a bit around here... Not that I'm expecting to be entertained. But it seems to me that you're a more outgoing person than either Pahls or me... and since you have a car perhaps we could do a bit of traveling around... At any rate, I am honestly looking forward to your coming here... Pahls' attitude is affirmative, though not enthusiastic... He doesn't seem to care very much either way... So cool it, fella... It's perfectly fine for you to come... We have lots of extra accommodations, as I said before... Charles has left, so the extra mattress will be yours...

Yes, Charles has left... he didn't really want to go home, but he felt he had to because he was falling in love with Barby Brock, Marty's girlfriend. And she wasn't exactly indifferent to him... This caused problems... problems which Charles felt would be best solved by his absence... The pity of it is he was right... Tis sad... I had hoped he would never go home again... I had hoped that perhaps at last he had flown the nest to start a life of his own and rehabilitate himself... Ah sigh... He says he's determined to get a job in Philadelphia and get his own apartment there... I hope to God he does... He still has a little mess on his hands with the Army... I hope he's gotten them off his hands by now... I'll have to call up my folks long distance and find out...

Charles and Marty didn't hit it off too well anyway... Marty got kind of pissed off because Charles drank all his vodka and wouldn't flush the toilet and puked in the laundry basket and got all his books and comics out of order and never did the dishes while we were at work. Of course, he had every right to be pissed... Charles is a slob... He doesn't give a damn about order and neatness and cleanliness and he's too thoughtless to care that he's drinking up all of somebody's vodka... Charles is very hung-up and very miserable... I think if he gets away from home there's more of a chance that he'll come out of it... I sure hope to God he gets a job and gets his own place...

The pictures of you and the dame were very interesting... She's a very typical healthy, American looking girl... Quite attractive, actually... You look like a suave, Latin playboy asshole... Both shots look like nightclub movie magazine celebrity type photos... I can almost read the captions under them... "Here's Mike and Ki at the Brown Derby after their recent engagement..." except that it doesn't look like the Brown Derby and you aren't wearing formal evening clothes... The pictures of Bert were funny... he looks very heroic and old and wise and noble... Ah! What a dog!! I'll send the pictures along with this missive...

Thanks for enclosing the article on old comic strips... Some beautiful stuff there... I especially liked the *Little Nemo*[1] page... *Little Nemo* is one of my all time favorite strips... McCay was a genius! Pahls and I got some Sunday pages of *Little Nemo* from a guy here in Cleveland... really beautiful!

Yeah... I saw that *Monocle* too... Yes, it is impressive but I didn't like it either, except for some of the artwork... Most of the humor is too sophisticated...

---

[1] Created by Winsor McCay, *Little Nemo in Slumberland* ran from 1905 to 1911 in the *New York Herald*, after which McCay went to work for Hearst, continuing the strip until 1914, under the title *The Land of Wonderful Dreams*. See bibliography.

You'll find a job here, long as you look for one... No sweat, really, I don't think... You have ability, skill... That's what's important...

You seem to have reached a pretty good understanding with your girl-friend... The relationship apparently has improved greatly... and well it should since you've been going together for more than a year...

Pahls and his job? Well, okay, Pahls writes newspaper ads for an employment agency... He tells young girls that they can find excitement and glamour in being a file cabinet slave... He tells guys they can be a big man and shoot right up to the top in fast-growing corporations... He's becoming quite a bullshit artist... or maybe that's how he got the job to begin with... He has a soft job... no pressures, no great tax on one's energies... about like mine... The two of us lead pretty soft lives...

No, I don't have any social problems any more... I guess I just don't give a damn as much as I used to... I spend most of my time working... drawing pictures and stuff... I find that keeping busy prevents me from thinking about the things I don't have... I'm not as hung-up as I used to be, I guess... One gets tired of wishing for something that one can't have... I just don't get as worked up about things as I used to... It's a great relief, boy! When Charles was here, he had the affect of sort of pulling me back to the way I used to be, because he's as hung-up now as I ever was... I haven't had much to do with girls of late and I find that for the first time in years I'm not all goddamn hung-up about them... I guess I'm just losing that old craving... Thank the fates... Oh, I still feel sorry for myself now and then...

I can see what's gonna happen to the world of rod-building... In twenty-five years it's going to be a very respectable, bushwah hobby... But it's true, it does have great possibilities as an art form and some of those guys have built some fantastic and imaginative pieces of baroque machinery... Every once in a while I go through the hot-rod magazines and look at them... I'd like to go to one of those shows where all the best home-made cars are exhibited...

I've shown the *Big Yum Yum Book* to everybody I know and alot of people I don't know... I almost feel like it's been published or something, so many people have seen it... Alot of people have suggested that I try getting it published, but it just ain't salable... and you'll agree when you see it... Pahls writes every once in a while... not very much... Actually, he has done very little on it since last spring... He's going through a period of doubt as to his motives and abilities... When he'll come out of it and what he'll do then I can't say...

Yeah, we still live in the approximate area of "La Cave" but neither of us have been around there in months... The place is a bore... Elonne was always there being her usual dopey self... She went to California about a month ago... The dope got a job with a card company in L.A...

Before I mail this I'll be sure to have a map enclosed so's you can find your way to our place... shouldn't be too difficult... I... I... I don't know...

Your Vigor for Life Appalls Me

Well, we'll be lookin' for ya, Britt... (gag, what a terrible dumb thing to say!)

Well, then, about the end of February, right? Okay! See ya then!! (gag choke puke vomit...)

~ 4 4 ~

June 22, 1968
San Francisco, California

Dear Britt:

Got your letter 's' morning... Glad you wrote... I'd still like to come up and stay with yiz, but we have not had no money for muntz! We're surviving on welfare and checks from *Cavalier*. When my book becomes a best seller, then I can jet-set around 'n' see everybody. The book is due out in September. Sure hope it sells.

Been trying to get *Zap*[1] no. 2 out for muntz also... It keeps dragging on and on... Sometimes I think it ain't worth the hassles... There'll be some work by other people in *Zap* 2... and in every other *Zap* to come out in the future... Namely Rick Griffin, V. Moscoso, both big-time poster artists who've had it with posters an' wanna do comics... Plus S. Clay Wilson, a crazy guy from Kansas who draws great pornograph comics... It's all great stuff but we can't seem to get it printed... Mostly it's lack of funds... moola... folding green stuff... Piz me off, man!

Another reason I haven't written is because I haven't written to anybody lately or drawn or anything except getting stoned all day and drinking wine. Never thought I'd see th' day. But it's alright, Ma! I've made my fame... Everyone loves me for my work... Now I've got to work on them loving me for myself! That's where it stands on this 2nd day of summer, 1968...

I'm going over to meet Janis Joplin tonight... CAN'T WAIT! Which brings me to another important point, which is my sex life has been sliding downhill lately so I'm trying to do something about that! The only girl I'm making it with is my wife, and gettin' tired of just her all the time...

What good has fame done me? I'm broke and girls still act aloof. Time has come for a change! Bwah howdy!

How come I never meet any chicks with money!? That's what y'get for hangin' around wid hippies, I guess...

Poor Dick Voll... I've never met anyone who benefited from shock treatment... I think it's a form of torture enacted by sadistic doctors on innocent freaked-out sensitive hurt people...

---

[1] Crumb self-published *Zap* Comics #0 in 1967. It was reprinted by Apex Novelty in 1968. Last Gasp continues to re-issue *Zap*, and this issue appears in *Complete Crumb Comics Volume 4*. See bibliography.

Hey, did you ever get your comics out here? That would be incentive enuff for me to go up there... Also I'd like to meet Basil Wolverton... Also mebbe talk to you, now 'n' then...

I haven't heard from Marty either so don't feel bad. I may go see him this summer... th' slob... Maybe I won't... He's really degenerated from his old degenerate self.

I thot sure I sent you a copy of *Zap* no. 1... Maybe not, though... I'd send you another one except they're all gone... I'm gonna buy some back from a chick who has a bunch of 'em in a box in her closet, so I'll send y' one then.

Could I come up there sometime in th' next coupla weeks? What're yer plans, Brip?

Love, Peace, Flowers,
Women, Pot & Wine,

R. Crumb

~ 4 5 ~   *June 1972*
                                      Potter Valley, California

Britt:

No notes!

Signed,
Crumb

P.S. Was good to hear from yo' again after all these years... Enclosed please find my latest masterpiece... chuckle, gloat...

Yeh, I'd like to see you again... I'd like to make it to Oregon... Ne'er been up that way before... But, if you get down dis way before I get up there, we're right off Highway 101 just north of Ukiah... Take 20 east and get off on the Potter Valley Road... Travel about 10 miles till you come to Hunter's Store... Turn left on the Eel River Road, go up over the foothills, keep left at top of mountain, go past ta' damn... We're on the right side of road... Ya can't miss it... It's ungodly hot up here this time o' year... Yesterday was 120° in the shade, but I just installed an air conditioner here in my cabin... Boy, wot o' difference!! Now I can work during th' day 'n' not go outside till the sun goes down!!

As for being "straight-arrow"... jeezis, Britt, don't worry 'bout it, bwah! This is America! You can be whatever th' hell y' wanna be! (except a capitalist exploiter)... I mean, there's no law sez you hafta smoke dope, fer chrizzakes!! Some o' my best friends are "squares"... yuk yuk...

Take Martin L. Pahls, f'rinstance. He won't allow dope in his house. Personally, I think he's overly paranoid, but that's his right. I just got back from a three-month tour around the country... Visited Marty in Chicago... Th' guy's more of a hermit than ever... Just listens to his old records all the time... And I do mean all the time!! It's unb'lievable!! He did a story for some shlock underground comic outfit in Chicago that wasn't too bad... but his drawing style wasn't changed much since 1959...

I was also in Philadelphia visiting my family. Charles is in a mental institution, as you might have guessed. Comes home on weekends. My mother watches tee-vee all the time and dotes on her pet cats. 'Tis sad... but my mother seems happier than she's ever been...

Maxon and Sandra both live in San Francisco. Maxon lives with his girlfriend and they collect welfare. A couple o' degenerates. Sandra lives in a house with a bunch of lesbians and queers and has a son named Avery or something and also collects welfare and is trying to get a divorce and support money out of Marty Pahls... Pitiful, huh? My fambly... wot o' mess!! (no notes)

Listen, I wish I *was* loved and ravished by some teeny-boppers! One or two would do!! Somehow, I've never managed to hit it with the girlies... I dunno... Guess I just don't have that animal magnetism... I've gotten real good at jerking off though... Once in a while I get laid... The situation between me 'n' Dana is weird... We still love each other, but she's given up trying to make me into a responsible husband and father, and got herself another ol' man... So we all live together in P.V.... I in my cabin, them and the kids in the big house... Cozy, huh? Is okay by me... And Dana manages th' finances... What a womin!!

I doubt if *Mr. Natural #2* has hit 100,000... I seriously doubt it! Probbly more like 50,000... Who tole you that figure? All the *Zap*s combined have sold almost a million in five years, which ain't too bad... Yes, I'm makin' th' big skins these days, 'bout $1500 a month... But, th' more y'got, th' more y' spend... This "farm" has alot of "costs"...

I'll do a cover for yer fanzine, but I dunno about full color... I can't color too good... but I kin do color separations with zip-a-tone overlays... So, gimme some idear of what you want... and when you need it...

I already got a Wolverton original... Actually, I'm not into c'llecting original art... What else you got? Any old comic books for trade? *MAD*s? *Pogo*s?

You still do any cartooning at all?

You can do posters if you want of my stuff...

I just bought a complete collection of *Little Lulu* comics up to 1954 for $200... mostly all in mint condition... Great stuff, those old *Lulus*... One comic is missing... no. 2, Feb-March or something, 1948... You got it, perchance?

Also, I still collect old records. If you run into any record collectors who'd like to trade for an original page, tell 'em to get in touch with me...

Have you seen *Fritz the Cat*[1]... I thought it was pretty depressing, but then, I'm probbly not in a position to be objective about it... If you saw it, wha'd you think?

Write... 'nuf sed!

Your old high school chum,
Bob Crumb

P.P.S. If dogs have a heaven, there's one thing I know... ol' Bert has a wonderful home!

---

[1] In 1972, Ralph Bakshi directed an animated movie based on Crumb's Fritz character. In response, Crumb killed off Fritz for good in the story "Fritz the Cat 'Superstar'," published in *People's Comics*, reprinted in the *Complete Crumb Comics Volume 8*. See bibliography.

~ 4 6 ~

July/August 1972
Potter Valley, California

Britt:

I got a copy of *Little Lulu* #2 from some jerk name o' Glenn Goggin who said he read I wuz lookin' for it in your famzime... Is this true? How come you don't send me copy of your fmz? Anyway, all this Goggin wants in return for *Little Lulu* #2 is a drawing by me of my idea of what a typical comic convention looks like!! Christ... A convention he wants... Shit... These comic fans are all punks... I went to the EC "con" in New York 'cause I just happened to be in town at the time an' Kurtzman got me in free... It was dizgustin... all these hero worshippin' little creeps groveling before the old EC artists and writers... Sigh... I'll probably be lookin' for those same creeps when I'm forty-five years old an' a has-been... Or maybe when I'm 35... Or maybe next week...

You say you're "trapped by society right now"... Liz'n, pal... I could write a book — I could tell you things — liz'n, I'm in so deep — I never believed it possible that life could get so complicated... As the godfather once said, "How is it possible that things could've come to such a state??"

Oh well, once in a while I get some peace and quiet here in my little house... You should come 'n' visit sumtime... Eventually, I'd like to come up there 'n' visit whichoo... Nev'r been up there...

Did you see that *Funnyworld* with th' article 'bout *Fritz the Cat*? A real incredible piece of journalism. It's all pretty accurate, if not a little boring...

Charles, my dear brother, now resides in a state mental institution... I just saw him this summer... He seems content... Beats livin' at home, he sez... No, my mom 'n' dad don't fight anymore... In fact, they hardly talk to each other at all... My mother watches TV all the time... A sad, sad situation...

Nah, I don't get no money from the youth-culture rip-off exploiters who turn my stuff into mass-produced garbage... I ain't complainin' though... I'm doin' real good financially... Probably in th' neighborhood of 1,500 dollars a month... just for doin' exactly what I like doin'... Pretty cushy, eh, Britt, ol' buddy? Ha ha!!

Listen, man, ya oughta get inta this "underground" cartoon racket!! This thing is gonna get bigger and it's a wise young cartoonist who starts now to develop himself in this field!! Yes, you too can make the big bucks in kartooning!!

Look for my latest hit *The People's Comics*[1] coming soon to your local hippie store!!

Also, I put out a 78 record through Krupp Comic Works... R. Crumb & His Keep-on-Truckin' Orch. on the Ordinary label... Got my finger in a lotta pies, boy!! When I got rollin' back into Milford, Delaware, I'm gonna do it in <u>STYLE</u>! Then they'll be sorry!! They'll be sorry they spurned me an' mocked me and scorned me!! I'll show 'em all!!

Maxon now lives on welfare with his girlfriend in San Francisco. Sandra is a lesbian and lives in a women's commune or something... I dunno if I told you all this before or not... Sandra hates my comics, of course... She told me that in five years the only people who will read 'em are cowboys in Wyoming, the last bastion of male chauvinism...

Toobad you lost that money investing it... That'll teach ya!!!!!!

Wal, I'm gonna go to bed... Write...

Yers,
Crumb

Westward ho the Foo Boys!

WIS

---

[1] Published in 1972 by Golden Gate, features collaborations with Maxon Crumb and Harvey Pekar. Other strips include: "The Confessions of R. Crumb," "The R. Crumb ucke$$ Story," "Patricia Pig in Patricia Stays at Home," and "Fritz the Cat, 'Superstar.'"

CITY AND COUNTY OF SAN FRANCISCO
DEPARTMENT OF PUBLIC WORKS

BUREAU OF
STREET CLEANING
AND
PLANTING

2323 ARMY STREET
SAN FRANCISCO
CALIFORNIA 94124

~ 4 7 ~   *January 21, 1977*

Dear Britt:

Nice to hear from you again... Sending out those freebooks has evoked letters from all kinds of unexpected places... Got a long tale of woe from Marty Pahls all about how it's been another bad year for him... and another from my brother Charles, who hasn't written me a letter in more than ten years... I visit Philadelphia about once every year or two, though, and talk with him then, but this is the first letter I've gotten since the Cleveland days about 1964 or '65... The weird thing is that the letter was almost the exact same kind of letter... reminiscing about the wrongs done to him in Milford... all that... Grim...

And then this from you... Oh man... Well, at least you don't have any kids, do you?? I'm pretty sure you don't... Count yourself lucky, my good man... If I get to telling you my troubles, it could fill ten pages, single spaced!! Alot of my woes are the price of fame... money troubles... crooked lawyers, alimony payments, income tax troubles... I owe the I.R.S. 28 thousand dollars... Yeah, that's right... But I won't go into it, except to say that I have a son nine years old who I haven't seen or talked to for two-and-a-half years, and it hurts... But that's life... I'm in the long drawn out process of trying to get a divorce from Dana (I dunno if you ever met her... I guess you did, around '67 or '68 in the Haight-Ashbury days) but it's very complicated... Property rights, child support, spouse support, the tax problem, her lawyer, my lawyer... The I.R.S. wants to take the property we bought in '69, where she now lives... I signed it over to her a long time ago, but the I.R.S. still considers both of us as one, so they might take it for the 28,000 owed... So we can't get the divorce until this tax thing is settled... Our lawyers have agreed that I should pay her 400 a month, which I've been doing for about a year now... Before that she was getting lots of money from my previous lawyer, who was also getting lots of money for himself by hustling guys who were using "Keep on Truckin'" without paying me... That gravy train finally fell through after a long succession of tedious litigations, trials, depositions, etc... A judge finally declared "Keep on Truckin'" to be public domain... I was relieved to be finished with all the legal battles... It was ridiculous... I was spending half my time answering questions fired at me by hack asshole lawyers... But the money stopped... and now there's this big tax debt... It seems my old lawyer wasn't taking care of business... except the business of lining his own pockets... I dumped him after he refused to help me with the tax debt which was at least as much his responsibility as mine & Dana's... All this happened after I had finally parted with the wife, summer of '74, I believe... That was the most painful thing I've ever done of my own free will, but hadda do it... so I can sympathize with your problem...

Anyhow, when Dana could no longer hit my lawyer up for a few thou' anytime she wanted, she pushed the panic button — and previous to this economic disaster, she was spending money, squandering cash at a rapid rate! New cars, additions to the house, horses, cows, boyfriends, jewelry, schemes to make money that failed, con-men, fast-talkers, mooches, bums, relatives... It was too classic... In fact, the whole situation is so typical it's banal... a tired old plot from a grade-B Hollywood movie...

So, she sends the sheriff after me with a paper demanding a thousand a month... I explained in detail to her lawyer how I'd have to work my ass off to make that much money and still stay alive myself... I had to fill out endless interrogatories, mountains of papers about every financial transaction I ever made in my life and every piece of property or object of value I ever owned, every bank account I ever had... It was endless... Dana had gotten used to living high and it scared her that it was over...

But, like I say, I won't go into it... This is just scratching the surface, believe me... The price of fame... How am I supposed to deal with all this shit and still draw comics is what I'm trying to figure out now... It's very difficult to get lost on one's art with all this crap going through your brain all the time, but I guess I better learn to live with it because it's not going to go away... It's an ongoing problem that I must live with, sort of like Marty Pahls' diabetes... Well, no... Actually, when I think of Pahls' situation, I count my blessings...

Oh man what a life, hah??

Crumb's a bumb, so's Britt... WIS

I'm living with another Jewish woman now named Aline Kominsky[1]... She's a cartoonist also, and has had some stuff published in *Arcade* and other places... I dunno if you keep up with the "underground" comic scene... If so, you might've seen her stuff... It's primitive but funny as hell... I think anyway... She's a good kid and pretty easy to live with, real smart and with a bitter Jewish-comedy-monologue that she keeps running all day for my entertainment and amusement... Also, she's a good fuck... We've been living together for two years now and things are still pretty mellow... I'm actually amazed at how little she gets on my nerves, after the succession of neurotic, psycho, mixed-up wives, mistresses and assorted girlfriends I've gone through... She's the most rational and mentally alert female I've ever been involved with... Women are generally a pain in the ass and a nuisance, and only good for one, or maybe two, things, at most, what with being so influ-

---

[1] Aline Kominsky-Crumb has contributed to anthologies such as *Arcade* and *Twisted Sisters* and collaborated with Robert on several projects, including *Dirty Laundry* and *Weirdo* (where she succeeded Peter Bagge — who succeeded Crumb — as editor). Most recently, the two co-created *Self-Loathing Comics* #1 and #2 (Fantagraphics Books, 1995-1997).

enced by hormones and other female bodily functions... I'd probably just live alone at this point if I broke up with Kominsky...

I was reading about Leonardo da Vinci recently... It seems he made it a point to avoid getting involved with females... was indifferent to 'em... and look at how much he was able to accomplish!!!

The fatal weakness, though, is the sexual attraction... I'm still so fuckin' obsessed with lust... can't live with 'em and can't live without 'em...

It's all Milford High School's fault... Those dirty —

Yer still collectin' those Disney comics, huh? I quit collecting comics years ago after a long period in which I was able to accumulate a big random sampling of all the better stuff and even some of those sleazy obscure 1940s and '50s byways of comicbookdom, except that I did buy up a complete set of *Little Lulu* up to 1955... I used to have all the early *MAD*s and lots of *Disney*s but I gave them all away one time in a LSD-induced trance in 1968... I wanted to shed all material burdens... "A fool there was..."

Now I just only collect records avidly, and accumulate other odd assorted items casually: knick-knacks, toys, books, all kinds of junk... You must come visit our little museum sometime...

How'd you wind up collecting old Victrolas? (or "graph-o-phones," etc.) Toobad you're not hip to what old records to look for... Grab anything that looks like hillbilly, blues or jazz from the twenties, but I also collect lots of different ethnic stuff from that period: Irish, Italian, eastern European, Mexican, Canadian... but you have to know what to look for... Maybe if I ever get up that way, you could turn me onto some "sources" places with old records for sale...

Do you ever actually listen to these old machines, or do you just like to look at 'em or what? I have an old beat up Victrola myself... works good... An ol' lady gave it to me... I'm saving it for when there's no more electricity available...

I do wanna get up that way sometime... I've never been up there at all, in the northwest... appreciate yer offer of a place to "crash" as we used to say in the hippie days...

I quit "doing" marijuana a coupla years ago... Now I'm "straight" again... I even go to the barbershop for my haircut...

If you ever wanna come here, you're welcome to stay with us... our phone number is:

916 · 662 · 3142

My younger brother Max lives alone in San Francisco. Lives on welfare and is a weirdo-hermit who eats sparingly and never does anything for pleasure... He's interesting to talk to...

My younger sister Sandra is now a fanatic lesbian "separatist" (won't allow a man in her house, although — bitter irony — she's got a seven year old son from her marriage with Pahls) living in Washington outside of Seattle... She hates my guts because I'm such a male-chauvinist (she's right, obviously) and because I'm "rich" and won't give her any money...

Such is life... Write and keep me informed of developments and let me know if you have a change of address, or a change of... Oh nevermind!! It was a bad joke...

Hope being a salesman doesn't get you down too much... Do you have to wear leisure suits on the job? I dunno, maybe you like leisure suits...

I dunno about comicons... I tend to avoid them, but I would like to see ol' Harvey... Maybe I'll try an' get up there, but stay away from the thick of the con fanboy action, if I can... I can't take the "fanboys"...

Which reminds me... it was thanks to your discerning eye that that guy Ferrigno finally got his money back for those forgeries of my work that he bought... Sheesh... He had to be BLIND not to see that they were fake... He sent me xeroxes of the stuff, and I immediately had my lawyer write a letter to Sandy Cutler (the dealer) demanding immediate recompense to Ferrigno of his 500 bucks and informing him that mailing forged artwork across state lines was a federal offense and to desist... I got clout in this world...

– Crumb

~ 4 8 ~

April 14, 1977
Madison, California

Britt:

Been so fuckin' buzy lately my head is spinning... Man, I gotta simplify my life somehow...

Hey, when is that comic convention in Portland supposed to be? I have to know so I can plan my trip up there... I'm s'posed to meet up with Kurtzman up there 'n' all like that... So, gimme some dates if you can, of when it starts and ends... It'll be the first time in years I've gone on a trip by myself... Hope I can afford it by then... The income tax debt looms ever closer like a big dark storm cloud over my head, about to burst any minute, raining paper, documents, demands, bureaucrats & sheriffs down on my head in a torrent...

Anyway, my divorce is just about settled... We've just about come to an agreement... I have to pay Dana four-hundred a month (includes child support)... I have to pay the tax debt... She gets to keep the property in Potter Valley... I get to keep all my copyrights and my artwork... Great deal, huh?? At this point I just sorta want to get it over with... It's been dragging on so long... I don't want to fight with her... At this point the main worry is what the I.R.S. is going to do... They're creeping along at a snail's pace as usual...

If they lay a really heavy demand on me, I just might have to resort to over-sized posters and stuff like that... Mr. Natural "Natural-Burger" fast-food franchises... something to get that thirty-thousand dollars paid off, or whatever it's going to be... Oh it's a cruel hard world out there...

No you didn't send me a calendar... Whatsis calendar? What calendar? Who's covering up?

Charles was in a crazy house for about two years... He's been out now for about three years, I think... They got him started on "medication"... heavy doses of downers every day, and he's been taking them ever since... Thorazine, stuff like that... The pills kind of keep him stable... at the exact level of mental energy or mental capacity that he existed on for years before his big "crack up" around 1971 or '72... In other words, he can't go forward... He can't develop past his hang ups, but he can't crack up either... He's just sort of static... I dunno if it's good or bad... I mean, maybe he was too far gone to get past his problems... maybe the medicine is good for him... I dunno... He got fat from taking it... The guy's a pathetic wreck, but he can still write interesting letters, I'll say that...

My brother Maxon is another case... The li'l Pollack we all knew and loved, who played in little league and built model airplanes, has become transformed into a wild-eyed, bony hermit, producing some of the strangest alien, out-of-this-world weirdo art work and writing I've ever seen... He has definitely turned out the strangest of anyone in the family... And I guess I told you about Sandra... being a raving fanatic lesbian who won't even allow a man in her house... except for her eight year-old son...

If you're serious about selling my artwork, you may be just the guy I'm looking for... I may very likely have to sell all I have left to pay off the I.R.S.... I've already traded off probably more than half of my original pages, but I have plenty left to sell... What would your "expenses" include... mailing costs and like that? Of course I'd give you some free artwork for your trouble, as I know it would be a time-consuming task, collecting the money and sending the stuff out... Are you pretty knowledgeable of the market for this stuff, the values, who buys... etc...?? Like f'r instance, I have alot of long stories, which would go for less per page than one or two-page items, right? It all depends on what the I.R.S. decides to do, but if I have to dump it all on the market, we should definitely get together on it and sort of loosely price everything, right? Do you think that having so much R. Crumb art for sale would be a glut on the market which would cause the value to drop? Anyway, I appreciate your offer to help me sell the stuff, as I may have to pretty soon, but won't if I can avoid it... But it looks like I will... I'll let you know...

The idea of reprinting *Foo* is interesting, but I feel kind of embarrassed about it... But if you really think you could get rid of 3 or 4 thousand copies... man, do it... I dunno... Hell, we couldn't even get rid of 300 when we first printed the 'zines... Oh man, what a shattering blow to our inflated little egos that was... Was good in a way, though... Milford was a lesson in the true hard-ass reality of America, doncha think? No? Oh... But, if you do re-print it and sell it, you can take half the profits for all your trouble... I'm sure it won't be very much... And, yeah, I'd like to write a little something... some kind of forward... And you can too... It'll be nice with those washed out black areas filled in... I remember how disappointed I felt when I first saw how shitty those first print-ed copies looked... Also, it was never properly trimmed after the printing... Those black areas on the cover are s'posed to bleed off the edge... So this time we'll do it right, ey? I'll send Charles a copy... Hell, I don't even have any copies of *Foo* #1 and #2 now... I have a tattered copy of number three...

I know what you mean about not being able to afford those high-priced collectors' items you need for your Disney collection... I had to stop buying expensive old records so that I can save some money to pay the taxes... It's hard to go cold turkey... I got very much in the habit of blowing two-hundred bucks a month on records... but it's good for me to stop... I mean, I got enough records (a couple of thousand)... If I didn't stop, sooner or later I'd blow it... The whole thing would get so unweidly, I'd end up having to get rid of it all... Anyway, after a certain point, you get more records than you could ever pos-sibly listen to in your life... Pahls was like that for a while... That guy had about ten million hours of music in his dingy basement apartment in Chicago... No way on earth could he ever have time to appreciate it all... And he was listening to <u>hours</u> of music every day... much more than I can handle... on 78, LP, tape, everything... Now he's selling off all his records... Needs the money... Can't find a decent job...

He was out here for a visit a couple of weeks ago, believe it or not... It's the first time he's ever been west... loved California and wants to move out here now... I kinda hope he does... It'd be good for him... I think he'd be hap-pier living in San Francisco than Chicago... His brother owns a bunch of prop-erty in S.F. now... He bought old Victorian houses in that town years ago when they were cheap and now they've all tripled or quadrupled in value... I think he could help Marty find a good place to live down there...

I recently sold my Victrola to a friend for $75.00... I kind of hated to see it go but it was just collecting dust out on the front porch... Mebbe when I'm up there we could spend some time looking in junk stores, if you have the time... I hear it's still possible to find good records in Oregon... only if you can spare the time... It's no big thing...

Well, goshes, Onckle Ted, guess I'll sign off... Lemme know when that fuggin' convention is... Write soon...

R. CRUMB

PS I'll bring some o' those old Milford note-books with me when I come up there... Should be worth a few laughs...

Dear Britt:

I've decided not to come to Portland during the convention but at a later time — in September most likely... The reasons are many... The first being that I have a hell of alot of work to do and a big trip in July will set me back too much... Secondly, I'm hearing from various comic fans that it's become common knowledge that I'm going to be in Portland during the "con," and I know there'd be alot of pressure for me to make an appearance, which I'm just not up to anymore... So I figure I'd just be better off not being there during the "con"... Thirdly, I am planning to take the train back east sometime late this year, so it seemed practical to combine the two trips... I'll go to Portland and spend a week or so there and then head east...

Is September okay with you? Lemme know if it is or it isn't... It'll be better for me both time-wise and economically to combine the two trips... I got a ton of commitments that have to get done in the next couple of months... Then I can quit cartooning for good... ha ha... Lotsa luck...

Pahls wants to move out here... He's in th' process of liquidating some of his vast collections, both to get money and lighten the load... It'll be good for the guy to get out of his dungeon... His brother is younger... He worked as a librarian in some university or something like that until recently... Now he's going into dealing antiques... He's your classic San Francisco-granny-fag-antique type... Actually, I've not seen him myself since about 1959, but from Marty's description, that's what he seems to be like... Marty wrote for a sleazy chain of tabloid newspapers for years... I guess you know about that... I dunno what he's gonna do for a living... He lost his job with the tabloid chain when he got diabetes and had to stay in bed for a couple of months... They fired him... He's pretty bitter about it... But th' guy's a pretty good writer... He could probably make a living just hustling the magazines... The sex mags especially... *Hustler, Swank,* an' all o' them... Did you know that he has to shoot insulin every day?... Grim... He does it right in front of everybody... Just pulls down his pants and jams the needle in his side... I think he gets a kick out of grossing people out doing that... Gives me the shivers... I can't look... Pahls' life is pretty depress-

ing, generally, but he's still a pretty funny guy... has a very bitter sense of humor about things...

Thanks for the xeroxes of *Foos* #1 and #2... They are pretty bad... kind of embarrassing... I don't know if you ought to print them... might not be worth the trouble of touching them up... Looks like alot of work to me... We can discuss it further when I see you...

That guy Sandy Cutler that did the forgeries that Ferrigno bought has pulled another hype on a hapless fan... Ferrigno wrote me about it... This time, though, rather than go to the trouble of trying to do forgeries, he just mailed the guy a package that had the appearance of having been torn open and the artwork stolen! On the outside of the package he had written in large print: "CAREFUL! VALUABLE ARTWORK!" Clever, ey? It's weird... Guys I know back east say that Cutler has a reputation of being a real nice guy, reliable, friendly... Pulling frauds such as these could really put th' guy in some bad hot water! Mail fraud — federal offense — felony — jail — F.B.I.... Bad business, Sandy, baby.

Mebbe I'll bring some 'riginal art with me to Portland and we'll see what we kin do...

Hope my change of plans doesn't hang you up or cause you any difficulties... Gotta get this work done over the summer...

~ 5 0 ~   *September 20, 1977*
                          Madison, California

Britt:

I'm still planning to make it to Oregon, but probably not 'til early October... I've been going through incredible shit with the I.R.S. lately, of which I will tell you when I see you... I will call you and let you know exactly when I'm planning to come up there and find out if it's okay with you an' everything a week or so beforehand...

You're welcome to come down here if you want to, although there's not much to do around these parts... But I like the idea of driving back up with you... I'd help pay for gas... Early October would be the soonest I can get away, though... How long's it take to drive the distance between here 'n' there, you think? How'd the "con" go? Did Harvey K. make it?

Looking forward to seeing you soon...

R. Crumb

Virtually all of Crumb's work is available in a variety of formats, including reprints of the original comics (predominantly from Last Gasp, which has re-released all the *Zap* issues and many of the vintage undergrounds, and Kitchen Sink Press) and book collections (including Fantagraphics Books, which to date has reprinted all of Crumb's comics work through 1992 in *The Complete Crumb Comics*). Of particular relevance to the periods discussed herein are *Crumb Family Comics* (edited by Maxon Crumb; Last Gasp, 1998); the first two volumes of *The Complete Crumb Comics*; *The R. Crumb Coffee Table Art Book* (Little, Brown/Kitchen Sink, 1997); and *The Big Yum Yum Book* (reprinted by Snow Lion Graphics in 1997). Fantagraphics' *R. Crumb Sketchbook* series also covers the period represented by these letters.

The following collections reprint material discussed by Crumb in this volume; given Crumb's perceptive taste, they form a useful primer of classic comic strips and comic books.

Barks, Carl. *The Carl Barks Library*. Another Rainbow, 1984-1998. (Unsurprisingly, Barks' Disney material has been endlessly reprinted, and is currently available in regular comics and in larger albums; although printed in black-and-white, the Another Rainbow edition is the most complete version extant.)

Bushmiller, Ernie. *Ernie Bushmiller's Nancy, Volumes 1-5*. Kitchen Sink, 1989-1991.

Caniff, Milton. *The Complete Dickie Dare*. Fantagraphics Books, 1986.

Capp, Al. *Li'l Abner: Dailies, Volumes 1-27*. Kitchen Sink, 1988-(ongoing).

Eisner, Will. *The Spirit*. Kitchen Sink (various collections, ongoing).

Feiffer, Jules. *Feiffer: The Collected Works, Volumes 1-3*. Fantagraphics Books, 1989-(ongoing).

Foster, Hal & Burne Hogarth. *Tarzan, Volumes 1-18*. NBM, 1993-1997.

Foster, Hal. *Prince Valiant, Volumes 1-34*. Fantagraphics Books, 1984-(ongoing).

Gray, Harold. *Little Orphan Annie, Volumes 1-5*. Fantagraphics Books, 1987-(ongoing).

Kelly, Walt. *Pogo, Volumes 1-9*. Fantagraphics Books, 1992-(ongoing). (Aside from this chronological reprinting of the earliest *Pogo* strips, other volumes are periodically available from other publishers.)

Kurtzman, Harvey. *Kurtzman's Jungle Book*. Kitchen Sink, 1986.

McCay, Winsor. *Little Nemo in Slumberland, Volumes 1-6*. Fantagraphics Books, 1989-1993.

Messmer, Otto. *Nine Lives to Live: A Classic Felix Celebration*. Fantagraphics Books, 1996.

Outcault, R. F. *R. F. Outcault's the Yellow Kid: A Centennial Celebration of the Kid Who Started the Comics*. Kitchen Sink, 1995.

Roth, Arnold. *Poor Arnold's Almanac*. Fantagraphics Books, 1998.

Segar, E. C. *The Complete E. C. Segar Popeye, Volumes 1-11*. Fantagraphics Books, 1985-1990.

Stanley, John. *The Little Lulu Library*. Another Rainbow, 1985-1987.

Wolverton, Basil. *Basil Wolverton's Powerhouse Pepper*. Fantagraphics Books, 1994.

Wolverton, Basil. *Basil Wolverton in Space*. Dark Horse Comics, 1996.

Various artists. *The Complete EC Library*. Russ Cochran, 1984-1998. (EC Comics, in particular Kurtzman's *MAD*, have been amply reprinted in both comics and album formats.)